HISTORY
OF
ABSTRACT
PAINTING

Cover Design: Xavier Barral
Design and Picture Research: Olivia Barbet-Massin
Translation: Jane Brenton

© Fernand Hazan 1989, Paris

Printed in Spain

ISBN: 2 85025 180 1

JEAN-LUC DAVAL

HISTORY OF ABSTRACT PAINTING

HAZAN

FOREWORD

In the 1950s there was an anecdote about Newman that became an anthology piece. Franz Kline and Elaine de Kooning were sitting at the Cedar Bar when a collector Franz knew came up to them in a state of fury. He had just come from Newman's first one-man show. "How simple can an artist be and get away with it?" he sputtered. "There was nothing, absolutely nothing there!"

"Nothing?" asked Franz, beaming. "How many canvases were in the show?"

"Oh, maybe ten or twelve — but all exactly the same — just one stripe down the center, that's all!"

"All the same size?" Franz asked.

"Well, no; there were different sizes; you know, from about three to seven feet."

"Oh, three to seven feet, I see; and all the same color?" Franz went on.

"No, different colors, you know; red and yellow and green... but each picture painted one flat color — you know, like a house painter would do it, and then this stripe down the center."

"All the stripes the same colour?"

"No."

"Were they the same width?"

The man began to think a little. "Let's see. No. I guess not. Some were maybe an inch wide and some maybe four inches, and some in between."

"And all upright pictures?"

"Oh no; there were some horizontals."

"With vertical stripes?"

"Uh, no, I think there were some horizontal stripes, maybe."

"And were the stripes darker or lighter than the background?"

"Well, I guess they were darker, but there was one white stripe, or maybe more..."

"Was the stripe painted on top of the background color or was the background color painted around the stripe?"

The man began to get a bit uneasy. "I'm not sure," he said, "I think it might have been done either way, or both ways maybe..."

"Well, I don't know," said Franz. "It all sounds damned complicated to me."

Thomas B. Hess,
Barnet Newman, MoMA, 1971

SUMMARY

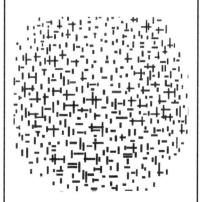

INTRODUCTION

"Our senses have a developmental age that is determined, not by our immediate surroundings, but by a moment in the history of civilization. That is far more significant than anything else we can acquire from the epoch itself. Development in the arts proceeds not only from the individual but from an acquired momentum, the civilization that has gone before. A gifted artist is not at liberty to do just anything. If he simply put his talents to work, and no more, he would not exist. We are not masters of what we produce. It is imposed upon us." (Matisse, "Propos à Tériade", *Minotaure,* no. 9, 1936) The significant point here is Matisse's insistence that it is receptivity to the broader spirit of the age that determines the direction of individual creative effort: art is the product of a historical moment, and never more so than in times of change and dramatic upheaval.

If the public at large has still not become reconciled to the concept of an art whose prime intention is no longer to reproduce an illusion of the external world, then that is indicative of a more general refusal to accept that the functions of art may change and be renewed. Timelessness may well be one of the marks of genius, and yet there is a huge gulf separating the Giottos of Padua and the Titians of Venice in the way they reflect their age... "One of the fundamental tasks of art," wrote Walter Benjamin, "has always been to create demand in an age where it could not yet be fully satisfied... The history of every art form consists of critical epochs where the form will strive towards producing effects not readily obtainable except after modifications of technique, in other words in a new art form." (Walter Benjamin, "The Work of Art in the Age of Mechanical Reproduction") The activity of any artist is motivated by concerns dictated by the needs and possibilities of a particular moment of history, but his activity, in its turn, alters the nature of these concerns and moves them in a new direction. Contemporary art forms have been transformed because few epochs have seen such upheavals as our own century.

The thirty years that preceded the First World War were particularly decisive; in philosophy, politics, sociology and ethics, as well as in the scientific, technological and economic spheres, changes occurred that even now profoundly influence our thinking and way of life. These changes came about as a direct consequence of the ideas that inspired the French Revolution: the goal of Liberty, the guiding principle of the Declaration of the Rights of Man, and its corollary, the responsibility to be absolute in its defence. But the inauguration of a new freedom was to be a long and arduous process. The progressive but definitive emancipation from the "values" of the past left the individual with no truths to fall back on other than those he could discover from his personal experience. And nowhere was that search for authentic experience pursued more eagerly than in the realm of artistic creation; while "official" art might continue to produce works calculated to satisfy and reassure, creativity was bound to lay the emphasis on expression and the opening up of new areas of exploration. In painting, Renaissance humanism had given rise to illusionism: the representation of a world in which the individual expressed his primacy by reducing the infinity of the universe to what lay within the scope of his optical perception. Yet that model of the relationship of man to his universe was constantly under pressure; every time the ideology and practice of a previous generation appeared inadequate to present needs, it became necessary to find new ways of justifying this world view. In the nineteenth century, not only was a new political equilibrium established, founded on universal suffrage, but industrialization, too, profoundly affected the conditions of life — even as scientific research, advancing pragmatically, revealed a hitherto unsuspected world, obedient to principles which directly challenged the reality of surface appearances on which man's domination of his universe was founded. All the ingredients existed for the invention of a new concept of pictorial space.

At its inception, the nineteenth century was split between the two opposing poles of Romanticism and Realism. Romanticism supplied the affirmation of subjectivity, embodying desire and passion, while Realism stood for direct experience and an empirical apprehension of the world. Apparently at war, these two tendencies nevertheless worked in concert to bring about an increasing emphasis on individual interpretation. Artistic creation was at the forefront of these changes: truth was held to reside henceforth in the absolute of self-expression. No longer was the artist the illustrator of a pre-existing order, an agent charged with setting out the details of concepts already established, rather he was the intrepid discoverer of new ways of seeing, feeling, understanding and expressing, his only guide his intuition. Innovation and originality became the measures of his activity. In parallel, the artist's role in society was also modified: where previously he had worked largely to commission, now with the establishment of the Salons, and later an exhibition network, he had for the first time the chance to present images that actually anticipated public demand.

The desire for freedom in life and thought was accelerated by the growth of formal education and the improved dissemination of information, which accustomed the public to the notion of progress. Equally, advances in science and technology proceeded at a staggering rate. The destruction of the figurative world was closely linked to the new perceptions imposed by these changes, as they cast doubt on the reliability of the visual observation of phenomena. Reality was now seen to lie beyond or beneath the visible, existing both at the microscopic level of the electron and in the infinite magnitude of the cosmos. The discovery of the atom or the exposition of a theory of relativity were not, of course, going to change men's minds overnight, but they insinuated themselves into the general consciousness, benefiting from a widespread readiness to sweep away the old ways of seeing and thinking: contemplation was no longer the order of the day in a society that was dominated by action and movement. Already new power sources like steam, electricity and petrol had transformed people's working lives and habits. New modes of transport and improved communications had broadened horizons from the scale of the village to that of the continent. At the same time, industrial and economic development favoured the town at the expense of the countryside. Men saw their lives in a new context, regarded work in a different light: nature, hitherto omnipresent, was blurred by an urban reality that at times threatened to destroy it altogether. Such a transformation was not to be without consequences for the life of each and every individual, the responses ranging broadly from nostalgia for a lost order to a blind desire for progress at all costs.

Nothing was immune from change. The artists of this society had no choice open to them but to construct from their own experience a response to a world whose outward appearance and structures were in the process of transformation, and which at the same time obliged men to take a different view of themselves. Of particular relevance, within the specific context of art history, was the still recent invention of photography, which was to have a direct influence on painters' attitudes. In 1839, the photographic technique was seen as a method of representation that exactly paralleled painting; in an age committed to realism, it appeared to provide an "objective" record — notwithstanding the presence of the man who selected, composed and regulated the shot. The painters saw themselves compromised, no longer essential to those functions of description, representation and illustration with which they were most readily identified. The threat posed by photography increased as a spate of technical refinements were introduced, culminating in the marketing in 1888 of the famous Kodak camera that mechanized the whole process, making photography accessible to all. With its ability to record a scene in a flash, to register the tiniest detail or the broadest pattern, it soon revealed a world invisible to the naked eye. By demonstrating that the reality of nature was not synonymous with the reality of human vision, photography provoked a crisis, one that was to be decisive in its effects. The painters, apparently rendered obsolete by the invention of a new method of reproduction that was not only speedy but cheap, were forced to re-examine the whole basis of their art in order to justify their existence.

Happily for them, the foundation of the great collections and the growth of the museums began to open the public's eyes to the possibility of an entirely different approach to creative art. By removing works of art from their former context and functions — a phenomenon discussed by Malraux in *Le Musée Imaginaire* — the museums helped to show that it was not so much *what* was represented that mattered as *how* it was represented. As the subject receded and was subsumed in the artist's translation of it, each creative work appeared in the light of a personal conquest, something wrested with great difficulty from the vast unknown of the universe. Reality came to be perceived as a global concept, something that could be glimpsed only in certain of its contingent manifestations: no single response could claim to be definitive. As people then began to reappraise the history of art in the light of this new analysis, it was only a step to regarding the work of art as having a reality of its own, subject to its own laws. No longer was painting subordinate to something outside itself; like any other language it served as a means of communication, but in addition it consisted of a structure of elements specific to it, whose expressive powers demanded recognition.

This novel concept crystallized in the public consciousness around 1860, the time when Japanese art came to Europe. Its perspective system appeared to call in question the convention of the "window on the world" adopted by Western painting, and at the same time it laid stress on certain constituents of painting such as zones of flat colour and line itself. At the dawning of Impressionism, painting appeared as a sort of inevitable "abstraction", a matter of uniting the three dimensions of reality on a surface. The flat plane of the image dictated the choice of a method of transcription that would supply the missing depth; everything else followed from that choice. Art continued to be guided by the desire to transcribe the visible, but painters began at the same time to lay emphasis on particular components of their repertoire: plane, line, composition, colour, pigment... exploring the potential of each and dwelling more on personal style. Art started to seek out its reality within itself. Little by little, arbitrary relationships set up between elements borrowed from nature were used as the means of re-creating the artist's "sensations" in terms of pictorial signs. As this happened, so the goals of painting itself shifted. In the view of Pierre Francastel: "The plastic image identifies and embodies aspects of the plastic and speculative experience of an age, but in addition it constitutes a sketch, a model that gives rise to new rules of conduct and brings forth new hypotheses. Thus, its reality consists in its figurative character, since it possesses, in just the same way as words, the power to provoke an active response in others. Figurative object or image, art is the domain in which works are developed out of common ideas and in their turn are suggestive of new experiences." (*Art et Technique,* 1964, p. 272)

Since artistic creation is inseparable from the age that nourishes it, the art of our own day is marked above all by its faith in evolution, and the belief that it is possible to transform the world through science. In every discipline, if a thing is new it is regarded as progress; we are embarked on an era of research for its own sake, of change and innovation; in artistic terms, this demand for continual invention has ushered in what might be called *the age of the avant-gardes.* But when the old is superceded, inevitably it is also destroyed; a work of art has ceased to be a fiction to set the imagination on fire, it has become a significant object in a civilization where artists and scientists are always alert for new phenomena, which they transmit in a form that is open-ended and capable of development. While the sciences are directed towards the study of life and its metamorphoses, technology and the requirements of modern life place the emphasis on activity. Everything is changing, on the move, in transformation. There is a new standard of measurement, that of space-time, a concept both fascinating and disturbing. The individual is aware that he no longer lives in a homogeneous world, one that is determined and fixed, he can no longer stand back and observe it from the sidelines; instead he is plunged into a reality that is without limits, constantly renewing itself, demanding his active participation. The traditional relationship of the object governed by the subject has become an impossibility; now subject and object form a couple whose relationship is constantly under review, never predetermined.

In the plastic arts, the liberation of intuition and imagination was achieved through awareness of the pictorial language. It then remained to develop an image that went beyond illusion: an image that was bound to consist either of elements borrowed from nature or of elements constructed *a priori.* A painting has never in fact been anything other than an abstract organization of plastic elements, but until the modern age only artists recognized that truth. Since 1880, the order of operations has tended to be reversed. We no longer proceed merely from perception to representation, but also from intuition to organization. This discovery of the expressive and communicative reality of painting has opened up, in Malevich's phrase, a new "window in which to see life": "I too was filled with a sort of timidity and I hesitated to the point of anguish when faced with leaving behind the world of conscious will and representation, in which I had lived and created and in the authenticity of which I had believed. But the feeling of satisfaction I experienced in the liberation of the object carried me ever further into the desert, to the point where nothing else was authentic except sensibility alone — and it was in this way that sensibility became the very substance of my life. That square I exhibited was not an empty square, but the sensibility of the absence of the object. I realized that the object and the representation had been regarded as the equivalents of sensibility and I understood the lie that is conscious will and representation." (Malevich, *Die Gegenstandslose Welt,* 1927)

J.L.D.

17

CHAPTER 1
THE WORK OF PAINTING

Cézanne:
Trees at the Edge of a Road,
1900-04

Liberated from a theological explanation of the world, the nineteenth century invented spaces of an increasing complexity, extending the traditional systems of "perspective" in the attempt to take account of recent scientific discoveries. But by 1900, the image of "nature seen through a temperament" had finally given way under the sheer pressure of technological advance, which seemed to offer the prospect of infinite progress to all. The preamble to the guide to the Paris World Fair illustrates very well the vein of visionary optimism then current: "The 1900 Universal and World Fair is the magnificent result, the extraordinary culmination of a century that has been the most fertile in discoveries, the most prodigious in the sciences, which has revolutionized the economic order of the universe... The exhibition shows, step by step, the march of progress, from the stage coach to the express train, from the messenger to the wireless and the telephone, from lithography to radiography, from the first search for coal in the bowels of the earth to aeroplanes that strive to conquer the airways." At this same period, intellectual giants like Bergson, Freud, Plank and Einstein published theories that obliged men to conceive of, in Jean Cassou's words, "unrepresentable cosmogenies, indeterminate logical systems, mysterious actions which, even in the shadowy depths of the psyche, operate in a precise and intrinsic way, outside the laws of classical logic as it is applied to the ensemble of natural phenomena". (*Sources du XXᵉ siècle,* 1961, p. 8)

These apparently conflicting discoveries and theories were to have one effect in common: the cultiva-

tion of a new spatio-temporal awareness. In the plastic arts this was to be superimposed on a changed concept of art itself, one which emphasized its organic reality at the expense of its power to create illusions. Since the picture was an object more than it was a representation, the painter was increasingly prepared to reveal his working methods: the creative process, the development of the work, how long it took, the materials employed. As artists from Constable to the Impressionists experimented with studies of water and atmosphere, they moved beyond perspective, and the transition was made from the representation of nature to pure painting.

In this process of experiment, Monet's role was decisive. From 1865 onwards he worked exclusively "from the motif", recording the changes in the appearance of objects in different lights and atmospheric conditions. Gradually the contrasts of light and dark, on which Western painting had been founded since the time of Giotto, gave way to a tension between hot and cold colour. Logically, this led in turn to a process of divisionism, as being the only technique capable of manipulating pure colour, replacing the impure blending of pigments by an optical mixture. Soon Monet's canvases were covered in dots and blobs of colour, each fulfilling an autonomous function. Working pragmatically, he arrived at the concept of the picture as a re-creation, in its own terms, of that decomposition of light that occurs in nature. At the same time he elevated colour to the primary role in painting. Seurat and his Neo-Impressionist friends were to go on to establish a scientific justification for colour materialization. Seurat's canvases are figurative, but his approach to painting was rigorously abstract; harmony was achieved through the physical organization of colour within a quasi-mathematical structure: "If I have managed to discover the law of pictorial colours, scientifically, by experimenting with art, am I not capable of discovering an equally logical, scientific and pictorial system by which the forms of the painting will be in harmonious accord, in just the same way as I have done with colours?" (*L'Art Moderne*, April 1891) Seurat was greatly influenced by the theories of his friend Charles Henry, whose *L'introduction à une esthétique scientifique* of 1885 (which anticipates so many of the ideas of "art concret"), demonstrates how scientific laws may be applied to art in order to control its

4

1. Monet:
   Haystack, Snow Effect, Morning,
   1891
2. Monet:
   Haystack, Snow Effect, Overcast,
   1891
3. Monet:
   Haystack, Thaw, Sunset, 1891
4. Monet:
   Waterlilies, Sunset, 1916-23
5. Monet:
   Weeping Willow (Tangled
   Foliage), c. 1923

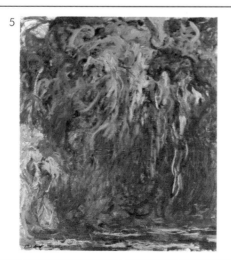

5

effects: "Who says science, says freedom... What science can and should do is disseminate what is agreeable both within us and outside of us, and in that regard its social function is enormous in these times of oppression and muted conflict."

It was with the great series he started in the 1890s, the *Haystacks,* the *Poplars,* the *Cathedrals* and finally the famous *Waterlilies,* that Monet advanced to the very threshold of non-figuration. In these paintings he placed such emphasis on colour as to obliterate the subject altogether. As early as 1890, he wrote of the *Waterlilies*: "I've turned again to more of these impossible things: water with grass waving in the background." For thirty or more years he worked on the theme, moving from general views to magnified details, from easel paintings to "environments" of the type now on display in the Orangerie in Paris, attaining ever more precision in capturing an instant of light, and arriving finally at a lyrical handling of the pigment that quite transcends subject matter. A paradoxical lyricism, however, since it was in the attempt to be more true-to-life, more immediate, more precise in his analysis of the natural world, that Monet ended up by blurring the boundaries of reality, or at least the stereotypes that passed for it.

Translating nature into colour, Monet was not properly understood until 1945, when he was greeted as the forerunner of Tachisme and Abstract Expressionism. Yet long before that, one of his *Haystacks* paintings had decisively influenced the course of Kandinsky's career, by revealing to him the first glimmerings of an abstract art: "Suddenly, in

1. Cézanne:
   Fishing, 1904-06
2. Cézanne:
   Foliage, 1895-1900
3. Cézanne:
   Mont Sainte-Victoire,
   c. 1900
4. Cézanne:
   Mont Sainte-Victoire,
   1902-04
5. Cézanne:
   Mont Sainte-Victoire Seen from
   Les Lauves, 1904-05

2

1895, I found myself in front of a painting supposed to be of a haystack, but which I did not recognize. This failure to understand bothered and upset me. I thought one had no right to paint in such an imprecise fashion. Dimly I was aware too that the object (the subject) did not appear in the picture. But I realized with astonishment and confusion that it did more than shock me, it imprinted itself indelibly on my memory and re-created itself before my eyes in all its detail... But what clearly emerged from it was the incredible power, unknown to me, of a palette that surpassed my wildest dreams. The painting seemed to me to be endowed with a fabulous power. But, imperceptibly, the object as an indispensable element of the work ceased to have importance for me." (*Rückblicke,* 1913) While retaining his links with the visible world, Monet had already established the primacy of the artefact in its own right: "One is not an artist unless one carries one's picture around in one's head before executing it... Art is a transposition that is achieved both by individual will and by sensitivity to nature." (Interview with Marcel Pays, *L'Excelsior,* 1920)

The liberation of painting from its role as a creator of illusions proceeded in parallel with the exploration by artists of the expressive potential of their medium. Gauguin was one of the first to claim for the plastic artist the same freedom as existed for the musician. He made this clear in an interview given in 1893, soon after his first visit to Tahiti: "If tomorrow a painter wanted to see pink or mauve shadows, there would be no reason to call him to account, as long as his

work was harmonious and provided food for thought... It's like music, if you will! By arrangements of lines and colours, with the pretext of some subject, borrowed from life or nature, I obtain symphonies, harmonies that represent nothing that is absolutely real, in the common sense of the word, expressing directly no idea, but which are designed to make you think in the way music makes you think, without the support of ideas and images, simply among those mysterious affinities that exist between our brains and such arrangements of colours and lines." Klee and Kandinsky were among the many other painters to cite the autonomy of music as a justification for abstraction, and it was the young Nabi Maurice Denis, a disciple of Gauguin, who summed up the mood of the times when he wrote, in his first published article of 30 August 1890, the sentence that was taken up as the creed of successive generations: "Remember that a picture – before it is a battle charger, a nude woman or an anecdote of some sort – is essentially a surface plane covered in colours assembled in a certain order."

Even more significant was the contribution made by Cézanne. Desirous of "making Impressionism something as durable as the art of museums" the Aix painter declared "art is a harmony parallel to nature". With that statement a turning point was reached in the history of representation, marking the determination once and for all of the direct dependency between nature and painting. True, Cézanne did not eliminate subject matter from his work – indeed few have gone so far in the analysis of the relationship of picture subject and object – but, as Merleau-Ponty wrote: "Cézanne saw no need to choose between feeling and thought, as between chaos and order. He did not aim to make a distinction between the fixed things that appear before our eyes and the fleeting manner in which they make their appearance, he wanted to paint matter in the process of acquiring form, order being born of spontaneous organization. He did not draw the line between 'the senses' and 'the intelligence', but between the spontaneous order of things perceived and the human order of ideas and science." (*Sens et Non-sens,* 1966, p. 23) And Cézanne did this in a way that brought out the integrity of the elements of painting. That "unfinished" look to his work, so often criticized, is in fact evidence of this struggle for picto-

rial truth, an obsessive search to make his medium respond to the difficult demands he placed upon it. Overwhelmed by the size, vitality and beauty of the world, Cézanne tried to express the multitude of possibilities inherent in nature by means of line, place, space, composition and colour, posing simultaneously the question of how to interpret the model and how to realize it. During his stay in Camoin, in 1903, he came to the conclusion: "Everything, above all in art, is a theory developed and applied in contact with nature." In his dream of uniting "the curves of women with the shoulders of hills", he redefined the relationship of form and colour: "Drawing and colour are not separate. Even as you paint, so do you draw; the more harmonious the colour, the more precise the drawing. When colour develops its full richness, form achieves plenitude."

Cézanne's legacy to succeeding generations was aptly summed up in a tribute issued by Maurice Denis after Cézanne's death in 1906: "In an age where the artist's sensibility was regarded almost universally as the sole justification of a work of art, and where improvization tended to destroy at a stroke not only the superannuated conventions of academicism but with them the necessary ways of proceeding, it was the art of Cézanne that proved capable of retaining for sensibility its essential role, while also replacing empiricism with reflection."

The rationale of representation was in crisis, a crisis that was to be made more acute by Matisse and the Cubists, with their increasing awareness of the expressivity of the painting medium.

3

4

From the time they made their appearance at the Salon d'Automne of 1905, the Fauves set out to startle, to induce in the onlooker a shock of the senses comparable to that they themselves experienced in confronting reality. They did this by projecting onto the confined space of the canvas the full force of their feelings, in orchestrations of brilliant colour/forms. Matisse went even further in pursuit of that congruence of feeling and painterly expression, suppressing all extraneous associations. In an article published in *La Grande Revue* in December 1908, he explained: "Expression, for me, does not consist in passion breaking out on a face or making itself felt in a violent gesture. It lies in the whole disposition of the picture: the area occupied by the bodies, the empty spaces around them, the proportions, everything has its part to play... In a picture, each part will be visible and will play the role appropriate to it, primary or secondary. Everything that is not of use in the picture is, by that token, detrimental to it. A work of art must be a harmonious whole: any superfluous detail would take the place of some other essential detail in the mind of the beholder."

As he strove to translate feeling into concept, between 1912 and 1916 Matisse hovered on the very brink of abstraction. It was the overall effect that mattered, not an individual detail or colour: "Feeling is independent of a change of colour. If a green is replaced by a red, the appearance of the picture may be altered, but not the feeling. As I used to say, the colours are energies. You have to arrange them so that they create an expressive whole. Just as in orchestrating a score, when you give a part to one instrument, you may decide to double it with another to augment the effect." (*Lettres Françaises*, no. 76, 6 October 1945) But Matisse never renounced figuration altogether, because it expressed something of his own relationship to the world: "Abstraction is but one method that has always existed, of which artists have always availed themselves. But we must not allow ourselves to be carried away by temptation, become the dupes of the methods we employ." (*Ecrits et Propos sur l'Art,* 1972, p. 252)

In their period of Analytical Cubism, Braque and Picasso stressed the primacy of pictorial construction, following Cézanne. But, although they appeared to connive at the elimination of the object, in reality it remained the starting point of their experiments. That

1. Picasso:
   Violin, 1913-14
2. Picasso:
   Man's Head with Hat, 1913

they preferred still life to any other genre is a measure of their reliance on a figurative dimension. To a very large extent it was because of this bias in their production that they emphasized space as something tactile and material, as opposed to the purely visual space of landscape. And once plastic realism had replaced illusionism in their work, it was not long before they began to incorporate elements of the real world. As Braque was to say: "They were forms which could not be deformed as they were flat surfaces, the letters existed outside space and their presence in the picture provided a contrast, allowing objects that were situated in space to be distinguished from those that were outside space." (Braque, "La Peinture et nous", *Cahiers d'Art,* no. 1, 1954)

For Braque and Picasso, collage was an inevitable extension of their working methods, marking the beginning, in 1912, of a period of Synthetic Cubism, where the emphasis was on using pictorial means to express a range of sensations. But in the plastic arts at large, the introduction of collage or assemblage provoked a veritable revolution in the language of painting. When Braque and Picasso created the first *object-pictures* incorporating elements of reality, they effectively subverted the accepted relationship of painting to life, whereby it was axiomatic that a painted image stood for the thing which it resembled. By including an actual musical score or a real newspaper, demanding that they serve as representations of themselves, Braque and Picasso destroyed the relationship of "signifier" and "signified". In plastic terms at least, there was no longer a distinction to be made between the real object and the representation of it. Thus the whole concept of the picture was revolutionized: reality resided no longer in the illusion of a thing, which itself had an independent existence, but rather in the object contained within the pictorial realization. Braque concluded: "Writing is not describing, just as painting is not depicting." The painted image had discovered its own logic, its own order of reality, its own independence; the evocation of real objects did not, of course, entirely disappear, but it became inextricably bound up with the elements of construction. Painting discovered within itself its raison d'être.

1

Robert Delaunay: Window, 1912-13

CHAPTER 2
PICTORIAL REALISM

If the brand of pictorial realism evolved by Braque and Picasso did not eliminate the representative function, it did call its necessity in question, and this at a time when scientists were demonstrating that the fundamental laws of nature itself lay beyond the reach of observation by the naked eye. In their commitment to a different apprehension of reality, the pioneers of Cubism had a very sure grasp of the consequences of that changed consciousness in terms of the practice of painting, but they did not develop their insights on a theoretical level. This was an omission rectified by other painters liberated by their example from the constraints of naturalism. Léger's writings are particularly instructive. In an article of 1913, he offered the following radical redefinition of realism: "The realistic value of a work is entirely independent of any imitative quality. It is essential that this basic tenet be accepted and taken as axiomatic in the general understanding of painting. I purposely use the word realistic in its purest sense, *for the quality of a pictorial work is a direct function of the quantity of its realism.* Of what does what we call realism in painting consist?... Pictorial realism is the simultaneous disposition of the three great plastic quantities: Lines, Forms and Colours." (*Fonctions de la peinture,* 1965, p. 12) Such a categorical assertion goes a long way towards explaining the zeal with which the artists of this generation focused on the constituent elements of painting; in laying them bare they hoped to make plain their elemental truth. Léger himself believed this change of direction was dictated by the alteration of sensibility induced by confrontation with the modern

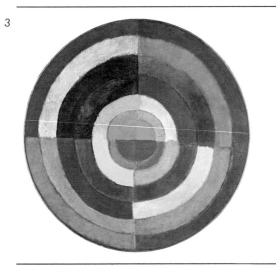

environment: "If pictorial expression has changed," he wrote in 1914, "it is because modern life has made that necessary. The existence of modern creative man is much more dense and complex than that of people in earlier generations. The pictured thing is less fixed, and the object too reveals less of itself than previously. A landscape traversed or riven by the passage of a car or fast train will lose in descriptive value, but it will gain in synthetic value. Modern man receives a hundred times more impressions than the artist of the eighteenth century; to the point, for example, that our language is now full of diminutives and abbreviations. The density of the modern picture, its variety, its formal disruption, these are the results of all that. Without doubt, the development of new forms of locomotion, and their sheer speed, must have crucially affected visual awareness." He went on to conclude: "Of course, to perceive in this break with everything sanctified by custom a justification of a new pictorial harmony, and a plastic means of expressing life and movement, was possible only for an artistic sensibility, which always anticipates the normal visual awareness of the masses." (*Op cit.*, pp. 20-21)

Inevitably, the artistic activity of this generation was to concentrate on those elements most in tune with the new sensibility: colour, rhythm and medium. Delaunay's *Circular Forms* or *Simultaneous Discs,* for example, are interpretations of a natural phenomenon, either fragmented or magnified, inspired by the discovery that light, in perpetual flux, creates forms independently of the presence of objects. As we see from the artist's autobiography, published in 1924, it was because Delaunay had moved so far beyond traditional perception that his painting, although it does not renounce figuration altogether, nevertheless has many of the attributes of abstract art: "Painting, then, should have its procedures, its laws of expression. It is colour, which as Apollinaire wrote is the fruit of light, that is at the heart of the painter's technical medium — and at the heart of his language. A painter thus works with the aid of physical elements which he must bend to his will in the whole. The colours themselves: being quantifiable, they are therefore apportioned over the picture surface, which is the only reference for the work as a whole, in terms of which it may be criticized or enjoyed — and in their interaction, these determine other quantifications... Consequently, the quantifiable

4
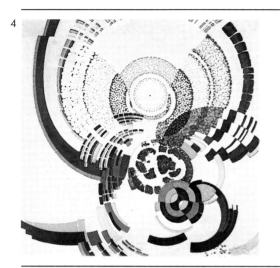

5

1. Léger:
   Contrast of Forms, 1913
2. Léger:
   The Discs, 1918
3. Robert Delaunay:
   Simultaneous Disc, 1912
4. Kupka:
   Around a Point, 1911
5. Kupka:
   The Cathedral, 1913

object we call the picture, a surface in two or more dimensions that are to be read simultaneously, is transformed into a multi-dimensional object; these multiple dimensions form groups, either setting up oppositions or neutralizing each other, the particular intensity of a colour, depending on what is adjacent to it and the total area it occupies, dictating the relationship with the rest of the colours." (Delaunay, *Du Cubisme à l'Art abstrait,* 1957, p. 60)

At around the same time, the Czech painter Kupka was similarly preoccupied with the intrinsic nature of colour. Progressively liberating it from form, he arrived eventually at a "subjectless" painting. His starting point was purely naturalistic, but as he decomposed the image, reducing it step by step to coloured planes and rhythms, in which figurative references were dispersed in a dialogue of colour and pure form, so at last, without conscious intention to do so, he found himself liberated from the concerns of representation.

In the years from 1910 to 1920, rhythm was another central preoccupation of painting, reflecting the interest aroused by the theories of the mathematician Minkowsky concerning the existence of the space-time continuum within a four-dimensional universe. His famous thesis *Raum und Zeit,* published in 1908, opened with the statement: "Henceforth space as such and time as such will disappear, giving way to a sort of union of the two that will stand alone." With the Cubist and Futurist generation, the gulf that for more than a century had divided artists and scientists was finally bridged, with consequences of great significance for painting. Pierre Francastel makes the point: "The fundamental opposition of rationality and geometry on the one hand, and spiritual and imaginative considerations on the other, simply disappeared, as a result of the new emphasis on irrational principles in physics and chemistry, and in mathematics, and as a result also of the intuitive apprehension in art of a non-Euclidian universe. The introduction of the fourth dimension, time, by offering us the opportunity to experiment and represent multiple points of view, or simultaneity, not only released us from the limitations of personal experience, it launched humanity towards the conquest of a whole new universe. Thus the fundamental opposition of reason and instinct was resolved into a new system of apprehending the basic truths of the universe, which permitted parallel modes of exploration and representation

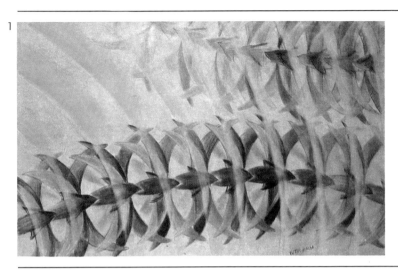

to be used in technology and art, both now subject in the same way to the new biochemical laws. Henceforth, as artists expressed movement, they felt themselves to be directly at grips with reality, they conveyed with hitherto unimaginable conviction the innate plasticity of a world reorganized by man." (*Art et Technique*, p. 54)

This conscious espousal of modernity is something we encounter again in the first *Futurist Manifesto*, published under Marinetti's signature in *Le Figaro* of 20 February, 1909. For the Italians it offered a means of breaking away from the weight of the Renaissance tradition of illusionist painting: "We proclaim that the splendour of the world is enriched by a new beauty: the beauty of speed. A racing car with its boot embellished with fat tubes, like snakes with explosive breath... a roaring car that looks as if it is charging into a hail of bullets, is more beautiful than the *Winged Victory*. We want to sing the praises of the man at the wheel, its central column like a shaft going down into the Earth as it circles in its orbit... We are on the very tip of the century!... What good is there in looking behind us, when the task we face is to batter down the mysterious portals of the impossible? Time and Space died yesterday. Already we live in the absolute, for already we have created eternal, omnipresent speed."

The introduction of movement into the system of figuration was to transform perspective: space now became a sphere of action for, with Futurism, the onlooker was projected right into the heart of the picture. The active role of space was stressed in the

4

5

Manifesto of Futurist Painters published in 1910 and signed by Balla, Boccioni, Carrà, Russolo and Severini. This sentence, for example, reflects the particular bias of Boccioni's work: "And indeed, the paving-stone in the street, drenched with rain, in the shine of the electric lights becomes an immense pit reaching down to the centre of the earth. We are separated by millions of kilometers from the sun; that does not prevent the house in front of us becoming embedded in the solar disc."

"The gesture we want to reproduce on the canvas," they declared elsewhere in the manifesto, "will no longer be a fixed moment in the universal dynamic. It will be simply the sensation of dynamism itself." With their goal of integrating all movement within the universe, the Futurists were still reliant at first on figuration, but later resorted to techniques such as chronophotography, or looked directly to science for their models.

Often the theories they evolved outstripped their ability to implement them, and it was not until 1912 that they finally succeeded in eliminating anecdotal reference from their work and addressed themselves to fundamental principles.

At times they went so far in their determination to undermine purely visual qualities – they wanted to include sounds and smells within the totality – that even Kandinsky was wary of them, judging at least by his letter of 12 November 1912 to his friend Walden, editor of the review *Der Sturm*: "If possible, do not push the Futurist painters particularly. You know my views about them, and the last manifesto (painting of tones, noises and smells) is even more crazy than the earlier ones... But art is indeed something sacred, you cannot treat it so lightly." Kandinsky implicitly rejects the interaction between art and life that was, in very different ways, the goal of both the Futurists and the Dadaists, and which was to be a crucial motivation for the Russian Constructivists.

This urge to integrate the whole range of sensual perception within the image is given a startlingly accomplished interpretation in Carra's *Inteventionist Collage*. Not only does he juggle with the contrasts between the various elements of the collage, which consist of scraps of old materials he has found, he also uses colour to reinforce the dynamism of the whole, and, beyond that, employs a sort of "nominal" figuration, quoting reality rather than presenting it;

the graphic inscriptions, and bold type, set up a kind of sonorous echo unprecedented in painting.

Marcel Duchamp and Picabia were also concerned with the expression of dynamism, and by their ironic reversal of figurative references achieved abstraction of a quite different order. In this pre-Dada period, the substitution of the machine for nature was little more than a way of "being modern", commenting sarcastically on the concerns of the Cubists and Futurists. Of the famous *Nude Descending a Staircase,* which created a scandal at the first avant-garde exhibition in New York, the Armory Show, Duchamp said the picture was not a painting "but an arrangement of kinetic elements, an expression of time and space through the abstract representation of movement". In the compositions preparing for the *Great Glass* he went further, replacing the romantic and sentimental expression of the Italian Futurists with a cold, mechanical and depersonalized formulation, which looked ahead to those anonymous objects he later elevated to the status of "ready-mades".

Duchamp's friend Picabia had an even more explicit purpose in using the machine — which he called ironically "the daughter born without a mother". In his first drawing of this type, which dates from 1913, the machine stands metaphorically for man; it was thus intended to mark a complete break with the subject matter of the past, the achievement of a sort of "second-degree" abstraction. In Duchamp's words: "To put it another way, painting should not be exclusively visual or retinal. It should also stir the grey matter, whet our appetite for understanding." Irony and absurdity were the most powerful weapons Picabia and Duchamp could muster to combat the enslavement to a traditional ideal, and, the better to condemn the past, they perverted all its effects in a deliberate spirit of anti-aestheticism. But in substituting the machine for classical motifs, they also destroyed the link between reality and representation. The image became no more than the free construction of an object — which could in fact be any object at all.

VOILÀ LA FILLE NÉE SANS MÈRE

Picabia

Kandinsky: Abstract Watercolour, 1910

CHAPTER 3

KANDINSKY AND THE INVENTION OF ABSTRACTION

Discussing the invention of abstraction in his *Concise History of Modern Painting* (1959), Herbert Read describes the radical break with the past that occurred in 1910: "This is the moment of liberation from which the whole future of the plastic arts in the Western world was to radiate in all its diversity. Once it is accepted that the plastic imagination has at its command, not the fixities of a perspectival point of view (with the consequent necessity of organizing visual images with objective coherence) but the free association of any visual elements (whether derived from nature or constructed *a priori*), then the way is open to an activity which has little correspondence with the plastic arts of the past. Of course, there are basic correspondences in so far as the plastic arts are *plastic* — that is to say, concerned with the manipulation of form and colour. In this sense, art has always been abstract and symbolic, appealing to human sensibility by its organization of visual and tactile sensations. But the vital difference consists in whether the artist in order to agitate the human sensibility proceeds from perception to representation; or whether he proceeds from perception to imagination, breaking down the perceptual images in order to re-combine them in a non-representational (rational or conceptual) structure. This conceptual structure must still appeal to human sensibility, but the assumption is that it does this more directly, more intensely and more profoundly in this new way than if burdened with an irrelevant representational function."

The transformation of perception, representation and expression that took place in around 1910 was

1. Kandinsky:
   In the Forest, 1911
2. Kandinsky:
   Brightly Coloured Field, 1911
3. Kandinsky:
   Drawing for Composition III,
   1910
4. Kandinsky:
   Drawing for Composition IV,
   1911
5. Kandinsky:
   Drawing, 1923

as decisive in its way as the invention of perspective in the early years of the fifteenth century. When the artistic geniuses of that era devised their system, they at the same time dictated a particular vision of man and his place in the universe; because theirs was a collective vision, differences in individual personalities or allegiances appeared trifling in comparison. In much the same way, in 1910 all the leading artists of the day felt the shadow of the inexorable phenomenon of abstraction looming over them, never mind to what particular "ism" they belonged.

For abstraction – or non-descriptive expression – was imposed as much by the evolution of society as by the logic of artistic development. Its sole prophet among the philosophers was Wilhelm Worringer, who in his famous essay *Abstraktion und Einfühlung*, published in 1908, interpreted it as a symptom of "discord between man and nature". But it was largely because of economic, technological and scientific advances that abstraction became inevitable: quite simply, reality had become a thing beyond the scope of human perception. Reflecting this altered relationship, the Modern Style had liberated line and colour, Matisse had moved beyond Fauvism in the direction of pure painting, the Cubists abandoned illusionism and stressed the reality of the created artefact, the Futurists were preoccupied with expressing such "invisible" concepts as speed, sounds, tones and smell, the Expressionists with the projection of inward states of mind... The inevitable drift of all this was towards abstraction, which would change once and for all man's traditional relationship with his environment.

Here we touch on a point of great importance that lies outside the scope of art history proper, but which the philosopher Michel Serres has brilliantly formulated in its general application: "My body, whether I like it or not, does not function in a single and particular type of space. It does its work in Euclidian space, but that is all it does within it. It sees in projective space, it touches, caresses and manipulates in a topological spatial type, suffers in another, hears and communicates in yet a different one. And so on, *ad infinitum*... Thus my body does not function in a single space but at the complex intersection of this large genus, in the totality of connexions and accords set up between these different spatial types. That intersection is not a given, it is not, if you like, always there and always the same... For a culture, in general, constructs in and

3

4

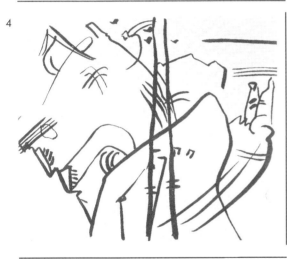

5

through its history its own intersection between such types of space, a nexus of connexion particular and specific to itself." (*L'identité*, Seminar led by Lévi-Strauss, 1977, pp. 30-31)

As the first painter to demonstrate both in terms of practice and theory the necessity and the potential of non-representative painting, Kandinsky played a decisive role. In straight pictorial terms, others had reached the same point, but it is to the Russian painter that the credit must go for inventing abstract art, since he alone developed the philosophical and ethical basis of artistic practice.

As we have mentioned, Kandinsky was inspired to make painting his career by seeing a picture by Claude Monet, which revealed to him the communicative and expressive power of colour. Studying art in Munich, he was further struck by certain ideas then current. Under the influence of Symbolism, painting had become a "subjective resonance", in which colour played a dominant role. Subject matter had waned in importance and many artists wanted to extend their skills into the realm of everyday life. Jugendstil emphasized decorative qualities above all else, and its theories cultivated a kind of abstraction, consisting in the use of certain plastic elements for their own sake, devoid of representative function. In 1903, in the famous review *Ver Sacrum,* Arthur Roessler published an article entitled "Abstrakte Ornament mit Gleichzeitiger Verwendung Simultaner Farbenkontraste". In it he put forward the idea that line was not only an element of construction, it was also an expression of emotion: "Artistic expression of an internal state is made visible in line." To prove his point, he then went on to draw numerous analogies between music and painting. Most of the leading decorative artists of the day held ideas very similar to these, creating an intellectual climate of opinion that was a crucial influence on Kandinsky.

The subsequent discovery of primitive art and Islamic culture had the effect of reinforcing the painters' interest in the emotional and ornamental qualities of the technical elements of a picture. The liberating influence of negro and Islamic art on the creative vision of the early twentieth-century painters cannot be too strongly stressed. It was in 1905 that, in France, the Fauves and Cubists first encountered negro art, at about the time the same discovery was made in Germany by the Expressionists of Die

Brücke; a major exhibition of Islamic art held in Munich in 1910 revealed to the German artists the wonders of Moslem culture. Objects previously regarded as no more than curiosities were suddenly recognized by modern painters as complex and satisfying works of art in their own right. They served to confirm a growing belief that the purpose of creation was not the making of an illusion or the description of the visible world, as Western tradition had for so long dictated. Kandinsky was as fascinated as the rest of his contemporaries by the discovery of these products of "exotic" civilizations, but the lessons he drew from the experience were not so much aesthetic as intellectual; chiefly, they confirmed him in his belief that no expression was possible unless dictated by an "inner necessity".

Kandinsky's move to Germany, in 1896, coincided with the arrival in Munich of his fellow countryman Jawlensky; the two painters found themselves attending the same studio and became firm friends. Jawlensky shared many of Kandinsky's ideas about painting but he was a more contemplative character, and remained greatly influenced by the formal simplicity and symbolism of the Byzantine icon tradition; as a result he concentrated largely on figurative representation. When the Munich Secession of 1909 rejected their submissions, the two painters joined forces with a number of friends to form a break-away movement, the *Neue Künstlervereinigung* (New Association of Artists), which held exhibitions at Tannhauser's Moderne Galerie. This group was to form the nucleus of the influential Blaue Reiter, which did not include Jawlensky. He was to develop in the direction of Expressionism and, through his repeated explorations of the human face, moved gradually towards a form of painting verging on non-figuration.

After travelling extensively in France, during the dominant period of Fauvism, from 1908 onwards Kandinsky spent much of his time in Murnau, in the Bavarian Alps. This small village was to become the focus of activity for the artists who later made up the Blaue Reiter group.

It was in Murnau that Kandinsky met Worringer, shortly after the publication of *Abstraktion und Einfühlung;* the two spent many hours in conversation, and Kandinsky was later to describe the philosopher as one of the spiritual fathers of the new painting. For Worringer, abstraction was evidence of a split be-

1. Jawlensky:
   Symphony in Black and Red,
   1929
2. Jawlensky:
   Twilight, 1916
3. Kandinsky:
   Landscape with Tower, 1908
4. Kandinsky:
   Romantic Landscape, 1911
5. Kandinsky:
   Impression IV (Gendarme), 1911

tween man and his world, whereas realism expressed a harmonious relationship between the two; he concluded that "pure abstraction is the only possibility of resolution amid the confusion and obscurity of the world of images". And, that pure abstraction would in turn engender "of itself, by an inner necessity, geometric abstraction". These were the very terms in which Kandinsky himself saw the future of abstraction. In *Concerning the Spiritual in Art,* written in Murnau circa 1910 and published in Munich in 1912, he discussed the dual nature of painting, consisting in expression and form. He recognized that: "The work of art is born of the artist in a mysterious way. Once detached from him, it acquires autonomous life, becomes an entity." But he also stated that "the artist must have something to communicate, for mastery of form is not an end in itself, that end being rather the adaptation of form to an inner expression". For him, the work of art must always be expressive, never dwindling into "a mere geometric decoration, something comparable to a carpet or a cravat".

In his Murnau landscapes, Kandinsky achieved a chromatic power unsurpassed even by the Fauves, but the links with the real world are far more tenuous, so that these pictures have a resonance that is personal and emotional more than it is visual. As painting followed painting, so Kandinsky moved closer to the expression of his central theme: the metamorphosis of life and the infinity of space. The stability of the landscapes is increasingly disrupted by a complex and seemingly infinite interpenetration of the planes; colour takes on an extraordinary significance.

1. Kandinsky:
   Lyrically, 1911
2. Kandinsky:
   Black Lines I, 1913
3. Kandinsky:
   Improvisation 26 (Rowing), 1912

In *Concerning the Spiritual in Art,* Kandinsky attempted to give a coherent exposition of his beliefs. He was a profound and original thinker, and this short text was to have a decisive influence on the avant-garde painters of the day, although, as time has distanced us, its all-pervading spiritualism sometimes makes the meaning less than clear. In a central passage Kandinsky writes: "And yet it is true that colour harbours within it a power as yet barely recognized but which is both real and evident and acts on the whole of the human body. The more so, then, can we not rely on the power of association to explain the action of colour on the soul. Colour, nevertheless, is a means of exerting a direct influence upon it. Colour is the keyboard, the eye the hammer that strikes it, the soul a many-stringed instrument. The artist, he is the hand that strikes the keyboard in this way or that to obtain the desired vibration in the soul. *Thus it is clear that the harmony of colours depends exclusively on the principle of efficacious contact.* The human soul, touched at its most sensitive point, responds. This fundamental concept, we will call the principle of inner necessity."

It was in 1908 that Kandinsky had an experience which acted as the catalyst for his determination to liberate "inner necessity" from the requirements of representation. "I broke off from my drawing, sunk in thought, and opened the door of the studio, when I found myself starkly confronted by a painting of indescribable and incandescent beauty. Stupefied, I stood rooted to the spot, fascinated by the work. The painting had no subject, it represented no identifiable object, it was uniquely composed of luminous patches of colour. At last I drew near, and it was only then I saw what it really was — a canvas of my own which was placed sideways on the easel... One thing suddenly seemed absolutely clear: objectivity, the description of objects, had no place in my canvases and was indeed detrimental to them." (Kandinsky, *Rückblicke,* 1913)

It was not until the famous watercolour of 1910 that Kandinsky found the courage to take the final step to non-objectivity. In this, the first non-figurative painting, he used forms and colours experimentally in a lyrical combination, always asking the question: if I dispose the constituent elements of painting quite arbitrarily, independently of representation, is what I am doing still painting?

3

1. Kandinsky:
   Improvisation 14, 1910
2. Kandinsky:
   Painting with a Black Arch, 1912
3. Marc:
   Genesis II, 1912
4. Marc:
   Landscape with Animals and
   Rainbow, 1911

To place the matter beyond doubt, he took the unprecedented step of allowing the final form of the work to be influenced by a degree of "automatism". The experiment proved conclusive: the validity of abstraction was established beyond question. Both practically and theoretically, he found his insights confirmed. Yet it was several months before Kandinsky was able to eliminate visual references entirely, for his work, like that of the other artists of his generation, was inspired at its very roots by a feeling for nature.

As he explained in an article published in 1913 in the review *Der Sturm,* his work was henceforth distributed between three distinct areas of experimentation, their differences reflected even in the titles given to the pictures: "1. A direct impression of external nature, I call an Impression. 2. A largely unconscious and spontaneous expression, of an internal and non-material (that is, spiritual) nature, I call an Improvisation. 3. The expression of an inner feeling, patiently formed and worked at over a long period in an almost pedantic fashion, I call a Composition. In it, logic, consciousness and a precise goal are capital elements. But there is no appearance of calculation, only of feeling... A work of art consists of two parts, the inward and the outward. The inward is the emotion of the artist's soul; this emotion has the capacity to awaken a similar emotion in the soul of the beholder. Linked to the body, the soul is accessible via the senses. The emotions are sparked off and touched by a particular sensation. That sensation therefore acts as a bridge, it is the physical link between the immate-

rial (which is the artist's emotion) and the material; from that the work of art results. And then once again, a sensation acts as the bridge between the material (the artist and his work) and the immaterial (the emotion felt by the beholder). The sequence is as follows: emotion (the artist's) ▶ sensation ▶ the work of art ▶ sensation ▶ emotion (the beholder's). The two emotions are similar and equivalent in precise ratio to the success of the work of art. And in that respect painting is no different from a song..." (*Op. cit.*)

To achieve his goal, Kandinsky devoted much patient preparation to his *Compositions,* as witness the numerous drawings and watercolours that accompany the oil paintings: the abandonment of visual objectivity in favour of inner freedom was a procedure fraught with peril, since the artist had no external reference point whatsoever and was obliged always to delve within himself. *Painting with Black Arch* is one of the most successful canvases of this lyrical period. Space here is of an unprecedented freedom and boundlessness, such that near and far elements combine in a dynamic, integrating these metamorphoses of reality within a quasi-biological rhythm. The work accentuates contrast and dissonance, celebrating the sheer complexity of the world, and at the same time it is suggestive of the equilibrium to which modern man aspires, rooted though it must be in conflict and fragmentation.

It was in 1911 that Kandinsky and Franz Marc founded the Blaue Reiter group, holding their first exhibition in December of that year at Tannhauser's gallery in Munich. Works were included by Kandinsky, Marc, Macke, Campendonck, Delaunay, Münter, the Douanier Rousseau, the Burliuk brothers and the composer Arnold Schoenberg. Klee was to join the group soon afterwards, and is referred to in the celebrated *Almanach* of the Blaue Reiter, published by Kandinsky and Marc in 1912.

Folk art and primitive or naïf painting were held in particular esteem, as being the forerunner of nondescriptive expression. In the preface to the second edition of the *Almanach,* Franz Marc wrote the following: "We have gone with a dowser's twig through the art of the past and present. We have shown only art that lived unaffected by the constraints of convention. Our love and attention were directed to any kind of artistic expression that was born of itself, living by its own merits and not relying on the crutch of custom.

1. Kandinsky:
   Study for the alamanac of Der Blaue Reiter, 1911
2. Kandinsky:
   The Last Judgement, 1912
3. Marc:
   Bull Resting, 1913
4. Klee:
   Composition 1914
5. Klee:
   View of the Harbour at Hammamet, 1914

Every time we discovered a crack in convention, we drew attention to it, because we wanted to discover the power that lay behind it, and which one day will come to light."

The name "Blue Rider" arose more or less by chance. "We both liked blue, Marc liked horses and I liked riders," Kandinsky was to recall in 1930. The group's artistic philosophy was based on the ideas already outlined in Kandinsky's book: "Painting in the present day finds itself in a new situation. It is in the course of liberating itself from a narrow dependence on 'nature'. Yet its emancipation has barely begun. If colour and form have already been used as agents of internal reality, up until now that has been largely unconscious. The ancient arts, as in Persia, knew and practised the surbordination of colour to geometric form. But building on a purely spiritual base is a task that will take time. It begins gropingly, proceeds by chance. The painter must not only educate his eye, he must above all render his soul capable of weighing colour on subtle scales, summoning up all its resources so that, on the day the work of art comes into being, it will be in a position not only to receive external impressions (and naturally, at times, to give birth to internal impressions as well), but also to act as the ultimate arbiter... We can say with certainty that we are but a short step away from pure composition."

By taking itself as its own subject, art no longer needed any justification beyond that supplied by its inherent capabilities; it rejected once and for all the notion of serving as a mirror to anything external. Kandinsky, by progressively eliminating figurative references in his own work, had pointed the way ahead for his colleagues in the Blaue Reiter, who declared: "The artist has not only the right but the duty to manipulate forms in the manner he judges necessary to attain his ends."

Schoenberg's contribution to the Blaue Reiter's activities is worth noting. Although he was an amateur painter, it was as a composer that his influence was felt, for, as we have seen, the non-descriptive art of music was regarded as the theoretical model for the liberation of painting. That is one of the recurring themes in Kandinsky's writings, and it was he who invited the musician to contribute to the *Almanach*. Schoenberg's article includes the following categorical statement: "One should concentrate on the effect a work of art is designed to produce, and not

3

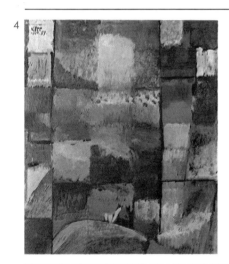

4

5

on whatever it may be that furnishes its pretext. The exact reproduction of events adds nothing to the aesthetic value of music composed after a poem, any more than the resemblance to the model adds to the value of a portrait, since no witnesses will remain after a century has elapsed to attest to that resemblance, whereas the artistic effect will survive indefinitely."

The measure of agreement that existed between Schoenberg and Kandinsky is itself instructive, as an illustration of the way new ideas are assimilated in the various branches of the arts simultaneously; Schoenberg's revolutionary influence on music was quite as decisive as Kandinsky's on painting.

It was in the months preceding the outbreak of the 1914-18 War that Kandinsky reached the height of his period of lyrical expression. Not long afterwards, Franz Marc, writing from the trenches only shortly before he was killed, gave the following account of his development as an artist: "Very early in life I already found man ugly, and animals seemed to me cleaner and more beautiful. But even in them I discovered much that was unacceptable and ugly, so that my art instinctively became... increasingly schematic and abstract." (in Myers, *Expressionism*, 1967) For Paul Klee, liberation came about during a trip to Tunisia where: "Colour has taken hold of me; no longer do I have to chase after it. I know that it has hold of me for ever. That is the significance of this blessed moment. Colour and I are one... I am a painter." (in Read, *op. cit.*) Not until that moment did the artist feel he had in his power the means to translate his intentions into painting: "Still more important than the primary vision remains the reality of form for which the true artist must struggle again and again. Form often develops of its own free will and strives to dominate with ever-increasing authority. Only with great effort can the artist control it. This is a real fight demanding strength and sound nerves. For a long time I could work but little, because the discord between first vision and ultimate expression was too strong to be overcome. I had to wait and wait — this was most difficult. Although it was painful, I preferred to do nothing until the purity of the form was assured and the picture tore at me..." (in Myers, *op. cit.*) It was the discovery of colour that liberated Klee — enabling him to produce rather than merely reproduce. "Art does not render the visible; rather it makes visible." (in Read, *op. cit.*)

CHAPTER 4
THE RUSSIANS AND THE
ABSENCE OF THE OBJECT

Although Kandinsky was the first to commit himself definitively to non-objective painting, his canvases were still rooted in the emotions and sensations elicited by nature. The confirmation of fully realized abstraction was to be achieved in Russia, Kandinsky's native country, where the avant-gardes ruled the day. In the past, Czarist autocracy had done little to encourage the individual creative artist, and it was not until the 1900s that a number of painters achieved a certain prominence, with the backing of discerning patrons. What brought new life to their work was the renewal of their links with the Russian tradition, of icon painting and popular decorative motifs, which had the same liberating effect on them as negro art on the Fauves, the Cubists and the Expressionists. A comparable boldness in the reinterpretation of tradition lay behind the triumph of Diaghilev's Ballets Russes and Stravinsky's music. In the pre-revolutionary ferment of the period leading up to October 1917, no field of human activity was untouched by the passion for radical reform.

Thanks to the activities of two collectors, Morosov and Shchukin, Russia also enjoyed a marvellous perspective on the international scene. Before the war, Shchukin alone owned 40 Matisses and 51 Picassos — and these phenomenal collections were freely accessible to the painters of the day. It is paradoxical that at this time it was easier to see avant-garde art in Moscow than in either Paris or Munich! Such patrons as these also smoothed the path of Russians travelling to the West by providing introductions to the most advanced painters. It was in this way that Tatlin saw

Malevich:
Yellow Suprematism, 1917

49

1. Larionov:
   Rayonism, 1912
2. Goncharova:
   Rayonism, 1917
3. Malevich:
   Suprematist Painting, Black
   Rectangle, Blue Triangle, 1915
4. Malevich:
   First exhibition of Suprematist
   paintings, Petrograd, 1915
5. Malevich:
   Suprematism no. 50, 1916

Picasso's first assemblages, even before they were exhibited. Intellectually, Russia was no longer isolated. Whether via returning political exiles or by other routes, all the new ideas were rapidly relayed to Moscow and St. Petersburg; there they were seized on eagerly, torn apart and reformulated with an apparently insatiable enthusiasm. In Russia more than anywhere else, creation became synonymous with originality and change; at the same time, an ingrained habit of intellectual rigour led to theoretical advances of sweeping radicalism.

The painter Mikhail Larionov and his companion Natalia Goncharova were the founding spirits of the first Russian avant-garde, which drew on the more revolutionary features of Cubism and Futurism. In 1913, on the occasion of the Moscow exhibition "The Target", they published the *Rayonist Manifesto,* in which they announced their programme: "It was necessary to find a starting point where painting, while retaining real life as a stimulus, could develop fully into itself." Taking pure colour as the "governing law", they concentrated on the expression of emptiness and space. The previous year, Boccioni had issued the following pronouncement: "Each object influences its neighbour not by reflections of light (the foundation of Impressionist primitivism) but by a real clash of lines and real struggles between the planes, according to the emotional law that governs the picture." In their declaration of 1913, Larionov and Goncharova extended this notion to include the perception of blank space and interval: "The style of Rayonist painting... has as its objective the spatial forms that result from the intersection of the reflected rays emanating from various objects and forms selected by the artist. Conventionally, a ray is represented by a coloured line. The essence of painting resides in a combination of colours reaching to the point of saturation, in the relationship of coloured masses and in the intensity of the ensemble."

Larionov's forceful personality and incisive ideas attracted the attention of Malevich and Tatlin. At this time Malevich was painting primitive mechanical figures, rather in the manner of Léger; yet, in that same year of 1913, while designing the sets for the Futurist opera *Victory over the Sun,* he produced his famous *Black Square on a White Ground,* the prototype of Suprematist painting.

The theory of Suprematism was made public in

December 1915 on the occasion of the exhibition "0.10", organized by Puni in Petrograd. Malevich showed 35 paintings and also distributed a pamphlet containing his manifesto, *From Cubism and Futurism to Suprematism. The New Pictorial Realism*. It was a historic moment: the idea of abstraction had been completely turned around. Where previously it had been seen as a process of reduction, laying bare the essentials of elements drawn from the visible world, now, with Malevich, abstraction was presented as a self-sufficient truth, capable of being developed in hitherto inconceivable directions.

As Malevich himself later wrote, the square he exhibited was not a "square but the experience of the absence of the object". In so saying, he effectively crossed a frontier at which many of his contemporaries had stopped short. Leaving behind "the world of purposefulness and representation", he opened up new horizons, "where nothing else will be authentic except sensibility alone". In the exhibition manifesto he stressed this point, right at the outset: "Sensibility is the only thing that counts and it is by this route that art, and therefore Suprematism, will achieve pure expression devoid of representation. Art arrives at a 'desert' where nothing recognizable remains except sensibility. The Suprematist square and the forms that have developed out of it may be compared with the signs made by primitive man..."

As Malevich recognized in 1920, it was the renunciation of the figurative that enabled him to give free rein to his intuitive powers: "Intuition brings you closer to the creative principle, but to attain it you are obliged to rid yourself of the figurative, you must create new signs and hand over the concern with figuration to the new art of photography and film. As for us, we must create in the same way as in the rest of our technological life. Having achieved the complete annihilation of the figurative in art, we will take the creative course of creating new formations, we will put behind us all that juggling with objects on the tightrope of art." (*From Cézanne to Suprematism*)

The victory over representation barely achieved, a flood of tracts, pamphlets and manifestos poured forth; these were so violent and extreme that even the traditional relationship of theory to practice was stood on its head. In a Russia seething with revolutionary fervour, the idea came first, a theoretical goal was pre-set that severely restricted the experimental

freedom of "praxis". Subjected to these "maximalist" theories, artists were in the end condemned to produce nothing, for it was not long before the idea was seen as an actual substitute for the artefact. Long afterwards, Gabo recalled this time with bitterness: "full of painful and rather tragic experiences." Initially committed to revolutionary change and co-author with his brother of the *Realist Manifesto* of 1920, he left for Germany in 1922.

By eradicating all reference to nature, Malevich opened up a whole host of possibilities which other artists were not slow to recognize. Many of these later developments were already implicit in the 1915 manifesto: "Creation exists only where form appears in the picture that takes nothing from what has been created in nature but derives from pictorial masses, neither repeating nor modifying the primary forms of objects in nature." One of the most perceptive chroniclers of the period was Nikolaï Tarabukin, who quickly saw the implications of this radical change of viewpoint: "While the old art, from Naturalism to primitive Cubism, is a 'representative' art, characterized by the link that exists between the pictorial forms and those in the real external world, the new art breaks this connexion, this dependent relationship, and creates autonomous objects... Art is 'fabrication', action, not a question of knowledge but of individual choice, for it establishes the primacy of creation over knowledge. The painter's vocation is not to 'represent' the things of the external world but to shape, make and create objects. It is not a 'representative' art but a 'constructive' art. It is this spontaneous impulse that distinguishes art from science, elevating intuition above all else." (*Towards a Theory of Painting*, 1916)

By limiting space to the surface of the canvas, and applying to it nothing but elementary forms and pure colours, Malevich effectively returned painting to its beginnings. As he wiped the past clean, he seized: "the world from the hands of nature, in order to create another of which man was master... Reproducing objects and little nooks of nature which have taken one's fancy, that is like a thief admiring his fettered legs. Only obtuse and impotent painters conceal their art with a mask of sincerity. In art, what you need is not sincerity but truth. Objects have vanished with the advent of a new artistic culture. Art progresses towards autonomy of creation, the domination of the forms of nature." (*Manifesto*, 1915)

1. Kliun:
   Untitled, 1916
2. Malevich:
   Suprematism, 1915-16
3. Tatlin:
   Synthetico-Static Composition,
   1914-15
4. Tatlin:
   Non-objective Composition, 1916

3

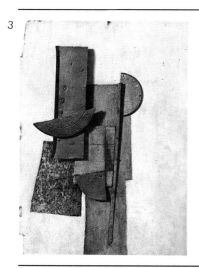

4

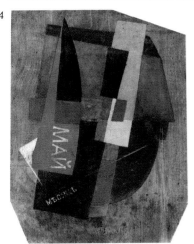

The race for novelty was such that Malevich himself was soon swept aside. His differences with Tatlin were already evident at the time of the "0.10" exhibition in Petrograd. Tatlin was showing his counter-reliefs, "real materials in real space", and had no desire to be taken for one of Malevich's disciples, who he attacked for resorting to the "fiction" of painting. These counter-reliefs were not so much paintings as assemblages, which existed in real space, and whose forms and colours were directly borrowed from reality. Tarabukin explains: "It is the material that dictates the form to the artist, and not the other way about. Wood, iron, glass, etc. impose different constructions. Consequently, a constructivist organization of the object is arrived at via the material..." (*Towards a Theory of Painting,* 1916)

A new concept brought in its train a new movement and a new name; through working on constructions of this type Tatlin evolved the theory of Constructivism, abandoning the flat picture plane and the materials specific to painting, rejecting the *abstraction* of painting in favour of the *construction* of reality itself. Tatlin's counter-reliefs marked the dissolution of the traditional genres and above all signalled a new synthesis of the arts and life, to be achieved through what he called Productivism. Once again we turn to Tarabukin for elucidation, in his famous text of 1923, *From the Easel to the Machine*: "If, in the past, the visual arts fell neatly into three typical categories — painting, sculpture and architecture — now, in the crucial counter-relief, in constructions possessed of volume, in 'spatial painting', we have an attempt to synthesize these categories. In the above, the artist combines the architectonics of the construction of material masses (architecture), the volumetric constructivity of these masses (sculpture) and their expressivity of colour, texture and composition (painting). It would seem that in these constructions the artist may regard himself as entirely liberated from the illusionism of representativeness, since he does not reproduce reality in them, but presents the object as an entirely autonomous value..., that is to say, as much by the forms as by the construction and the materials he employs, the artist brings into being an authentically real object."

It was at the "Magazine" exhibition of 1916 that Rodchenko first came to prominence; his three line drawings, done with the aid of compasses, were enthusiastically received by the more seasoned con-

1. Exter:
   Non-objective Composition, 1918
2. Popova:
   Non-objective Composition,
   c. 1916

tributors. Not sharing Malevich's idealism, he allied himself with Tatlin, coming to be regarded as one of the bolder spirits of the Constructivist movement, and later an influential exponent of Productivism.

Among the Russian avant-gardes we notice now for the first time a substantial number of women. Apart from Goncharova and Sonia Terk, who married Delaunay, there are also Alexandra Exter, Varvara Stepanova, Olga Rozanova and Liubov Popova, all highly original creative artists. Of particular note are the latter's paintings of 1917 onwards, dynamic compositions in which the form/colours are rendered with the utmost purity.

Colour was central to the Russian imagination. Malevich declared "the coloured surface is the real living form", and in 1919, in a manifesto published to coincide with the Tenth State Exhibition, held in Moscow, he went on to develop that idea: "Suprematism may be defined as a method that allows colour to pursue its long course of growth. Painting is born of a mix of colours, of the transformation of colour, in the crucible of aesthetics, a chaotic brew. With the great painters of the past, objects were used as the source of painting. I have discovered that he who most nearly approached the phenomenon that is 'painting' was that artist who was most successful in making objects lose their identity, by breaking them up, in this way arriving at another order of conformity to the laws of painting. It is becoming clear to me that the new sources of pure painting in colour need to be such that they respond to the demands of colour alone. Secondly, I have realized that colour should no longer be a pictorial mix, but must tend towards the condition of being an independent unity, part of a collective system yet still individually independent. A system creates itself in time and in space, without any recourse to the canons of aesthetics, or experimentation, or the various modes. It is more what one might call a philosophical ensemble of colour, which takes in my new ideas as they occur and combines them in a coherent scheme." This manifesto effectively sums up Malevich's pictorial legacy, a progression through colour that led back finally to white itself, the origin of all the colours. It was at this exhibition of 1919 that he showed his famous *White Square on a White Ground,* both a supreme and dignified act of pure painting, and at the same time the expression of a limit beyond which it was impossible to go...

And yet Rodchenko did just that. At the same exhibition he showed a *Black on Black*: "My period of growth began with the demolition of all the 'isms' hitherto known to painting," he was to say. "It is to the tolling of the passing-bell for colour painting that we now bear to its resting place the last of the 'isms'; all last requests and love itself go up in a puff of smoke, and me, I leave behind me the season of dead truths." (in *Rodchenko,* German Karginov, 1975). There was only one last step to be taken, one last frontier to cross, and this Rodchenko did at the exhibition "5 × 5 = 25", where he showed three monochromes, in red, blue and yellow. In the catalogue he described his revolutionary career: "1918: at the exhibition 'Non-Objective Creation and Suprematism', I first presented spatial constructions, and in painting, *Black on Black.* 1920: at the State exhibition no. 14, I first presented *Line*, as a factor of construction. 1921: in this exhibition are presented for the first time the three pure colours of art." It was, as Tarabukin at once recognized, the death of painting. At a conference he convened on 20 August of that year, under the title "The Last Picture", he declared that non-objective art had reached its critical breaking point, that of the absolute purity of the painting material; all that remained was to discover the consequences of attaining this absolute by which the act of painting was condemned. These consequences he later examined in his analysis of the evolution of Constructivism. "Every time the painter has tried to rid himself entirely of representation, it has been at the price of the destruction of painting and his own suicide as a painter. I am thinking of a canvas recently shown by Rodchenko... This is not a stage, that will be followed by other stages, it is the last step, the final step in a long progress, it is the last word, after which painting must be silent, the last 'picture' executed by a painter. But the death of painting, the end of easel painting, does not mean the death of all art. Art continues to live, not as a determinate form but as a creative force." (*From the Easel to the Machine*, 1923)

In *From Cézanne to Suprematism,* published in 1920, Malevich made his position clear: for him, abandoning the figurative system was a means of rediscovering the universal qualities of man, once he was liberated from "nature and the elemental forces, so that they no longer plagued him with disaster and anxiety". He went on: "I strive to overcome the ele-

1

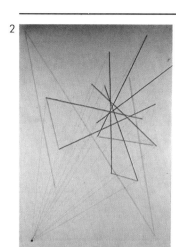

2

3

mental forces in humanity, for humanity is a thousand times more powerful and disruptive than the elemental forces of nature; my goals are fraternity and unity, so that through fraternity and unity I shall achieve calm and plenitude."

But for Tatlin, Rodchenko and their Productivist colleagues, painting no longer provided an effective means of shaping the sensibility of the new man; art had to become part of life. They no longer wanted to paint but to construct everyday reality: cities, houses, domestic objects. They wanted to influence men by their example, reflected everywhere, offer mankind a new equilibrium founded on a notion of egalitarianism that did not exclude tension or contrast. Rodchenko declared: "The artist of our day is the man who knows how to organize his life, his work and himself. You have to work for life, not for palaces, churches, cemeteries and museums..." The critic Alexei Gan took up the theme, in 1920: "A communist town, as conceived of by the Constructivists, is a first attempt towards an organization of human consciousness, the first step towards a clear notion of collective property. The time for pure applied art is passed. It has been superseded by an age of social experiment. We will bring into being the utilitarian object, in a form appropriate and acceptable to all. Nothing will occur by chance, nothing will be accidental." By achieving abstraction, and building on that achievement, the Russian Constructivists succeeded, most certainly, in supplying art with a new function beyond representation... but in so doing they destroyed the very justification of painting itself.

Mondrian:
Composition in a Square with Red,
Yellow and Blue, 1921-25

CHAPTER 5
MONDRIAN AND
DENATURALIZATION

An account of Mondrian's development as an artist is like a summary of all the stages that led up to abstraction, starting with early Cubism and ending with Russian Suprematism. In 1909, as a young Symbolist painter, Mondrian joined the Theosophical Society in Amsterdam, seeking an explanation of the world that was intellectually as well as emotionally convincing. Like Kandinsky, he believed creation should express a spiritual message. His intuitive faith in an eternal order received confirmation in the theories of the Theosophist Schoenmaekers, of whom he became a disciple. It could have been Mondrian himself who wrote: "We want to penetrate nature to the point that the innate pattern of reality is revealed to us." Or again: "However lively and capricious it may appear in its variations, basically nature functions always with absolute regularity." This search for underlying patterns was gradually to lead Mondrian away from a form of representation that still echoed the real world, and towards the exploration in his art of a more fundamental unity. By the time he saw an exhibition of the paintings of Cézanne and the Cubists, held in Amsterdam in October 1911, he was already receptive to their message.

"After several years my work unconsciously began to deviate more and more from the natural aspects of reality. Experience was my only leader; I knew little of the modern movement." (Mondrian, *Towards the True Vision of Reality,* 1941). But once that crucial encounter had taken place, he knew he had to go to Paris. Cézanne and the Cubists pointed him in the direction of pure construction; nevertheless he had

1. Mondrian:
   Still Life with Ginger Jar II, 1912
2. Mondrian:
   Apple Tree in Blossom, 1912
3. Mondrian:
   Composition with Lines, 1917

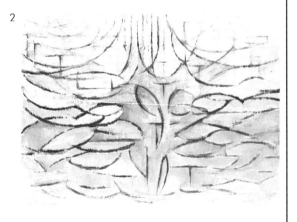

his reservations: "This desire of the Cubists to represent volumes in space was contrary to my conception of abstraction, which is rooted in the belief that the said space must be destroyed. That is how I arrived at the idea of utilizing planes." From systematic transformations of landscapes, he moved towards variations of pure plastic elements, gradually eliminating any visual reference that interfered with the final structure. No longer was it a question of painting a tree, a pier or a bell-tower, but of constructing an order that transcended nature and at the same time expressed its universal harmony. Starting out from a type of Analytical Cubism, Mondrian worked towards constructions where the subject — though still there — was no longer identifiable, was indeed no longer related to its final form by a logical sequence of transformations. Whatever the original motif that served as an initial pretext, the end result was always a geometric structure, illustrating an idea of Schoenmaekers: "We now learn to translate reality in our imagination into constructions which can be controlled by reason, in order to recover these same constructions later in 'given' natural reality, thus penetrating nature by means of plastic vision." (in Jaffé, *De Stijl*, 1956)

During this phase of simplification, Mondrian reduced the universe to a fundamental opposition between verticality (the expression of purpose) and horizontality (the symbol of repose). This contrast was multiplied many times over, so that it occupied the whole surface of the canvas, reflecting Mondrian's belief that the principle held true throughout the whole of the universe and not merely up to the line of the horizon separating the plane of the earth from that of the sky. To make his intentions even more clear, he moved away from a topographical view to "close-ups". When he returned to Holland at the outbreak of war, Mondrian pursued his quest for elemental reality. Finally he concluded that, whatever subject he started with, the outcome was the same. And since the simplified form of any motif was, in plastic terms, identical, the obvious next step was to abandon any reproductive function of the picture and experiment with the elements that constituted the image itself. In the series of *Blacks and Whites* of 1917, in which he experimented with vertical-horizontal oppositions, he started out from the belief that the plane of the canvas was a reality. It followed that the surface to be paint-

3

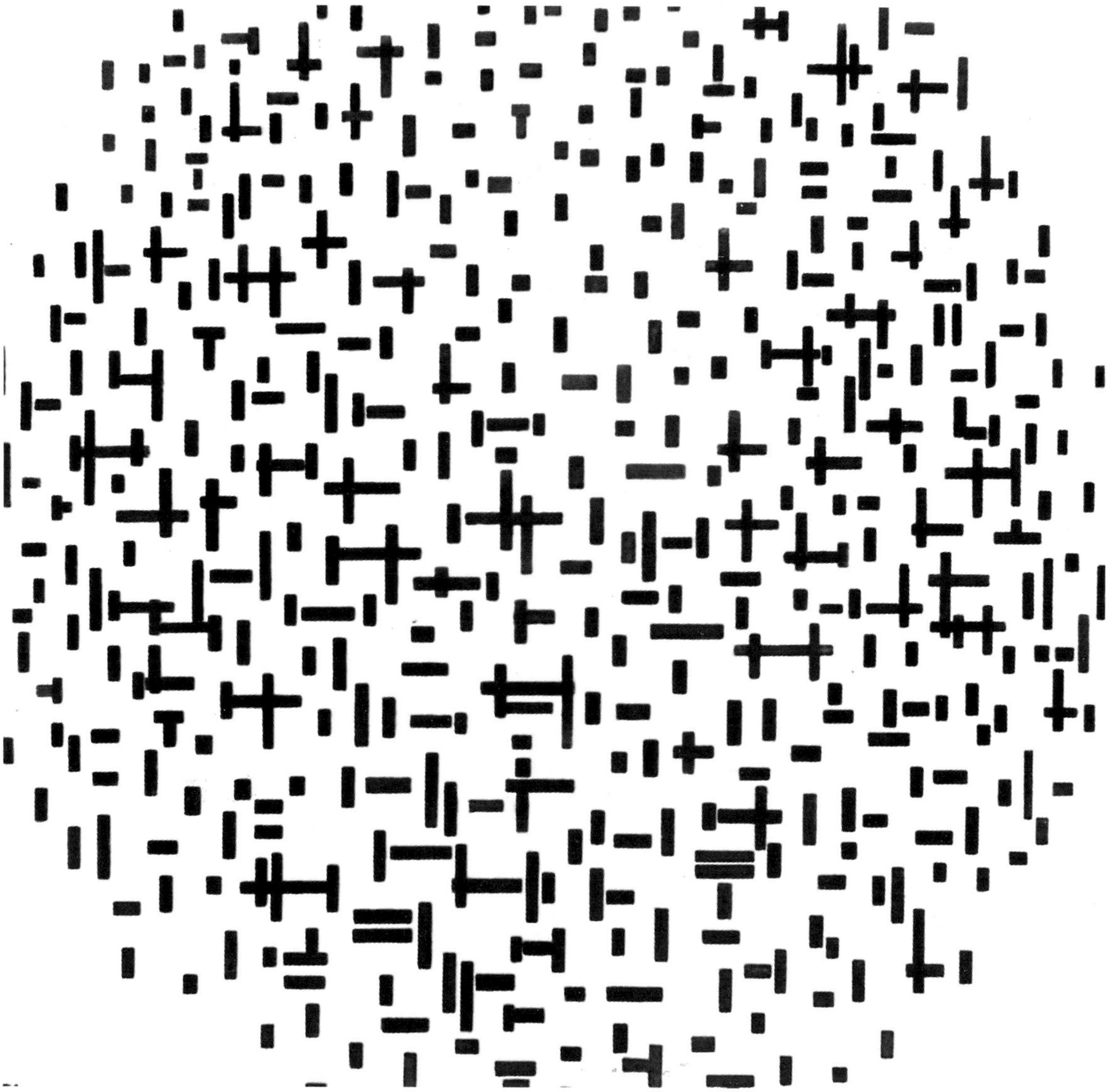

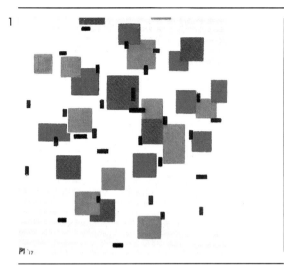

PM '17

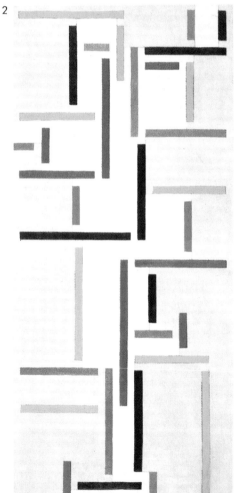

ed defined the size of the elements within it. But the surface, whether in a non-colour (black or white) or, as later, in a tone of pure colour, itself produced a particular effect, seeming either to advance or recede, so that it actually destroyed the plastic unity.

Seeking to re-create an equilibrium out of his oppositions, Mondrian experimented systematically with the different effects that could be obtained from coloured surfaces, sometimes enclosing them, sometimes not; in so doing, he moved from an almost infinite subdivision of the surface to compositions that concentrated on just a few elements. Neo-Plasticism was the name he gave to this search for a "painting that demands nothing but the expression of the relationships between line and colour".

Back in Holland, Mondrian joined forces with van Doesburg, an active publicist as well as a painter, poet and architect, and with Bart van der Leck. Together they founded the review *De Stijl*, which appeared in October 1917, and which was subsequently to publish most of Mondrian's theoretical essays. According to Seuphor (*Le Style et le Cri*, 1953), all three shared the belief that: "a work of art should arise in a collective spirit and aim at the integration of the various disciplines. It should henceforward be present in everyday life, conceived of as a synthesis of the plastic arts." Thus, although starting from very different premises, the Dutch painters of De Stijl had the same desire as the Russian Constructivists to transform the traditional values of art, substituting construction for lyricism, machines for workers, and collectivism for individualism.

Like the Russians, by 1922, Mondrian saw the painting of the past in the light of a laboratory experiment, made necessary by circumstances but no longer justified: "Plastic equilibrium can foster the plenitude of humankind and become the goal of art. To an extent, art has already begun its own destruction, and indeed the end is in sight. The regeneration of art by life is no longer possible, another kind of art is needed for our times... With the old materials, we cannot build a new art..."

After eliminating all reference external to painting itself, Mondrian concentrated purely on effects of line, surface and colour. From 1919, the white background plays an architectural role, and line organizes the surfaces, while the relationship of occupied to empty space is the material expression of that "equilib-

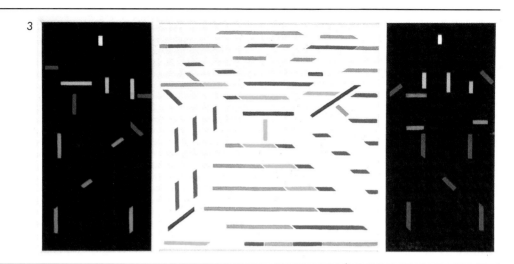

3

1. Mondrian:
   Composition in Colour A, 1917
2. Van Doesburg:
   Rhythms of a Russian Dance,
   1918
3. Van der Leck:
   Composition 1916-4
   (Mine Triptych), 1916
4. Mondrian:
   Composition. Checkerboard,
   Bright Colours, 1919

4

rium of duality" which was the ultimate goal of Mondrian's work.

As the painting surfaces grew larger, so they began to call in question the frame that defined the surface. Marcellin Pleynet (*L'enseignement de la peinture*, 1971) makes the point: "If colour is matter, and white is emptiness, what remains of the object (or picture) but an architectural structure — which however allows its objectivity to be compromised by being encroached upon by the very space it is its function to mark, in short, losing its autonomy by being placed in a relative situation." In other words, as the constituent elements — which echo the shape of the frame — extend outwards, so the picture is overrun by its content, for its edge slices arbitrarily across surfaces in such a way that in your mind's eye you extend these surfaces. It is in the *Compositions in Diamond Shape* that this reversal of normal pictorial status is most apparent. In works of this type, the orthogonal rhythm (vertical-horizontal), on which Mondrian was now to concentrate, is set up in contrast to the frame, which cuts diagonally across it and cannot therefore enclose it, so that the beholder is encouraged to push it out in his mind beyond its material limits. If previously painting had condensed the reality of the external world within the dimensions of its frame, now in Mondrian's work, the constituent elements dictated the organization of the containing space, forcing it out beyond its limits. This effect is particularly marked where Mondrian, obedient to the inner logic of his work, utilizes only a small number of complementary elements.

1. Mondrian:
   Composition with Yellow Lines,
   1922
2. Van der Leck:
   Composition, 1918-20
3. Van Doesburg:
   Arithmetic Composition, 1930

Mondrian saw it as the goal of art to liberate man from the disorders of the world, by means of "denaturalization". Today it is hard to comprehend the almost blind hatred he felt for anything to do with the representation of the natural world. It was a hatred born out of the unyielding mystical beliefs he referred to in numerous articles. For example, in the *Cahiers d'Art* of September 1926: "And so composition in the style of natural appearance had to be abandoned in painting, so that it could become a truly new painting. Through continuous hard work, an arrangement was arrived at that was a composition based exclusively on the *equilibrium of pure relationships,* derived from *pure intuition,* brought about by the union of an intensified sensibility with a superior intelligence. Although these relationships in nature and in our spirit are created according to the same universal laws and principles, *in our time* the work of art manifests itself differently from nature. Because, in our time, in the work of art we must attempt to express what is essential in nature, and what is universal in man."

In 1926, Mondrian quarrelled with van Doesburg, who had recently published a manifesto in *De Stijl* in praise of the line rotated through an angle of 45°. For Mondrian, this represented a dynamism tantamount to "natural appearances", and was a purely frivolous form of expression. He was moved to write the following: "Denaturalization being one of the essential factors of human progress, it is therefore of absolutely capital importance in Neo-Plasticism... To denature is to abstract. Through abstraction is obtained pure and abstract expression. To denature is to intensify. Denaturalization occurs both consciously and unconsciously. Proof of the latter is provided by the development of fashion; do we not see clothes assuming a shape that is not only more pure but also in direct contrast with nature? And cosmetics, do they not prove the disgust we feel for the natural flesh?" Sweepingly, he concluded: "And man? Nothing in himself, he will be but one part of the whole, and when he has lost the vanity of his insignificant and petty individuality, he will be happy in the Eden he has created." (*Le Home, la Rue, la Cité,* 1926)

Immured in his beliefs, Mondrian lived through the war years without any trace of these terrible events being reflected in his work.

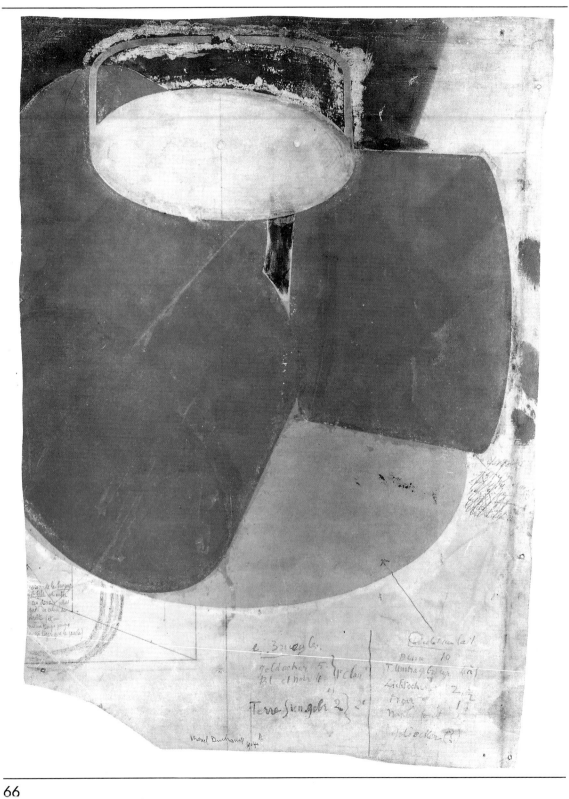

CHAPTER 6
THE ABSTRACTIONS
OF DADA

Marcel Duchamp said: "I regard painting as a means of expression, not as an end in itself. One means of expression among many, not something destined to take up your whole life." That effectively sums up the attitude of the Dadaists to abstract art: only one weapon among the many available to their moral crusade against Western civilization. If anything they tended to have a distrust of painting. Breton wrote of Duchamp: "The practice of drawing and painting seems a fool's game to him: it leads to a stupid glorification of the hand at the expense of everything else... It's the hand that's really the culprit, and how can you accept being enslaved to your own hand? It is unthinkable that drawing and painting should still occupy the same position today as handwriting did before Gutenberg. In the circumstances, all we can do is unlearn how to paint and how to draw. Duchamp has never been in any two minds about that since." ("Phare de la Mariée", *Minotaure* no. 6, 1935)

In the end concerned not so much to destroy art as the accepted idea of art, the purposes for which it was used and the values attributed to it, the Dadaists — whether in New York or Zurich — were characterized by their refusal to adopt a style and the desire to find novel means of expression. At a time when the avant-gardes were espousing abstraction as a means of asserting the autonomy of art, they sometimes seemed bent only on achieving its humiliation. All that counted for the Dadaists was liberation from the old restraints and traditions. But because abstraction represented a new and revolutionary approach, they

Duchamp:
Study for the Chocolate Grinder, no. 2, 1914

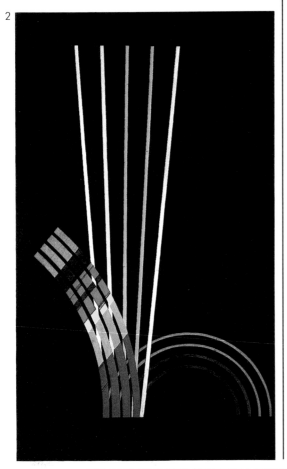

were prepared to make use of it, in their own terms, to "sweep away and clean up the debris in the great task of destruction that lies ahead", to quote Tzara in the *Dada Manifesto* of 1918.

Dada was essentially a way of life, the expression of an anarchic spontaneity, founded in a desire for rebellion, a hatred for and denunciation of conventional attitudes. Huelsenbeck was among the fiercest of these rebels: "The Dadaist should be a man who has fully understood that one has no right to have ideas unless one knows how to put them into practice – a genius of action, who lives only by doing, because he knows that is the means by which he will achieve knowledge." (*En avant Dada,* 1920) It is to the Dadaists that we can trace back that recurrent opposition in contemporary art, between those who express themselves through art and those who use art as a weapon to transform man and society...

We have already discussed how Marcel Duchamp and Picabia used drawings of machines as ironic condemnations of illusionism. Duchamp was later to move on to a full-frontal attack on representation through his experiments with "trompe-l'œil" – which he translated into a sort of deception of the mind and the senses. Hitherto the lines of debate had been drawn between illusionism and abstraction; the Dadaists complicated matters by introducing a fourth dimension of their own, that of psychological reality, an elusive phenomenon so neglected and suppressed by civilization and custom that it had all but withered away; the liberation of that faculty was one of the goals of the Dadaists and Surrealists.

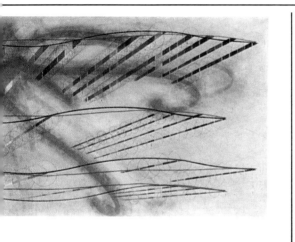

1. Duchamp:
   You-Me (Tu m'), 1918
2. Picabia:
   Music is Like Painting, 1914-17
3. Picabia:
   Hydraulic Press, 1921-22

3 PRESSE HYDRAULIQUE

Francis Picabia

Picabia has explained that the key to his mechanical assemblies lies in the substitution of the subjective for the visual: "All our desire and our need to project ourselves, all our subjective impulses, can be expressed in hundreds of different ways, but to express these desires we need to find a medium of absolute formal purity, and, in painting, it is impossible for form to suggest any resemblance to an abstract idea: it is left in a state of cosmic suspension, with a hidden significance that exists just between ourselves. In the first place we create objectivity and then we superimpose our subjective intent; so that our work then becomes the mental and metaphysical expression of the external world — that is to say, it becomes a living object in its own right, possessed of its own expression. In my work the title is the subjective expression, the painting is the object. And yet this object is up to a point subjective, since it is the imitation, the outward appearance of the title..." Picabia's titles, indeed, are never tautologies, they always supply a meaning or an ironic twist to the appearance of something that, in itself, is no more than an abstract construction, a travesty of reality. Abstraction there is, but not where one has become accustomed to look for it.

As far as Duchamp was concerned, the only way he could liberate himself from the image was by abandoning painting altogether. In his last canvas, *You-Me,* painted in 1918, he subtly introduced elements of illusion, or allusion, suggesting the presence of a fourth dimension. To quote William Rubin (*Dada and Surrealist Art*): "Duchamp explains very simply that if a shadow is a two-dimensional projection of a three-dimensional form, then a three-dimensional object must itself be the projection of a four-dimensional form. The most ordinary object thus holds the possibility of an epiphany; given the right insight into its nature, one need only single out the object and detach it from its ordinary context to make manifest its meanings." After this last painting, Duchamp worked exclusively with transposed objects or non-painted images (such as the *Rotoreliefs*).

Man Ray, who regarded himself as Duchamp's closest friend, appears to stress the role of intuition, being more concerned with the act of producing the work than with its ultimate aesthetic effect. From drawing pictures of machines, he moved on to the invention of a painting machine. It is him we have to thank for introducing the spray-gun or pistol-painting into

1. Man Ray:
   The Rope Dancer Accompanies
   Herself with Her Shadows, 1918
2. Arp:
   Dada Collage, 1918
3. Arp:
   Enak's Tears (Terrestrial Forms),
   1917
4. Arp:
   Travel Kit of a Da, 1920
5. Max Ernst:
   Dadaville, 1923-24

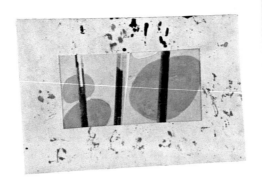

the realm of serious art. With the aid of these tools he created some novel effects of monochrome; but they also brought into play the element of chance, so raising much the same questions as projections. Man Ray was a first-rate publicist, and it was his experience in advertising that gave him the idea of using the spray-gun. In *Self-Portrait,* the autobiography he wrote in 1963, he looks back to the genesis of *The Rope Dancer*: "I worked in gouache on tinted or white cardboards — the results were astonishing — they had a photographic quality, although the subjects were anything but figurative or rather, I'd start with a definite subject, something I had seen — nudes, an interior, a ballet with Spanish dancers, or even some old miscellaneous objects lying about which I used as stencils, but the result was always a more abstract pattern. It was thrilling to paint a picture, hardly touching the surface. A purely cerebral act, as it were."

If the Dadaists arrived by routes such as these at abstraction, it was abstraction of a very different kind from what had gone before; reliant on chance rather than considered construction, the picture became not so much a statement as a revelation of the unknown. The Dadaists, and later the Surrealists, made use of many different forms and techniques, but the underlying purpose of their work remained always the same, to bring to light a hidden face of reality.

Hans Arp, for example, was the originator of a whole genre of forms that find particular favour today. Exiled to Zurich during the War, and deeply affected by the wholesale destruction, he rejected the supposedly "rational" view of the world that had led Europe into a terrible conflict. Since cultural attitudes had created the war, it was culture itself that had to be reformed: "Revolted by the butchery of the Great War of 1914, we in Zurich devoted ourselves to the service of the Arts. While the cannons boomed in the distance, we put all our efforts into singing, painting, making collages and writing poems. We were looking for an art of elementals that would cure man of the folly of the times, for a new order that would restore the balance between heaven and hell." (Richter, *Dada,* 1964)

Collage, the technique invented by the Cubists, supplied the Dadaists with the means of liberating themselves from past traditions. But with Arp in particular, it took on an additional dimension of abstrac-

tion, or at the very least became divorced from figurative reference. Relying on his intuition, reacting spontaneously, welcoming chance inventions, Arp soon arrived at those characteristic biomorphic forms so welcome to the Surrealists as a means of circumventing the opposition of figuration-abstraction. He also invested the constituent elements of the work with an infinitely greater power of innate expressivity than had ever been possible in painting, not so much discovering the forms and combinations of his collages as serving as the vehicle for their expression. The traditional relationship of the artist or spectator to the work of art was turned on its head.

Arp retained a formal purity in his work that made him a respected ally for even the most intransigent of the abstract painters. Setting out his ambiguous forms, born of chance, against a non-illusionist background, making no literal allusions, he pointed the way to a new relationship of occupied to empty space: no longer did the background mimic the infinity of space itself, rather it was an environment, the point of encounter of these first forms produced by what the Surrealists were to call "psychic automatism".

Arp sought to define the significance of this process that enabled him to create "like nature": "Dada denounces the infernal ruses of the official vocabulary of wisdom. Dada is in favour of the senseless, which is not the same as non-sense. Dada is senseless in the way that nature is." Arp was to concentrate exclusively on collage and assemblage, regarding the natural beauty of the objects he produced as "intrinsic to them, like the beauty of a bunch of flowers picked by children". In them he found a way of escaping from any "ridiculous resemblance to the appearance of something else".

Max Ernst made frequent use of collage, but in a far less abstract spirit, without abandoning the relationship of signs and sense. Most of his productions had a specifically autobiographical character. Looking into his memories for the subjects and substance of his work, he used art as a kind of Freudian analysis. It was he who invented most of the automatic techniques of Surrealism as he pursued a path of self-discovery via the association of ideas, in a manner highly reminiscent of psychoanalytical technique. Within an entirely abstract architecture, he allowed images to coalesce until they assumed the form of his "hallucinations", or else led to "the chance encounter

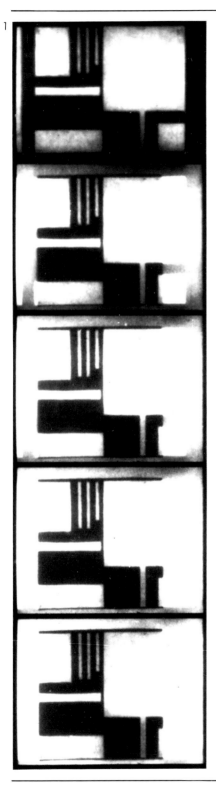

1. Richter:
   Photogram from the film
   Rhythmus 23, 1923-25
2. Eggeling:
   Photogram from the film
   Diagonal-Symphonie, 1921-24

of two distant realities in an inappropriate context". In spite of their differences, Ernst joined with Arp to found a Dada group in Cologne; but he was to play no more than a subsidiary role in the evolution of abstraction, except perhaps on the level of pictorial technique. For him, art was essentially a secondary activity, less an autonomous process than a means of recording the states of his inner consciousness.

When they returned to Germany from Zurich, the former Dadaists Viking Eggeling and Hans Richter were to embark on a period of full-blown abstraction. Their radical explorations of time and space led them towards cinematography, and they made the first ever non-figurative films. "In 1919," Richter recounts (*op. cit.*), "basing our ideas on what Eggeling called the *Generalbass der Malerie,* we produced our first scroll-pictures, variations and formal themes drawn in pencil on long scrolls of paper: Eggeling's *Horizontal-Vertikal-Messe* and my *Präludium.* Developing the idea of motion implicit in these scrolls, in 1920 we began our first ventures in abstract film... Although both abstract, these films were very different in spirit and in approach, as Eggeling started out from line and I began with the surface. Eggeling orchestrated and developed his forms, while I renounced form altogether and tried to articulate time to a variety of different tempi and rhythms."

It was collage again that provided Kurt Schwitters with the catalyst he needed to develop his work. The moment of discovery occurred in 1918: "All through the war, inspiration was hard to come by. What I had got from the Academy was of no use to me at all. The

2

new things I could use were still very much in the early stages, and all about me there was this appalling conflict about things that left me indifferent. Then suddenly, it was the glorious revolution. (I don't hold much brief for that sort of revolution. Men need maturity for that. It's like when the wind blows fruits off the trees before they are ripe. Wholesale devastation.) But at the same time, at least all that duplicity that men call war was over and done with. I left my job without giving notice, and, on with the show! It was only then that inspiration really began to bubble. I felt free, I wanted to shout my joy to the world. To do just that, and as a means of economizing, I used whatever I could find. The country was terribly impoverished. You can create things perfectly well out of rubbish, and that's what I did, sticking and nailing it together. I called these objects *Merz,* and that was my personal prayer in celebration of the victorious end to the war, since the victory was the peace, yet again. Anyway, everything was destroyed, and it was a matter of constructing something new out of the rubble." (in W. Schmalenbach, *Schwitters,* 1967)

It was both chance and necessity that led Schwitters to collage, but in it he discovered a new way of creating painting, and indeed abstract art. With absolute integrity and originality, he pursued his exploration of the technique as far as he could take it. With hindsight, Schwitters has been credited with all sorts of sociological intentions, but it is far from certain that he had any conscious desire, for example, to attack the consumer society by confronting it with its discarded waste. He was unlike the other Dadaists in emphasizing, not so much the significance of objects brought together by chance, but rather the plastic effect they created. Most of his scraps of paper are cut rather than torn, and the pieces of rubbish he collected are transformed in his work into form/colours organized in a way that makes them into complex and satisfying compositions. Having started with a vision comparable to that of the Cubists and Futurists, he very quickly arrived at an authentic non-figuration, in which letters and materials were made to function as pictorial elements. His concern was less to telescope sense than to construct a new space.

Again and again he refers to his desire to make painting out of materials not designed for it. As, for example, when he explains the origin of the word "Merz", which he used as a title for many of his

1. Schwitters:
   Merz 600 Leiden, 1923
2. Schwitters:
   Disjointed Forces, 1923
3. Schwitters:
   Revolving, 1919
4. Schwitters:
   Merz Picture with Candle,
   1925-28

works: "Merz was the name I gave to my new manner of working with, in principle, any material to hand. It is the second syllable of Kommerz. The word presented itself to me in a Merz picture in which, among the abstract forms, had been stuck the word Merz, cut out of an advertisement... Indeed I saw no reason why one couldn't use old travel passes, bits of wormy wood, cloakroom tickets, pieces of bicycles, buttons and all that old junk you find in attics or on rubbish heaps, just as well as the pigment that is specially prepared for painters. That was something you might call taking up an attitude to society, and as far as art was concerned, it was also a personal delight, but above all it was following the thing through to a logical conclusion." (*Merz*, no. 20, 1927)

The review Schwitters founded in 1923 at first reflected what was in effect a Dadaist view of the world, but it was not long before the publication became a sort of meeting point for Dada and Constructivism. Theories of Neo-Plasticism and Productivism also found a wider currency in its pages, because of the friendship that came about between Schwitters, van Doesberg and El Lissitzky. After 1925, Schwitters himself began to develop more elaborate forms of pure construction, using collage to explore the ultimate possibilities of contrast and opposition. Oil painting had been invented to serve the demands of illusion; real materials, borrowed or salvaged, now proved highly effective elements in a form of expression that rejected imitation but wanted to convey a modern order of reality.

Fundamental abstraction, inaugurated by Malevich and Mondrian, was soon to spread way beyond the immediate circle of their friends and colleagues. In France, as early as 1918, it was the basis of the ideas advanced by Amédée Ozenfant and Charles-Edouard Jeanneret (who was to take the name Le Corbusier in 1927). In *Après le cubisme,* issued to coincide with an exhibition at the Galerie Thomas, the two painters, although they did not exclude figurative reference, nevertheless stressed the importance of the individual pictorial elements. They called for: "rigorous procedures, rigorous figurations, rigorous architectures, highly formalized, as purely and simply as machines." Above all they strove to find a way of developing beyond Cubism by using mathematical, geometric and organic constructions: "Scientific perfection and the progress of beauty go hand in hand; as it sheds new light on nature, science allows art to progress, by alerting our senses to mechanical harmonies, and to feelings that remain unawakened right up to the very threshold of beauty itself. Science and art are collaborators." They concluded: "Painting is significant for the intrinsic quality of the plastic elements, not for their representative or narrative potential... The work of art should not be random, exceptional, impressionistic, inorganic, challenging, or picturesque, but rather, general, static, expressive of permanence... Every freedom is permitted to art, except that of not being clear." Ozenfant and Jeanneret went on to develop their ideas in the review *L'Esprit Nouveau,* forging close links with De Stijl, the Bauhaus and the Russian Constructivists.

Lissitzky:
Proun 4B, 1919-20

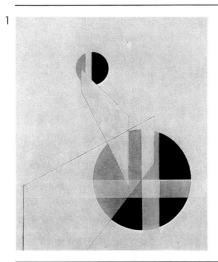

In the political, economic and social ferment that followed the defeat of 1918, Germany was to become the crucible of the new art, the crossroads of Europe, where innovatory ideas from North, South, East and West, came into productive collision. The Hungarian Moholy-Nagy, who arrived in Berlin in 1921, revealed himself rapidly as one of the most original thinkers on the artistic scene. Only ten years younger than the first generation of abstract artists, he subsumed within his work influences from pure painting, De Stijl, Suprematism and Constructivism. One of his inventions, which he called *Em,* to denote a way of creating abstract pictures over the telephone, had profound implications for the future of painting. "In 1922 I ordered by telephone from a sign factory five paintings in porcelain enamel. I had the factory's color chart before me and I sketched my paintings on graph paper. At the other end of the telephone the factory supervisor had the same kind of paper divided into squares... One of the pictures was delivered in three different sizes so that I could study the subtle differences in the color relations caused by the enlargement and reduction... My belief is that mathematically harmonious shapes, executed precisely, are filled with emotional quality, and that they represent the perfect balance between feeling and intellect." (Moholy-Nagy, *The New Vision and Abstract of an Artist,* 1947) By eliminating entirely the artist's manual function, Moholy-Nagy demonstrated that the object counted less than the process by which it was created, in other words that the concept was more important than artistic virtuosity...

1922 was also significant for other reasons, two events in particular marking the international rise of geometric abstraction: first the exhibition of Russian art staged by El Lissitzky at the Dienen gallery in Berlin, and secondly the Düsseldorf Congress of 29 to 31 May, attended by Moholy-Nagy, El Lissitzky, van Doesberg and Hans Richter, all responsible for publications devoted to abstract art — *MA, Veshch, De Stijl* and *Gestaltung...* This encounter was to lead to a convergence of views, effectively setting the seal on the dominance of geometricism over lyrical abstraction: its significance appeared more universal, both because it employed a vocabulary of plainly stated forms that reflected the rational processes of the world, and because it produced images sympathetic to the spirit of science and industry. Above

1. Moholy-Nagy:
   Composition A XX, 1924
2. Moholy-Nagy:
   Composition A 19, 1927
3. Klucis:
   Axonometric Construction,
   c. 1920
4. Peri:
   Spatial Construction in
   Three Parts, 1923
5. Vordemberge-Gildewart:
   Construction in Red, 1924

all, its formal neutrality lent itself to the devising of a simple, effective language accessible to all, fitted to express the preoccupations and aspirations of a modern technological age.

The dream of all these artists was to integrate art with life, but it was only in painting that they found the freedom to explore their ideas to the full. El Lissitzky, Moholy-Nagy and Laszlo Peri were to go furthest in their experiments with space and the use of novel materials. Like Mondrian, they sought to make a painting extend beyond its frame, and, by the sheer force of its projection, or rayonism, occupy the whole space of the wall on which it was hung. El Lissitzky created many *Proun* paintings of this type and even environments such as the *Proun Room* exhibited at the Grosse Berliner Kunstausstellung of 1922. For these artists, a painting was no longer a plane surface, it extended into the dimensions of the space enclosing it, by means of the tension of its forms, the intensity of its colours and the dynamism of its contours.

The influx of foreign painters supplied a welcome encouragement for the indigenous German abstract artists, who were still few and far between. Among the latter were Vordemberge-Gildewart, who attempted a radical synthesis of Dutch and Russian influences, and Baumeister, who in 1918 began to evolve a highly personal abstraction of forms and materials. But it was above all within the context of the Bauhaus that abstraction was to find a new direction and new impetus. Established by Gropius in Weimar, in 1919, the school was dedicated to bringing

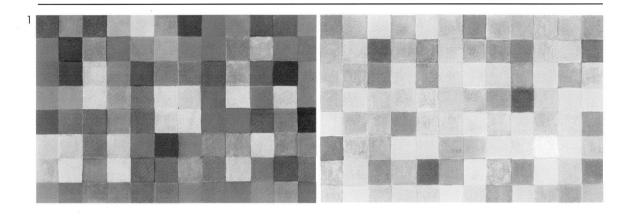

1. Itten:
   Colour studies
2. Schlemmer:
   The Nightingale's Song, 1929
3. Kandinsky:
   Thirteen Rectangles, 1930

about a revival in the arts, founded in the collaboration between the various disciplines and inspired by a spirit of conscious modernism. At the end of his life, Gropius recalled his original intentions: "I wanted to concentrate my effort on ideas of integration and coordination — welcoming everything, excluding nothing — for I was deeply conscious that the salvation of architecture depended on the close and harmonious working of a busy team, whose collaboration was essentially a reflection of that organism we call society. Thus the Bauhaus opened its doors in 1919. It saw its specific task as being the achievement of a modern architecture which, like human nature, would encompass all things. Its efforts were principally directed to what had now become an urgently pressing need — ensuring that man does not become a slave to the machine, while at the same time safeguarding mass-production and the workplace from mechanical anarchy, and giving them life and meaning. Indeed, what the Bauhaus taught was the equality of rights of all the creative modes, and their reciprocal relationship in the modern world. We were guided by the following idea: the creative instinct belongs no more to the realm of the spirit than it does to the physical world, it is simply an integrating principle of the vital substance of a civilized society." (Gropius, *Architecture*)

Influenced initially by the Expressionists, Gropius was soon drawn to the ideas of van Doesberg and Moholy-Nagy. He attracted a formidable body of teachers to execute his programme: Feininger and Itten, and later Schlemmer, Klee, Kandinsky and

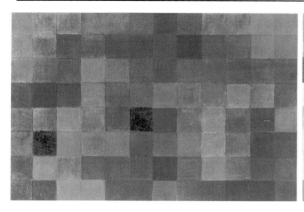

3

Albers... By the time the Bauhaus transferred to Dessau in 1925, it had become a major centre of artistic activity and a focus for the dissemination of Constructivist theories. In his inaugural lecture to mark the opening of the new building, Gropius declared: "... today we can take pleasure in the fact that the ideas of the Bauhaus have set in train a movement that extends well beyond these frontiers, one which reflects the structures of modern life. It was born out of the clear thinking and enthusiasm of the teachers and students. The more we succeed in making our enterprise a truly collective enterprise, the easier it will become, starting from this kernel of the collectivist spirit, to establish a relationship linking industry, crafts, science and the forces governing spatial organization."

The Bauhaus was to revive the notion of functionalism, the belief that creativity should have a utilitarian purpose, and that this should be achieved by using the most up-to-date techniques. Various approaches were tried out in the studio devoted to studies of "volume", and some of these were taken up and given a wider application in industry. In 1927 a new architectural faculty was opened, in which the virtues of "design" were extolled, defined by Gropius in the following terms: "Each thing is determined by its essence; to conceive of it in such a way that it will function correctly, you must make a thorough study of this essence, for it must serve its purpose perfectly, or in other words fulfil its practical function, be durable, of good value and well made."

In their teaching, Kandinsky and Klee developed theories that were to have profound repercussions for

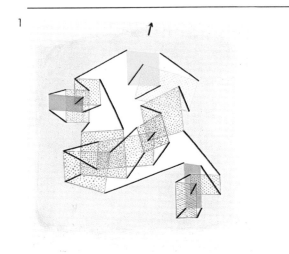

1. Klee:
   Hovering, 1930
2. Kandinsky:
   On White II, 1923
3. Kandinsky:
   Upward Tension, 1924

painting. Never before had their own work been so purely abstract, or, to use a term coined by van Doesberg, so "concrete" in its nature. It was in 1930 that van Doesberg rejected the vague description "abstract", which he regarded, with some reason, as an essentially negative epithet, indicating that painting was progressively moving away — or abstracting itself — from nature. In replacing "abstract" with "concrete", he marked the distinction between art that was still, fundamentally, inspired by the external world and art that derived purely from the imagination or from human feelings, and which had its own intrinsic reality.

Klee himself found it almost impossible to distinguish between inspiration and realization, subjectivity and objectivity. For him, the work of art sprang directly from the subconscious, although its gestation was complex, involving a process of observation, analysis, meditation and craft-skill: "A knowledge of the rules is valuable, as long as you guard against being too schematic, confusing the bare principle with the living reality. Such misapprehensions lead to construction for its own sake, the obsession of nervous asthmatics who give us rules instead of works of art. You must understand that the only point of trying to establish general principles, when you are dealing with works of art, is to discover how these latter succeed in being distinct from the works of nature without becoming merely arbitrary. You must understand that the laws are merely the substructure that is common to both nature and art." (Klee, *Bauhauszeitschrift für Gestaltung,* 1928)

If, for Klee, creation was indistinguishable from actualization, for Kandinsky the crucial question was the process by which mind determined matter. Exposure to the Suprematists and the Constructivists had freed him from any last desire to seek inspiration in the external world, and when he arrived at the Bauhaus in 1922, having just returned from Russia, his overriding concern was to find a way of making form express its inner necessity. His work was now fundamentally different from what it had been even ten years earlier. This he recognized in an interview given on July 21: "After the Revolution, I painted quite differently. I experienced a great spiritual calm. Not at all a feeling of tragedy, something very calm and organized." At that time, he was working towards a metaphorical language that would serve to express, by analogy, the metamorphosis of natural

forms, the dynamism of the world and the infinity of space revealed by science. Trusting to his intuition, he established correspondences between his feelings and certain plastic forms that were their precise echoes. As he did so, in the quest for universality, he increasingly suppressed any response he deemed to be merely idiosyncratic. The title of the book he produced in 1925 is revealing: *Point and Line to Plane.* "The aim of all research is the minute examination of each phenomenon in isolation, the reciprocal effect of the phenomena, synthesis, and the general conclusion that follows from the two previous stages. It is only by means of such a microscopic analysis that the science of art can lead us towards a vast synthesis which, going beyond art, will reach into the realms of 'Unity', the 'Human' and the 'Divine'. That is the perceptible though still distant goal of 'today'." As Carola Giedion-Welker makes clear, in her admirable critique of this work, it is when signs become symbols, when the point and the line are transposed like the colours before them to the autonomous realms of pure logic, that modern art is born.

A pupil at the Bauhaus before he joined its teaching staff, Josef Albers too aimed to achieve impersonality in his work. Concentrating on the interaction of positive and negative aspects of form, eliminating all that was superfluous, he offered his own interpretation of the pictorial elements and of their psychological significance. By repetition of simple structures, and basic colours and values, Albers constructed analytical spaces in which he explored the essential nature of the elements that made up his equation. The systematic, serial nature of his work makes him one of the precursors of kinetic or optical art, and it enabled him to study in some depth the physiological effects produced by the various forms and colours; this in due course became his exclusive concern.

By 1927, geometric abstraction could claim to have a truly international public: the Hanover Museum opened a special room devoted to abstract painting, and Malevich was warmly received in Poland before he moved on to the Bauhaus. In Warsaw, Kobro and Strzeminski, early members of the Unovis movement, achieved a type of painting that could almost be called minimalism, surpassing even the stark effects of the Russians in its bare simplicity. It was through their efforts that, in 1932, the museum in Lódź opened two rooms devoted to abstraction. The

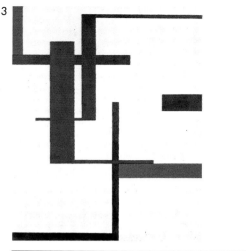

1. Albers:
   Violin-pegs, 1935
2. Strzeminski:
   Architectonic Composition 13c,
   1929
3. Hélion:
   Tensions, 1932
4. Pasmore:
   Square Motif (Indian Red) no. 1,
   1959

installation remains in place today, a profoundly moving testimony to the early origins of concrete art.

But with the economic crisis that began with Black Thursday on the Wall Street Stock Exchange (24 October 1929), and above all with the rise of totalitarianism, a direct threat was posed to the most revolutionary artists. For the abstract painters life became fraught with difficulty. After 1928, most of them found their way to Paris, the last bastion of European freedom. There they sought to regroup their forces and defend themselves as best they could.

The Montevideo-born painter Torres-García became the catalyst of this abstractionist avant-garde. Soon after reaching Paris, he joined forces with van Doesberg, and in November 1928 at the Salon d'Automne met Jean Hélion (apart from Jean Gorin, the sole French exponent of geometric abstraction). Through Mondrian and his circle, Torres-García came to know the critic Michel Seuphor, with whom he founded the "Circle and Square" group. Before long membership had swelled to eighty and a review was published bearing the same name. The first issue appeared on 15 March 1930, and an exhibition was held that April at Galerie 23 in the Rue La Boétie. "Circle and Square" had as its goal the defence and promotion of abstraction. Torres-García declared: "To introduce some order would be an achievement, but that is not enough, what we need is to create a new order altogether."

"Circle and Square" was a short-lived phenomenon, but it was succeeded by a larger group called "Abstraction-Creation", which united all the various

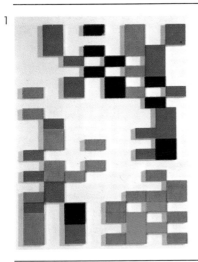

1. Taeuber-Arp:
   Aubette, 1927
2. Nicholson:
   Painting (Trout), 1924
3. Domela:
   Composition A VII, 1923

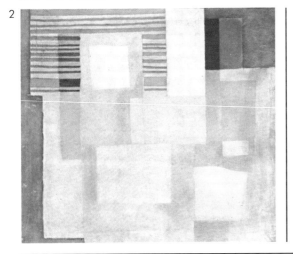

Constructivist tendencies. Founded in February 1931, in a few years it had acquired over four hundred members, and through the review of the same name attracted wide support. At the heart of all these activities were Arp and his wife Sophie Taeuber, who by then was working with very simple, bare forms.

Abstraction reached England not long afterwards through Ben Nicholson, who met Mondrian in 1934. Even in the United States, "Abstraction-Creation" could soon count thirty active members. The free world was only too ready to welcome dissidents from Eastern and Central Europe, obliged by the worsening political situation to seek refuge in the West.

The architect Hannes Meyer, who took over from Gropius the directorship of the Bauhaus, was summarily dismissed because of his leftist views. He was succeeded by Mies van der Rohe, who in 1931 began to promote technical education at the expense of the creative disciplines, leading Klee to offer his resignation. In 1932, the Nazis won a majority on the town council in Dessau and closed down the Bauhaus. Mies van der Rohe tried to save the foundation by turning it into a private school; with the help of Albers and Kandinsky, he moved with sixty-eight students to Berlin. On 11 April 1933, the Berlin premises were raided by the police and the SA. The school was dissolved and its staff harassed, so that most were forced to emigrate. A veritable diaspora took place, sending the members of the Bauhaus far afield, to Paris, London and the U.S. In 1933, Paris became the *de facto* — if temporary — international capital of abstraction. Significantly, Zervoy's famous review *Les Cahiers d'Art* had only recently published a major feature on abstract art (nos. 7-8, 1931). The views expressed revealed a somewhat uneasy and tense situation; in his contribution, Mondrian appeared to foresee the impasse that would soon be reached, in the atmosphere of doubt engendered by the economic and political crisis: "All plastic art has until now been able to develop and move towards the achievement of pure plasticity. Yet once this has been achieved, we can go no further in art. But will art always be necessary? Is it not but a poor artifice, while beauty in life itself is absent?"

3

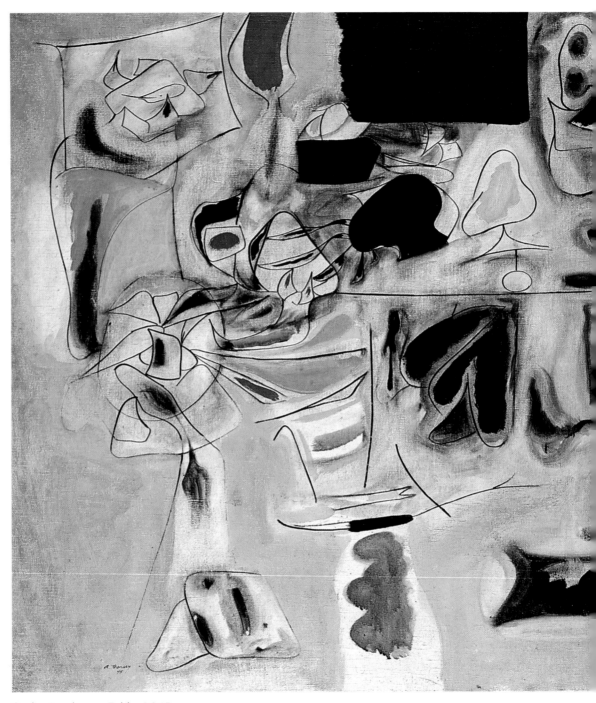

Gorky: Landscape-Table, 1945

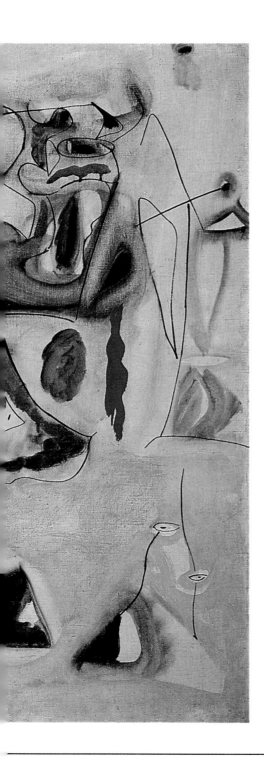

CHAPTER 8
THE SURREALIST CONTRIBUTION

Surrealism was to give rise to another type of abstraction altogether, one that was the absolute antithesis of concrete art. The Surrealists had nothing in common with the idealism and Utopian dreams of the Constructivist tradition. Like Arp, they sought inspiration in chance events. Their abstraction was a response to the promptings of the unconscious , and it was rarely free of figurative reference, except occasionally in the work of Miró. They had none of the Constructivist desire to educate and proselytize, being more concerned to shock and disturb.

Because Surrealism is more an attitude of mind than an artistic movement as such, it does not play a major role in the history of abstraction, except in terms of the contribution made by the first generation of its adherents — Masson, Miró and Ernst. Painting for the Surrealists was a means, not an end, and indeed André Breton, the founder and spiritual father of the group, always had a preference for those who "imagined" with the unconscious, as compared with those who regarded the unconscious purely as the motivating force for a painted image. It is significant that Breton did not develop a real interest in painting until the late twenties, by which time Masson and Miró had distanced themselves from the group, to be replaced by Tanguy, Dali and Magritte, each of whom found a way round the dilemmas of contemporary painting by developing a sort of "abstract" poetry of images accessible to a more conventional understanding of painting, and which consisted in the creation of illusionist spaces transformed in significance through the translation of objects into images.

Dali explains: "All my ambition in painting consists in materializing, with the most imperialist rage for precision, the images of concrete irrationality. Making the imaginative world and concrete irrationality as self-evidently objective, of the same consistency, the same hardness, the same persuasive cognitive and communicable density, as the external world of phenomenological reality." (*La Conquête de l'Irrationel,* 1935)

When the *Surrealist Manifesto* appeared in 1924, it contained no reference at all to the abstract painters. It was as though André Breton was still oblivious to their existence. Much later, he wrote: "From 1918 to 1921, you might say that there was more or less nothing going on at the cutting edge of artistic experiment, there was a total 'crisis of the model'. The old-style model, taken from the external world, was no more, it had lost its will to survive. That which was to succeed it, taken from the internal world, had not yet been discovered." (*Genèse et perspective artistique du surréalisme,* 1941) Yet the fact is these "new models" were discovered largely through the development of techniques of painting that were abstract in nature.

The particular form of collage practised by Max Ernst since 1919 was one of the earliest attempts at using "automatism" as a route into the unconscious; soon afterwards he also developed the complementary process of frottage. It was, however, with the widespread adoption of automatic writing that Surrealist painting found its most productive vein.

In his first *Manifesto,* André Breton offered the following definition of Surrealism: "Pure psychic automatism, by which an attempt is made to express,

3

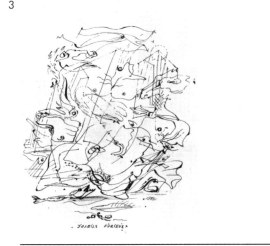

« SOLEILS FURIEUX »

4

either verbally, in writing or in any other way, the true functioning of thought. The dictation of thought, in the absence of all control by the reason, excluding any aesthetic or moral preoccupation."

Painters responded with enthusiasm to this call for freedom. André Masson was the first to experiment with the unrestrained expression of line and gesture, and was soon followed by Miró. By 1925, both these artists had revealed in their work the potential of pictorial automatism as a means of conveying a state of "innate primitivism". Their compositions were the more disconcerting because they were like nothing that had ever been seen before, and hence lay outside the scope of the usual aesthetic criteria...

Masson concentrated largely on pen-and-ink drawings, and did not practise automatic writing in painting until 1927. As he held the pen, his role was that of a medium; the line spoke for itself, possessed of its own movement and its own lyricism, until at last from out of its interweavings emerged biomorphic forms, or states of metamorphosis, which the painter lingered on and accentuated. In letting himself be transported by the élan of his gesture, Masson anticipated the Expressionism of the American painters of Pollock's generation. His hand was like a seismograph which, without being controlled in any way, recorded all its impulses and counter-checks. Looking back to these Surrealist drawings, the earliest of which dates from 1924, Masson recalled: "What characterized them, in their spontaneity, was chance association. It was not a matter of bringing incongruous objects together, nor of collages assembled in a spirit of humour, it was the emergence of beings 'in process', always in the throes of change. Naked metamorphosis, beyond the accepted images of fable, traditional myth and folklore." (Masson, *Métamorphose de l'artiste,* 1956) This quotation indicates the benefits the Surrealist painters gained from their reliance on the unconscious workings of the mind: freedom to escape from stereotypes, expressivity of line, which revealed its meaning only as it was traced, a means of making the "signifier" into the "signified". Breton was not to recognize this until much later. He made no comment at all on these early Masson drawings, but in 1941 wrote: "Now the painter's hand truly *flies*: no longer is it that which transfers the forms of objects, it is that hand which, carried away with its own movement and with that alone, describes invol-

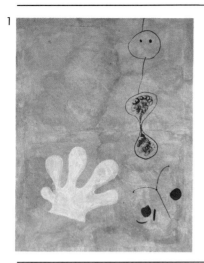

1. Miró:
   Untitled, 1925
2. Miró:
   Untitled, 1927
3. Max Ernst:
   Grey Forest, 1926
4. Max Ernst:
   False Positions, 1925

untary figures in which, experience shows, these forms feel the urge to regroup themselves. The essential discovery of Surrealism is indeed that, its intention already predetermined, the pen that hastens to write, or the pencil that hastens to draw, *extrudes* an infinitely precious substance, perhaps not entirely the matter of transference but appearing, at least, to be charged with all the hidden emotion of the poet or painter." (Breton, *Genèse et perspective artistique du surréalisme,* 1941)

In terms of painting, Miró went further, and faster. During the winter of 1924-25, he concentrated on a form of abstract and spontaneous gestural expression, which liberated him from the strict architecture of Cubism by exposing the actual processes of painting. Out of this concentration on the sweep of the brush, on colour and pigment, out of the interplay of gesture and sign, came pictograms of biomorphic forms, novel figurations charged with that erotic force the Surrealist writers were then attempting to infuse into their own work. Miró painted directly onto the canvas; eliminating preliminary sketches, he gave himself up to the immediate expression of the working of his innermost being. His painting became the screen for an instantaneous projection, the surface on which being was metamorphosed into painting. Working in this way, he reversed the traditional order, whereby the artist started with an idea around which he then organized the image; his method was to start with nothing, to assert that it was nothing, and only then to take possession of it, obedient to instinct alone. Later Miró could not resist the urge to accentuate the signs he discovered, but his painting always began with this plunge into the unknown.

A great technical innovator, Max Ernst combined automatic writing with the process of frottage, which he discovered during the summer of 1925; this consisted in taking a rubbing of some real thing which would then act as a trigger for the operations of the unconscious mind. Of this "objective chance", Max Ernst said: "The process of frottage does not depend on anything other than the intensification of the excitability of the mental faculties by the appropriate technical means, excluding any conscious mental input (of reason, taste, morality), reducing to the minimum the active role of that person who has hitherto been referred to as the 'author' of the work. The process was already known under the name of

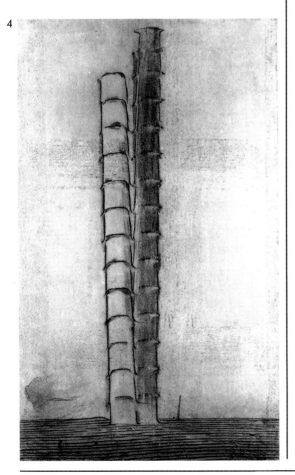

automatic writing. It is as a spectator that the author is present, indifferent or enthusiastic, at the birth of his work, observing the stages of its development..., the role of the painter is to focus and project what presents itself in him." When the method was later applied to painting (using for example grattage, scraping colour on a prepared ground set over an uneven surface), it produced, typically, such canvases as the *Forest* series: "By adapting the process of frottage to the technical procedures of painting, although at first it had seemed applicable only to drawing, while all the time trying to restrain my own active participation in the evolution of the picture so as to increase the active functioning of the hallucinatory faculties of the mind, I succeeded in being present *as a spectator* at the birth of all my works... Swimming blindly, I made myself see. *I saw.* And I was surprised to find I was in love with what I could see, and wanted to identify with it." ("Au-delà de la peinture", *Cahiers d'Art,* nos. 6-7, 1936)

The automatic writing of the early Surrealist painters was to find its echo in the work of the second generation: Paalen, Seligmann and Matta.

It was Wolfgang Paalen, a member of the group from 1935, who introduced the technique of "fumage". This consisted in laying smoky traces over the picture surface with the aid of a lighted candle, and then carefully picking them out so as to reveal the visible images of the unconscious mind.

Kurt Seligmann practised a form of automatic writing very close to Masson's original procedures. Coming from Basel, he gravitated naturally towards the themes of heroism and battle favoured by the painters of the Rhenish Renaissance. When war was declared he emigrated to the States, where he enjoyed considerable influence as a teacher.

Originally trained as an architect, the Chilean artist Matta discovered Surrealism on the occasion of the major exhibition held in 1938 at the Galerie des Beaux-Arts, in the Faubourg Saint-Honoré. It was this experience that made him a painter. Obsessed with space, he began to paint powerful metaphors of the creation of the world, using automatic-writing techniques: these vast landscapes that emerged from his psyche, he called *Inscape.* In painting them, he drew on every conceivable technique of automatism: dripping paint, spontaneous gesturalism, chance juxtaposition of blobs of colour, spreading the pigment with a

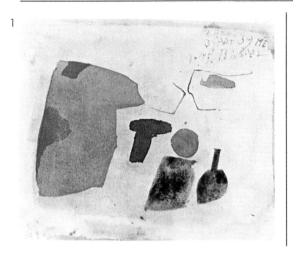

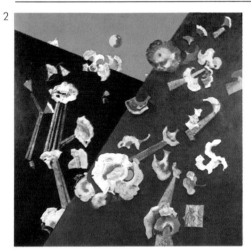

rag, etc. Like Masson, he sought refuge in the United States during the war, and there received an enthusiastic welcome from the younger painters. New York, indeed, became the new stamping-ground of Surrealism. In 1939, discussing the most recent tendencies of the movement, Breton declared prophetically: "Surrealist painting in its latest manifestation among men young enough not to have to take account, artistically speaking, of their personal antecedents, is exhibiting now a marked tendency towards a return to automatism..."

When the European exiles arrived in the United States, they helped to lift the atmosphere of disillusionment that had taken hold of American painters. Barnett Newman has described how, in 1940, he had come to feel painting had no reality any more. For him, the new ideas represented an awakening, with "all the excitement of a revolution." In addition, there were already hints of changes on the horizon, far-reaching changes that would lead eventually to the abandonment of focused space and the transformation of the canvas into a field of action.

Arshile Gorky was one of the precursors of the new movement in painting. His career had followed a course that enabled the Surrealists, when they arrived, to greet him as one of their own. Entirely self-taught, Gorky had studied the moderns at length to discover the true potential of painting. In circa 1936 he began to experiment with a free graphism that was not unlike the inventions of Masson and Miró. The emphasis on gesture led, once more, to the creation of biomorphic forms, but in Gorky's case these embodied a highly personal mythology.

Gesturalism is a striking feature too of the work of Mark Tobey, who drew heavily on his experience of Oriental painting and studies of Eastern mysticism and religion. Tobey evolved a system of "white writing" with which he created works of a transcendent graphism, much in the spirit of the inspired calligraphy he had first seen in Japan. Working independently, on the fringes of the American School, he exemplified that Zen influence which was to become increasingly attractive to succeeding generations.

In Europe, shortly before the war, the German painter Julius Bissier had also arrived at a highly original form of sign-calligraphy. A friend of Baumeister, he turned to abstraction in 1929. Soon after that date: "The first psychograms were born, produced

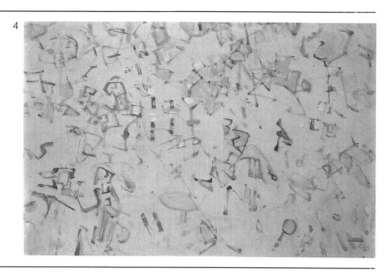

1. Bissier:
   3 February 1959, 1959
2. Max Ernst:
   Snow Flowers, 1929
3. Matta:
   Untitled, 1947
4. Tobey:
   Composition on Blue, 1955
5. Tobey:
   The Search, 1954

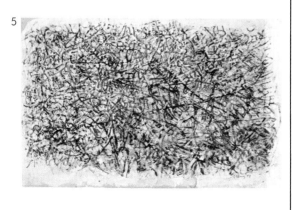

almost unconsciously. In the years from 1933 onwards, these were transformed as if in a sort of game into signs possessing a purely personal significance, but the comforting thing about them was that I absolutely had to write them, under pressure of some sort of inner compulsion." (Extract from Bissier's diary, exhibition catalogue, Galerie Pauli, Lausanne, 1984) The paintings he produced are of great delicacy and refinement, rather in the manner of Oriental washes. Bissier remained in Germany during the war years, and thus found himself almost totally isolated. Yet, as we see from his diary entry for 23 March 1943, he was very much in the forefront of modern thinking: "In three strokes of the brush, in truth, everything should already have been said: the man who writes them, together with his constitution and his temperament, etc., the age in which he lives and, in a general way, his attitude to life. If everything is not contained within these 'three strokes', it will not be any more so in the whole picture."

We cannot conclude a discussion of Surrealism without reference to Josef Sima, who worked at the periphery of the group. Initially he developed a mythical imagery with biomorphic forms, and later went on to produce mystical landscapes that became further and further removed from all significance. In these, within space that is highly structured, he reduced to their luminous essences the four elements of fire, air, earth and water.

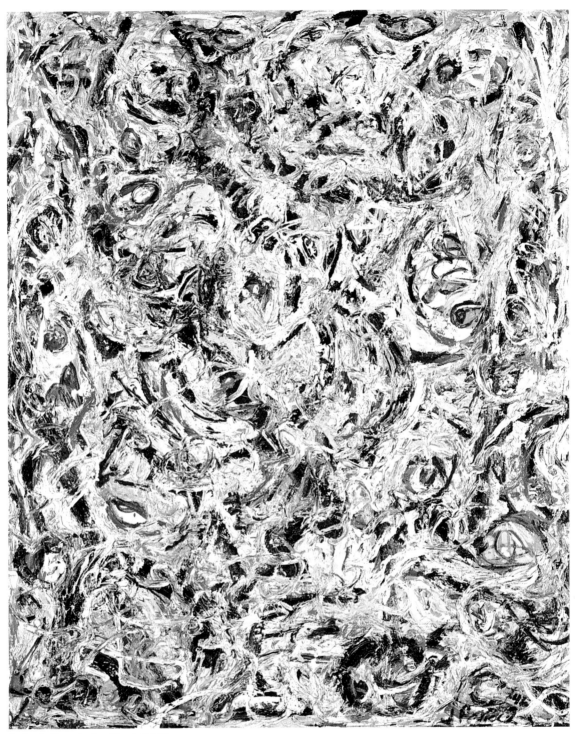

Pollock: Eyes in the Heat, 1946

CHAPTER 9
ABSTRACT EXPRESSIONISM

It was in the United States that abstraction gained its second wind. Taken up by another generation of painters in a continent where the weight of history was less oppressive, it triumphantly recovered its creative élan, carrying all before it. Yet this liberation from past tradition was achieved precisely through the expression of direct and intense human experience; only out of a multiplicity of deeply-felt personal responses was a universality of significance attained. It was a huge change, and could not possibly have occurred except as part of a wider modification of behaviour affecting other areas of life as well, a more general move to question the traditional relationship of "signifier" to "signified".

Through Impressionism, the "sign" had become increasingly imprecise, dissolving finally into a mist in Monet's late works. Progressively, the relationship of form to substance had been overturned, so that the substance had become the true "subject" of the picture, and the beholder was obliged to choose his interpretation from within a complex configuration, where a plurality of "signifieds" coexisted within the one "signifier".

In *The Open Work,* a book that was profoundly influential at the time of its publication in 1962, Umberto Eco emphasized the close relationship that has always existed between the approaches adopted by the arts and the sciences. The "formlessness" that surfaced at this time in the cultural sphere was thus the direct counterpart of the application of the "uncertainty principle" and techniques of statistical probability to the contemporary scientific interpreta-

tion of natural phenomena. In every sphere the principle of causality was under attack. Eco declared: "Art wants to be, and should be considered as the response of the imagination to the vision of the world put forward by science: art is a structural metaphor of that vision." In particular, Eco based his argument on the physical law of "complementarity" which, in stating that every phenomenon must have its opposite, effectively called into question the validity of synthesis as a method. "Although an artistic form is not an exact substitute for a scientific fact, nevertheless one can see it as an epistemological metaphor; in every age, the way in which the various forms are structured in art, reveals — in the broad sense, by simile or metaphor, the reduction of concept to figure — the way in which science, or at any rate contemporary culture, sees reality." Thus, uncertainty having become: "... a category of knowledge, within the cultural context a new poetics emerges, in which the work of art no longer has a necessary and predictable goal; in which the freedom of the interpreter becomes another form of this same principle of discontinuity, which for modern physics represents not a setback but the inevitable statement of a fundamental truth, at least at the subatomic level." (*Op. cit,* p. 29)

In terms of the plastic arts, there was now no logical reason why the "signifier" should not operate without any pre-existing notion of the "signified". It was a conceptual advance that was to have profound consequences for painting, above all in the United States. A key element in all this was the opening by Peggy Guggenheim of the Art of This Century Gallery, in October 1942. Here were presented side by side the works of the Surrealist *émigrés* and those of the young American painters. It was the time when Pollock, Rothko, Motherwell, Gottlieb, Still and Gorky were looking within themselves to find the subject matter of their work. "Thereafter, they sought the true dimension of their vision within themselves," explains Pierre Restany, "in the direct relationship between their affective response and the environment. Their ambition was matched only by their ethical consciousness. To live fully the modernity of their time, they had to search down into the depths of their being. Painting was a moral act, the painter was the philosopher of his own action." (*La Grande Histoire de la Peinture Moderne,* T.V., 1982)

In their enthusiastic espousal of Surrealism, these

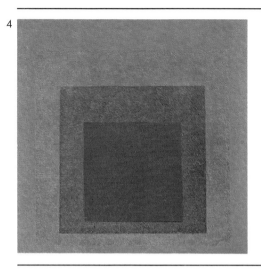

1. Gottlieb:
   Descending Arrow, 1956
2. Still:
   Untitled, 1951
3. Gorky:
   Agony, 1947
4. Albers:
   Homage to the Square:
   Ritardando, 1958
5. Hofmann:
   Cathedral, 1958

American painters saw Masson's violence of gesture as being synonymous with an inner rebellion. They were convinced that gesture was the means of representing a pure psychic automatism, and that, in its spontaneity, it was the most absolute expression of the self. Subject neither to the operation of reason nor to the laws of aesthetics, it was the expression of the being in contact with the cosmos. The euphoria that was to greet the defeat of the Nazis could not hide the fact that the human soul was riven with contradictory impulses, but it did help establish a mood of confidence in human potential, creating an audience susceptible to the implicit philosophy of the new approach to painting. This was a booming society, of economic expansion and thrusting advertising campaigns. For the United States, victory was more than a testimony to its military might: in the post-war years the country extended its hegemony over the Western world to the political and economic spheres as well. Before long it also exercised a cultural dominance. Where America had been a consumer of foreign art, now it was to export its own products, their independence and vitality fuelled by an expansionist art market which would stamp its authority worldwide.

The U.S. had laid the foundations for its emancipation by absorbing the lessons of certain earlier emigrants such as Hans Hofmann and Josef Albers, whose teaching helped painters detach themselves from regional or realist traditions, and at the same time instilled a greater awareness of technique. With the advent of Abstract Expressionism, the abstract-figurative debate was settled once and for all. This was

"action painting", in which the reality of the work was defined by physical modes of intervention.

Jackson Pollock was to play a major role in the years 1946 to 1956, with a phenomenal period of activity from 1947 to 1951, when he effectively dominated the American scene. His work *was* Abstract Expressionism. Almost singlehanded, he opened up a new future for automatism, by redefining the concepts of "picture" and "object". Marcellin Pleynet makes the point: "It was through this idea of automatic writing or psychic automatism that the American artists arrived at their synthesis of Expressionism, Cubism, Matisse, geometric abstraction and Surrealism. But if Surrealism was the key, it operated now within an altogether broader social context than had existed for the original Surrealists... Breton's cultural politics were quite different from the beliefs of the New York artists. This turn-of-the century politics of the *tabula rasa,* in which the 'sur' of 'realism' spiritually transcended its historical limitations... could not be taken on board until it had been modified by American pragmatism, which retained the method of automatic writing from the Surrealist programme, but situated it within an evolutionist context. In fact, it was not so much the ideas of Surrealism as its techniques that the American artists requisitioned." (*Paris-New York*, exhibition catalogue, Musée National d'Art Moderne, Paris, 1977)

Since the early years of the century, pictorial experiment had focused increasingly on the act of painting itself. The artist's participation in his work had come increasingly to dictate the situation of the work in time and space – after Cézanne, that could no longer be viewed as something external, rather it was directly embodied in the picture, a reflection above all of the painter's emotional state. With Pollock, this personal input became almost paroxysmal. In 1947 he invented his famous technique of dripping paint, of which he said: "When I am in my painting, I'm not aware of what I'm doing. It is only after a sort of 'get-acquainted' period that I see what I have been about. I have no fears about making changes, destroying the image, etc., because the painting has a life of its own. I try to let it come through. It is only when I lose contact with the painting that the result is a mess. Otherwise there is pure harmony, an easy give and take, and the painting comes out well." ("My Painting", *Possibilities* 1, 1947-48)

1. Pollock:
   Drawing, 1947
2. Pollock:
   Gothic, 1944
3. Pollock:
   Convergence, 1952
4. Pollock:
   Greyed Rainbow, 1953

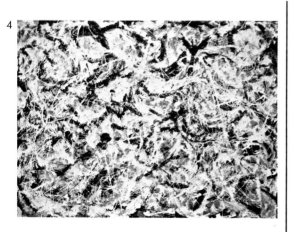

Pollock's decisive contribution to Expressionism lay in his treatment of the picture as a limitless field, on which the image arose directly out of the act of painting. The autonomous space thus created was real but it was also abstract, because it was formed solely from the marks of the painting and the gestures of the painter. Pollock soon stopped using brushes altogether, employing instead a trowel or a stick, or even his fingers, allowing the colour to run as it would. He also replaced traditional oil paints with industrial colours — Duco enamel paint — exploiting their qualities of ease of application, good covering power and quick drying, by pouring the colour rather than painting it on. So Action Painting was born, achieving its full potential when Pollock took the crucial step of laying his canvas out horizontally on the floor. The pictorial space then ceased to be something abstract, accessible largely through the visual sense, it became instead a physical space, a terrain to be traversed. The painting surface was no longer pre-defined; the canvas extended over the whole floor and was not cut to size until later, when the painter was exhausted from his mortal combat with colour. Moving around and across the surface, Pollock allowed the trails and swirls of paint to flow, often from perforated paintcans. One "projection" was built up over another, so that a complex universe was created in which form was indistinguishable from background. The artist applied no sort of reason, he acted instinctively. And yet Pollock's "marks" are distinctively his; what he produced in no way resembles the work of his imitators; his "drip" is as personal to him as his physical

make-up. A further characteristic of this form of expression in which drawing equals painting and form equals colour, is "all-over" space, that is to say, space that is infinite, both in breadth and in depth, created out of the superposing and juxtaposing of an inextricable network of blobs and splashes and drips, which assume a pattern that is the direct reflection of Pollock's own organic being. The vital intensity of these pictorial fields is indicative not only of cosmic and synthetic aspirations but of a meditative, even mystical, cast of mind.

That de Kooning was able to move apparently at will between gesturalism and figuration can be ascribed to his fundamental adherence to the "active" principle of Action Painting, the term coined by the critic Harold Rosenberg to describe Pollock's technique. He had much the same relationship to the work in progress as Pollock, completely immersed in the painting process until the moment of completion. If the picture worked, he would keep it, if not, he threw it away. De Kooning's work is dominated by violent gesture and a powerful use of colour, but the underlying personality is hard to grasp because of his swings between abstraction and figuration. By 1950 he had arrived logically in his work at non-figuration, but his dramatic feeling for emptiness and space, and his roots in Expressionism, made him reluctant to accept any limitation at all. By 1952, he had already discovered, rather to his surprise, that he could not do without a subject: "It's really absurd to make an image, like a human image, with paint, today, when you think about it... But then all of a sudden, it was even more absurd not to do it... It [*Woman I*, 1952] did one thing for me: it eliminated composition, arrangement, relationships, light — all this silly talk about line, colour and form — because that was the thing I wanted to get hold of." (*De Kooning*, exhibition catalogue, MoMA, New York, 1968)

The painter's desire to participate physically in his work is characteristic also of Kline and Still. Unlike the other Abstract Expressionists, Kline did not pass through a stage of Surrealist automatism. Around 1950 he switched abruptly from realistic paintings to a type of gestural art that relied on the bold statement of sign/gesture against its background. Clyfford Still, on the other hand, moved to abstraction via paintings of dark, brooding totemic figures; later he was concerned less with the expressivity of gesture

than with establishing a new relationship between form and ground, emphasizing organic unity, and imparting new intensity to the colour fields.

Motherwell was to have a major influence on the development of collage. He worked principally in the area of colour field and the relationship of form to ground, suppressing half-tones and accentuating surface and the zones of flat colour set against a uniform background, often white. His work stands somewhat apart from the rest of the movement, spontaneity of gesture being always allied to the requirements of a fine aesthetic sense.

Sam Francis was another who pursued a relatively independent course, while profiting from the aesthetic and subjective freedoms offered by Abstract Expressionism. Marked by his experience of Europe and the Far East, he began to explore abstraction sometime before 1950. Although he believed the true character of a canvas did not reveal itself until the element of conscious will had been entirely eradicated, he nevertheless retained landscape as a conscious influence. In his work he invented subtle pictorial equivalents to express the rhythm of the seasons and the changing light, space itself and the atmosphere of the natural world. Through explorations of the relationship between the coloured "stain" and the white of the painting surface, he returned eventually to composition, in the late fifties; empty space, formerly delineated by a few swift brushes of colour, became now the principal subject of the picture, as it was once in Cézanne's watercolours.

For imagination, the Abstract Expressionists had substituted experience. "It is only when I lose contact with the painting that the result is a mess," wrote Pollock. "Otherwise there is pure harmony, an easy give and take, and the painting comes out well." But, with this surrender to action there was one central question that demanded an answer — a question posed by Motherwell in 1950 in the course of discussions held at Studio 35: "When is a painting finished?" As Hubert Damisch points out in his account of the debate (*Fenêtre jaune cadmium,* 1984): "Elevating the question of the rule for knowing when a work is finished above all other considerations in effect brings you back, in a quite unprecedented way, to the logical nature of the creative process and, *a fortiori,* the whole rationale of abstraction: something that might be thought to have been settled with Sur-

1. De Kooning:
   Woman I, 1950-52
2. De Kooning:
   Night Square, 1950-51
3. Kline:
   Painting Number 2, 1954
4. Motherwell:
   Elegy for the Spanish Republic
   no. 34, 1954
5. Sam Francis:
   Blue Figure, 1960

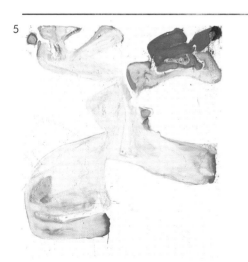

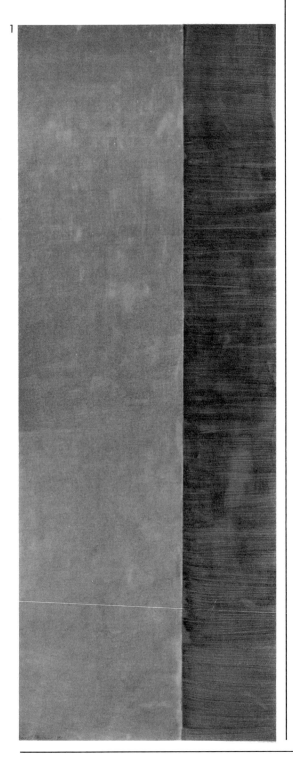

1

realism... To draw a simplistic and deliberately ideological parallel, you might say that at the point where the artists of the past started out, with an idea, a theme, a form and above all a pre-determined 'subject'..., the painters of Pollock's generation found themselves in a very different situation. This it fell to Baziotes to define, which he did, significantly, in terms of gambling..." The point Baziotes went on to make was that the artist of his day had no choice but to see himself as a gambler — all he could do was put something down on canvas and take a chance that something worthwhile would emerge.

In 1955, Rosenberg identified two opposing tendencies in American art, the one exemplified by Pollock's spontaneity, the other by the colour fields developed by Newman and Rothko, which firmly returned painting to its place on a wall, and, by virtue of size alone, gave it more the character of an environment.

It was shortly before 1950 that Newman began to paint his colour fields, vast expanses of monochrome, unbroken except for a column or caesura of another colour. Painting for him was a deeply considered act, of a mystical significance. His study of history had determined him to opt for a modernism that would attain universality by projecting the present into the future. He wanted to convey the idea of creation itself: the cycle of birth, life and death. As his colour fields became ever more vast, so they enabled him to work in "real space"; this he then broke, or framed, with stripes which, by virtue of their colour, occupied space in depth. Colour was not on the surface, rather it created a sort of timeless surface, in which the "zips" or glued strips, either painted over or left blank, were poignant interruptions. Profoundly influenced by the Jewish faith, Newman regarded his images in the light of revelations. Later he abandoned automatism altogether to work patiently on his empty spaces, seeking to create unity out of the contrasts and ruptures he brought together in a secret symmetry. In his later notes towards a "Prologue for a New Aesthetic", he summed up his approach: "Everyone says the important thing in painting is space. The story of modern painting is always told as a struggle for or against space — deep space, shallow space, positive and negative space, cube space, the space of 'infinity', etc. What does all the clamor over space mean? It is all too esoteric for me... Is painting crawling over a canvas in a great paroxysm of intoxicated

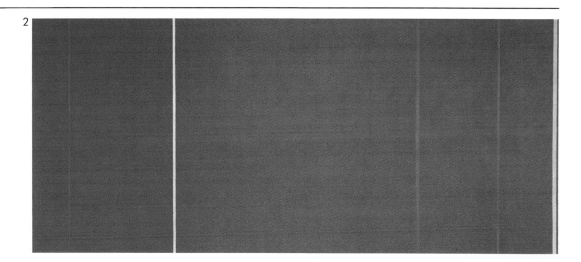

1. Newman:
   Ulysses, 1952
2. Newman:
   Vir Heroicus Sublimis, 1950-51
3. Rothko:
   White and Green in Blue, 1957

improvisation, like a collection of hot jazz players? Everybody says that the important thing in painting is the image — the real image, the imagined poetic image, the whole image, the automatic image of chance, the broken Surrealist image, the pure, universal image of the material itself, the *coup d'œil* image. My paintings are concerned neither with the manipulation of space nor with the image, but with the sensation of time. Not the *sense* of time which has been the underlying subject matter of painting, which involves feelings of nostalgia or high drama; it is always associative and historical..." — but rather, he goes on to say, a time created out of work, out of study, out of tensions, and which, through these things, becomes timeless. Such simplicity of effect, thought made pictorial space, appeared like a deliberate provocation. All it actually sought to provoke was silence and contemplation, but that did not prevent it being subjected to a formalist interpretation and used subsequently as a justification of Minimal Art.

In his explorations of the density, transparency and texture of colour, Rothko followed a very similar path : "Pictures must be miraculous; the instant one is completed the intimacy between the creation and the creator is broken. He is an outsider." His fluid paint becomes at times translucent and seems to seek its way through to penetrate the surface, elsewhere it gains in intensity from the superimposed veils of pigment. Rothko never knew in advance what would be the nature of his paintings, he discovered it only as he worked. "They begin as an unknown adventure in an unknown space," he explained. "It is at the

1. Ad Reinhardt:
   Blue Painting, 1953
2. Rothko:
   White Stripe, 1958

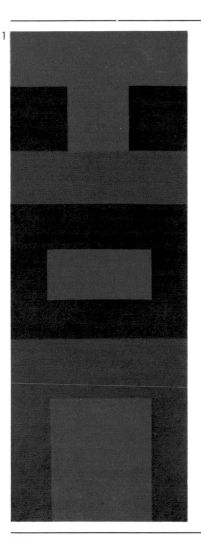

moment of completion that in a flash of recognition, they are seen to have the quantity and the function which was intended. Ideas and plans that existed in the mind at the start were simply the doorway through which one left the world in which they occur." *(Possibilities* 1, 1947-48) To Rothko it was entirely irrelevant whether he was abstract or figurative, for: "It is really a matter of ending this silence and solitude, of breathing and stretching one's arms again." And: "The familiar identity of things has to be pulverized in order to destroy the finite associations with which our society increasingly enshrouds every aspect of our environment. Without monsters and gods, art cannot enact our drama : art's most profound moments express this frustration."

With Rothko, colour asserted its primacy. It dissolved form and lent new vigour to the space/plane of the picture by penetrating into it, dilating it. To make this effect more marked, the painter often used canvases of enormous size that seemed to engulf the spectator. "I paint very large pictures...," he explained. "The reason I paint them, however — I think it applies to other painters I know — is precisely because I want to be very intimate and human. To paint a small picture is to place yourself outside your experience, to look upon an experience as a stereopticon view or with a reducing glass... However you paint the larger picture, you are in it. It isn't something you can command." *(Interiors,* May 1951) It was this desire to show colour to advantage that led Rothko to present some of his later shows as environments, co-ordinated displays in which each work had a specific resonnance within the overall intensity — rather like an orchestral setting composed of the unique contributions of each instrument in the orchestra.

We rediscover something of this same meditative intensity in Ad Reinhardt, who used minimally contrasting colour fields which seem to aspire to the condition of monochrome, within severe geometric compositions; these he regarded as representative of a type of universal painting that was unmannered, beyond style and free of artifice. Pictures have a life of their own, the more so, however, in the work of this generation of painters, whose canvases are often so large that they exceed the spectator's field of vision, and so seem to immerse him in a world where colour acquires new significance.

1

CHAPTER 10
INFORMAL ART

2

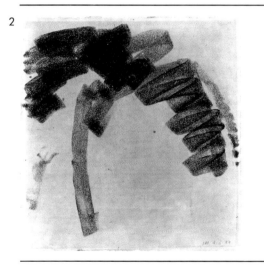

1. Hartung:
   Untitled, 1956-59
2. Hartung:
   Untitled, 1924

In *The Open Work,* which explores the dimensions of creativity in the post-war years, Umberto Eco notes: "The crisis that overtook bourgeois civilization related in part to the average man's inability to adapt to systems of acquired forms, presented to him from outside, and which he had not discovered for himself through the conquest of reality... It becomes legitimate to ask the question, whether contemporary art, by accustoming us to the continual disruption of models and schemas — by adopting as model or schema the innate perishability of all models and schemas, and the necessity of their modification not only as between one work and another but actually within the context of each single work — whether that might not fulfil a precise pedagogical function, namely a function of liberation. If that were the case, then it would be true to say that the scope of contemporary art now extends beyond taste and aesthetic structures, and takes its place as part of a much wider debate, so that it represents for modern man a possibility of salvation, a means of rediscovering autonomy, a dual level of perception and intelligence."

This element of disruption, the necessity for pure experimentation without pre-set goals, was also imposed by changes within the civilization as a whole, as was recognized by one of the leading French abstractionists Georges Mathieu: "If in the artistic domain we are experiencing the dissolution of all the classical values, an equally fundamental and parallel revolution is taking place as well in the scientific domain, where the recent discrediting of old concepts of space, matter, parity and gravity, and the

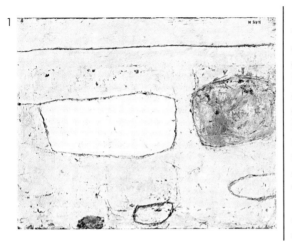

1. Scott:
   Composition, 1955
2. Bryen:
   Crinane jaune (no. 41), 1953
3. Fautrier:
   Sweet Woman, 1946
4. Fautrier:
   Hostage: Head, no. 1, 1944
5. Fautrier:
   Little Square, 1958

resurgence of ideas of uncertainty, probability, contradiction and entropy, now create the real prospect of a renaissance of mysticism and the achievement of a new transcendence." ("D'Aristote à l'abstraction lyrique", *L'Œil*, April 1959) Such a parallel has of course always existed between the approaches adopted by scientists and artists, but if our own age has been forced to come to terms with the fundamental revision of attitudes that has occurred in the mainstream of science, it has often been reluctant to accept that the same must hold true for the arts, where the logic of change is equally compelling.

After the war, Paris remained the only European capital spared from the general devastation, the only arena in which the battle for a new consciousness in the arts could be waged; yet circumstances were less propitious than in the United States, for tradition continued to weigh heavily and realism had gained a new currency from the rearguard action against the Social Realism of the Communist bloc. Above all, the public was more hostile to the avant-garde, because the great generation that included Matisse, Picasso and Braque was still active.

It was within the luxurious confines of the Galerie René Drouin, Place Vendôme, that the first intimations of a new and different art were felt, later to be characterized as "art informel". After that first Dubuffet exhibition of October 1944, the same gallery showed in the following year Fautrier's *Hostages* series, works by Wols and Dubuffet's "hautes pâtes". Then in 1947, at the Galerie du Luxembourg, Michel Tapié and Georges Mathieu staged an exhibition of the works of Wols, Hartung, Mathieu, Riopelle and Bryen, marking the first appearance of a school of Lyrical Abstraction. The emphasis of these artists on gesture was not markedly different from the comparable American phenomenon, except that it was much more firmly rooted in drawing and not therefore concerned to question the "closed" space of the picture. But for the European artists, like the Americans, the act of painting and the expression of creative freedom had become the subject matter of art: "The painters of the past started with a meaning and found signs for it. The new painters start with signs, and all that remains then is to discover a meaning," noted Jean Paulhon (*L'Art informel*, 1962).

Dubuffet, Fautrier and even Wols do not by any means exclude all reference to the visible world, but

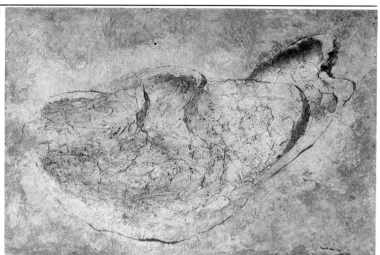

as Damisch emphasizes: "What the 'informal' painter rejects is first and foremost a particular conception of the picture as a reflection, or repetition, of a reality or a model, of a sketch even, that has been laid down in advance. The informal is opposed in principle to all forms of representation, imitation or verisimilitude: and if an image emerges at the end of the pictorial process, that image in no way resembles a copy or a portrait. Rather, by doubly emphasizing the signifier, it works by analogy, an analogy that may be premeditated but which relies more on the materials of painting than on any reference that the pigment, through its excesses and accidents, gives rise to in the mind." (Fenêtre, ibid.)

Started in 1942, the Hostages series marked the culmination for Fautrier of a long exploration of the expressive potential of his medium. First covering sheets of paper with thick glue, he would then apply the pigment with great freedom, creating a highly textured surface which, for him, was the picture's flesh. He confided to André Vernet: "I wanted to discover for myself a palette distinctively mine, a system in which drawing had a place, and an important place, so that colour and impasto did not disrupt its meaning." In their sheer physicality, these broken images directly convey the quality of Fautrier's own profound emotion, but they are in no sense a description of the horrors he witnessed. With its emphasis on expression, as opposed to geometry, this type of painting changed the whole conception, in France, of what abstraction could mean.

Although laying great stress on the "signifier", by

1. Dubuffet:
   Landscape with Bat, 1952
2. Dubuffet:
   Terre courde, 1959
3. Dubuffet:
   Mire G 49 Kowloon, 1983

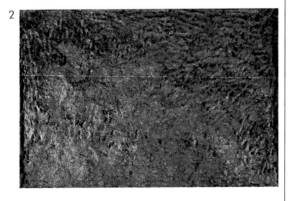

the liberties he took with his medium, Dubuffet did not sever himself from reality, any more than Fautrier did. Using forms, colours and materials with a boldness and freedom hitherto reserved for primitive painting or the artistic expressions of the mentally disturbed, he evolved a type of "art brut" ("uncultured art") that rapidly found great favour with the Americans. His search for contact with life made him look first to the world to provide him with his material. A true poet of nature, fascinated by themes of germination, to convey his sense of the universe, he drew freely on those things that were in effect nature's rejects: in so doing, he liberated Western painting once and for all from the constraints of aestheticism. This "other" art, which preferred to manipulate materials rather than create visual illusion, revealed to his contemporaries the vast expressive potential of texture and materiology; Tàpies and the supporters of *arte povera* were among those who were quick to follow where he had led. Trying always to transcend his own limitations, Dubuffet revived long-despised forms and found new ways of appropriating real life and the real world to his purposes: "The picture will not be regarded passively, simultaneously taken in at a glance by whoever sees it, it will be re-experienced in the way it was made, it will be re-created by thought, I go so far as to say, it will be re-enacted. All the gestures made by painters will be reproduced in the viewer." (Dubuffet, *Prospectus T,* 1) In his desire to communicate, Dubuffet was alert to the promptings of chance and instinct, and this led him to develop a distinctive form of automatic writing, consisting exclusively of anthropomorphic forms. The automatism of the Surrealist painter Miró culminated with the image of a man; in the Dubuffet of *L'Hourloupe,* the *Theatres of Memory* or the *Psycho-sites,* it is that image that is fundamental, as though he had chosen, in Daniel Abadie's words: "to make these silhouetted figures bear the weight of identifying the focus of some apparently indeterminate action. Not without ambiguity, and in spite of the inevitable distortions of scale, these figures, deposited apparently arbitrarily in space, imparted to that space a hitherto undreamed-of coherence." (*Mires,* exhibition catalogue, Venice Biennale, 1984) In the *Mires,* Dubuffet seems almost to obliterate the human image in a last instinctive act of liberation, producing the most purely abstract works of his whole career. But for Dubuffet, ab-

1. Wols:
   The Butterfly's Wing, 1947
2. Wols:
   Untitled, 1949
3. Riopelle:
   Follow the Guide, 1969
4. Hartung:
   T 1936-10, 1936
5. Schneider:
   Untitled, 1960

straction and figuration are in the end no more than intellectual categories, incapable of containing the reality and the mystery of man's exploration of his world. Dubuffet has never become identified with any school, it is his individual thirst for freedom that has paved the way for a type of expression emancipated from all stylistic constraint; he thus appears as the direct precursor of the return to free and instinctive painting that has characterized the eighties.

In France, the painter who pursued non-geometric abstraction to its limits was Wols, whose real name was A. W. Schulze. Of German origin, he had attended the Bauhaus and thus knew most of the leading abstract painters; when he went to Paris, he earned his living at first as a photographer, but while interned during the war years developed a highly personal and distinctive style of painting, of great dramatic intensity. The major exhibition of his work at the Galerie Drouin in 1947 marked the climax of his career — he was to die aged only thirty-eight. Energizing Surrealist automatism with Expressionist violence Wols evolved an inspired calligraphy, sign and background setting up a powerful interaction in a manner that was entirely new. Something of that style finds an echo in the paintings of the poet Michaux.

The exhibition staged by Tapié and Mathieu in 1947 offered its own alternative approach to painting, namely, that form of instinctive and improvisatory self-expression described by Mathieu as Lyrical Abstraction. This type of painting became so popular that, in his book *Morphologie autre*, published in 1960, Michel Tapié counted 108 painters practising "art informel", for whom gesture was the product of "psychic improvisation". Mathieu, who was familiar with the work of the Abstract Expressionists, developed a particular interest, circa 1951, in exploring the points of comparison and contrast between the two schools. In general, it was true that the painting of the artists who lived and worked in Paris tended to be less vehement and dramatic, and to distinguish them from the Americans they soon came to be grouped together as practitioners of the "informel" (Michel Tapié, 1956) or as "tachistes" (Charles Estienne, 1954). For these painters, soon to be joined by Soulages and Riopelle, the picture was the field of expression of states of feeling, in both their physical and psychic manifestations.

Georges Mathieu was both the catalyst and the

spokesman for this embryonic movement. In his own work he developed a form of calligraphy inspired by Far Eastern models. To encourage spontaneity of gesture he worked very rapidly, and regarded each painting as a performance, which he was quite prepared to enact under the public eye. In Tokyo, for example, he painted a picture twelve metres long in just twenty minutes! But his provocative approach and impassioned gesture did not prevent a degree of mannerism entering his work, a pitfall avoided by Hartung, who largely retained his youthful vigour and inspiration. From a very early age he had been interested in drawing and by this means had arrived intuitively at a form of spontaneous gesturalism. In 1937 he painted his first canvases in the manner later described as Lyrical Abstraction and, abandoning any attempt at formalism, developed a gestural expression of great emotional force. For him, painting was "acting on canvas"; what he sought to express was man's emotion in the face of his destiny. Grappling with ever larger painting surfaces Hartung experimented with different tools, but whether he used an artist's brush, a decorator's paintbrush, a spatula or a spray-gun, his concern was always to make his dynamic calligraphy appear to erupt out of an infinity of space, its violence echoing the harshness of the times.

In general, the European artists had difficulty in dispensing with the aesthetic considerations the Americans had simply sidestepped, by broadening the scope of their concerns, elevating the "making" of the picture over the end result, however raw.

Tachism became so fashionable and "tasteful" that in the end only a few exceptional personalities have survived the test of time. Soulages, in objectifying Hartung's gesture and supplying it with an architectural dimension, arrived at an organic conception of space. Gesture became identified with surface, in a type of chiaroscuro construction where the true "subject" of the picture was light. A metaphorical distillation of his sensations, Soulage's painting presents itself simply as a moment of life, begging all considerations of abstraction or figuration. He said: "I do not start out with either an object or a landscape, which I then distort, nor on the other hand do I try to conjure these up by painting their appearance. Rather what I hope for is rhythm, that beating of forms in space, the intersection of space by time. Space and time cease to be the medium within which the painted forms have their existence, they have become the instruments of the canvas's poetry... What happens in a picture, which from being an object in the course of fabrication suddenly becomes something living, that I can find no words to describe." (in J. Grenier, *Entretiens avec dix-sept peintres non-figuratifs*, 1963)

A similar quality of direct emotion emerges from the canvases of Gérard Schneider, although his works are more violent and tragic in mood. He was an original and independent artist, who largely escapes classification by sheer immediacy of gesture and stridency of colour, which seem to subsume in an instant's conflagration the traditional categories of painting: subject, emotion and presentation.

Similarly lyrical in spirit are the first abstract works by Messagier, who drew inspiration from the elemental forces of nature and its powers of continual regeneration. He arrived at plastic equivalents for these themes through constructions in which spontaneity of gesture is integrated within an architecture of complex organic space. Degottex adopted a more Oriental approach to painting, rejecting any notion of a pre-existent image in favour of signs he devised for himself. The marks of his calligraphy cut through silent space in such a way as to emphasize emptiness and infinity. "Painting," he said, "is an emotional language which is opposed to everything fixed that belongs to conventional language... What attracts me about the unconscious is its boundlessness, in other words precisely that area which goes beyond what you might

3

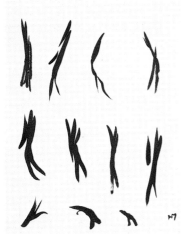

1. Soulages:
   Untitled, 1956
2. Degottex:
   Suite la rose (IV), 1959
3. Michaux:
   Movement, 1950
4. Michaux:
   Face, 1958

4

expect to find in the individual unconscious." (*Quadrum* no. 10, 1961)

A painter of calligraphic signs, Degottex adds another dimension to automatism, as a way of capturing the profound truth of an inner world. That same quest for the images of an internal abstract reality preoccupied Henri Michaux from the time he began to publish his writings, in 1927. "Painting, composing, writing, exploring myself. That is the adventure of being alive," he wrote. It is probably because he regarded all these branches of activity as interconnected that Michaux has remained a marginal figure in the history of painting. And yet his washes and watercolours articulate the forms of the unconscious in signs that have an extraordinary supercharged intensity and phantasmagorical power. Gifted with an almost mediumistic power of expression, his hand reacts with the sensitivity of a seismograph to the struggles and dramas enacted in the landscape buried deep within the artist's consciousness.

Since the ringing declarations of the Futurists, Italy had ceased to play much part in the evolution of abstraction. Only Magnelli continued to pursue the goal of pure pictoriality, building on the early Cubist experiments. It was many years before he eliminated figurative reference, since he saw no real distinction between figuration and abstraction, never having regarded it as the role of painting to copy external objects. Inspired by the masters of the *quattrocento* he painted compositions in which colour was one with matter, of which his friend Arp wrote: "Magnelli's canvases are not deceptions, imitations of the world. They are pure

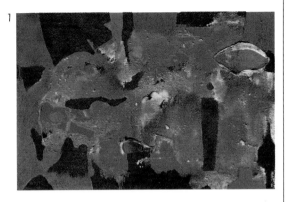

1. Burri:
   Sabbia, 1952
2. Tàpies:
   Collage with Rice, 1969
3. Tàpies:
   Rectangle and Oval, 1967

and full of reality... They are natural ornaments, without presumption or virtuosity." (*Magnelli*, exhibition catalogue, Galerie Drouin, 1948)

In the fifties, however, the breakthrough of gestural painting led to some spectacular developments in both Italy and Spain, centring on the figures of Burri and Tàpies. Each in his own way exemplified the particular feeling of Southern painters for colour/matter. Alberto Burri was among those who were to go furthest in the exploration of tangible space. Using the roughest of materials, old sacking, charred wood, rusty metal, and later plastics, he created compositions that were charged with intensity — as the Americans were quick to recognize. A similar visceral feeling for raw materials characterized also the Catalan Antonio Tàpies, enabling him to take the crucial step beyond gesturalism. His works have the look of walls that are as old as time itself, full of rich and complex textures, bearing a few boldly inscribed marks that could be taken as scrawls of graffiti.

For Tàpies, "the reality that meets the eye is but a poor shadow of reality"; the act of creation was determined simultaneously by an emotion stirred in the depths of the artist's innermost being and his response to a particular historical, geographical and cultural situation. In Catalonia, long oppressed under Franco's dictatorship, Tàpies's painting was like the sudden vision of a living land, bearing the marks of extortion and suffering, yet still fertile, still possessed of a future. Initially Tàpies was influenced by the Surrealism of Miró, but his work was transformed in circa 1953 by the discovery of abstract art: "Then one day, I reached out to find a direct expression of silence. More resigned, I submitted myself to the necessity that governs every profound struggle. The thousands of scratches turned into thousands of grains of sand... A whole new landscape, as though *Through the Looking Glass,* was suddenly available to me, opening up the innermost essence of things... And my greatest surprise was to find one day, quite suddenly, that my pictures, for the first time in this whole voyage of discovery, had been transformed into walls. By what strange route had I arrived at precisely these images? And why was it that I, the first to set eyes on them, trembled with emotion before them?" (Tàpies, *The Practice of Art,* 1974)

A parallel, although very different development occurred in France with the growth of another form

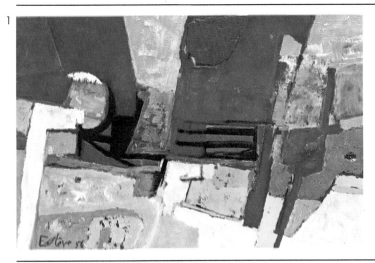

of abstraction — or, more accurately, of non-figuration. The pioneers of the movement made their first appearance in 1941 as the *Peintres de la tradition française,* expressing their united opposition to the Nazi Occupation. The principal members of the group were Bazaine, Lapicque, Manessier, Estève and Le Moal: they regarded themselves as the true heirs of Bonnard and Villon. Several of them had been taught by Roger Bissière, who, after many years of silence, had a major exhibition at the Galerie Drouin in 1947. From his study of folk-art he had evolved a radically different style, a transposed expression of nature marked by its sheer primitivist vigour.

Bazaine became the *de facto* theoretician of these painters of the new "School of Paris", who continued to regard as central the expression of an emotional reaction to the world. The object as a pretext for description had ceased to have any validity, yet they saw the dangers of becoming cut off from life altogether. As Bazaine noted: "... in princely solitude, guided and limited by his intelligence alone, our modern man has become one-legged. And he has lost his second face, the one that is turned towards the outside world." In his *Notes sur la peinture d'aujourd'hui* (1953), Bazaine set out what was effectively the programme for the whole group: "For more than half a century we have seen painting trying to rediscover its incarnation, trying to recapture the object that remains always elusive, trying, in other words, to achieve that penetration, that profound resemblance that exists between man and his world, without which there is

1. Estève:
   Sioule, 1956
2. Hayter:
   Yellow Flight, 1953
3. Bazaine:
   Noon, Trees and Rocks, 1952
4. Tal Coat:
   Vein of Flint, 1959
5. Zack:
   Untitled, 1954-55

no living form." What they now sought was: "a presence that would be, in itself alone, the sign of all reality: a deepening of the means of expression to take in a content that exceeds it, a move from explanation to significance. Undoubtedly, the ultimate form exists in another sphere, a realm where the question of figurative and non-figurative is simply irrelevant, but where this essential Presence may be found once more. A world which in all its details, in all its signs, reflects the whole of the world." Art has "always remained for man that more or less unconscious need to discover himself, to be aware of his inner life or the power he has, through the visible extension of himself, to objectify his inner universe. Art is temperament seen through nature: man's expression is always of himself and through himself."

It was this deeply felt belief that underlay the determination of these artists to enrich themselves with the experience of the world, and then to find a pictorial equivalent made up of forms and colours, whose rhythms and material presence would reflect a new consciousness, an awareness of the infinity of space and life. The success of such an enterprise thus depended in large measure on the subjective emotion and sensual response of the artists concerned.

Like the Impressionists, Bazaine and Manessier were captivated by the changing intensity of light, and both combined painting with an exploration of the techniques of stained glass; Estève experimented with slabs of form/colour, in a generally more classical spirit, while creating unusual and bold chromatic harmonies. Olivier Debré and Léon Zack sought in

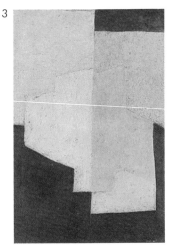

their work a pictorial equivalent of the changing face of the days and seasons; as too did Tal Coat, whose exploration of the relationship of space and light led him eventually away from signs to monochrome. Notably, this "landscape abstractionism" provided the classically educated painter Zao Wou Ki with a means of renewing his links with his Oriental roots. Through the self-expression of gestural painting he arrived at a form of calligraphy set in deep space, in which the sign was invested with a new spatio-temporal significance.

Vieira da Silva was one of the rare women painters of her generation. In abstraction she found the means of constructing a world made up of allusions and tensions, guiding the onlooker into labyrinths of light and life in which space appears to be infinitely expanding; here the aspirations of the mind seem perfectly in tune with the experience of the senses.

Three other artists working in France are largely unclassifiable since they arrived at new forms of abstraction by independent routes. Bram van Velde used the canvas to objectify and universalize the states of his own personal unhappiness and depression; within the convoluted arrangements of form and colour, each element is the mark of his own *Angst.* Van Velde's pictorial creations are in the end indistinguishable from his acute sensibility, for, with an absolute integrity, he lived each canvas as he lived every moment of his life. The element of chance that he allowed to intervene in his painting, he saw as directly comparable to those occasions in life when accident or fate obliges the individual to react, to assume the choice of a course of action that will determine his future. The rejection of fixed models, the failure he courted every time he started afresh with a new canvas, made Samuel Beckett describe van Velde as a hero of the malaise of contemporary life; isolation and the inability to communicate, transformed into signs and colours, inspired one of the most original and complex pictorial quests of our times.

Poliakoff's compositions were more finite: he made space a unity, giving matter/colour a timeless iconic and spiritual dimension; while the incomparable Nicolas de Staël, in the course of his short life, explored every medium of expression with a quite dazzling intensity. In its richness and many-sided complexity, its inspired combinations, his *œuvre* transgresses all the accepted boundaries.

4

5

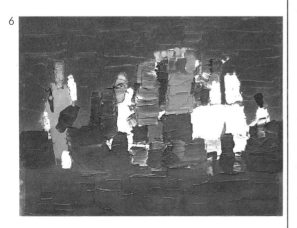

6

It was while in Nice during the war that de Staël learned about abstraction from such pioneers of concrete art as Magnelli and Sophie Taeuber-Arp. From the start, his work was dynamic in its handling, with a strong feeling for the expressivity of paint. As gesture was translated into a powerful calligraphy, within the ever-larger formats that sought to contain it, so he began to apply the pigment with a palette knife, closely identifying gesture with the picture space and surface.

By December 1949, de Staël had already posed the question: "Can a picture be a coloured mark and nothing else? I do not know the answer." In his canvases, fragments of the real world began to show through the paint; matter, form and colour were as one, in an architecture that cried out to be called by the name of the real element of which it was the perfect plastic equivalent, be it earth, sea, wall or sky... Finally he arrived at the discovery of pure colour as he also identified the object with its coloured mark, making the "subject" of the painting synonymous with its "object". This "reinvention" of figuration was greeted with blank incomprehension at the time, as it anticipated later developments on these lines by some twenty years. Surrounded by the landscapes of Sicily, and lightening his palette in response, de Staël produced paintings even more intensely alive and glowing, for in practice it is not when colour is at its maximum intensity throughout that it appears most brilliant, but when it is used sparingly, so that its stridency lights up only a few selected areas. In his last pictures, de Staël worked at "the limits of the void". In the violence of

their contrasts, these paintings seek to express the multiplicity of nature buried within the vastness of its shifting realities; the return to the forms of the visible world has been accomplished without any diminution of the expressive potential and freedom of action that characterize modern painting. Insisting always that felt personal experience was at the heart of the performance that was painting, de Staël conveyed all the immediacy and dynamism of that act. For him, execution was the expression of power as well as the power of expression.

Fierce expression and the retention of figurative allusions are also the hallmarks of works by the COBRA group. The name was made up from the initials of the Northern capital cities: CO(penhagen), BR(ussels) and A(msterdam). The founder of the movement was Asger Jorn, and his colleagues included Appel, Jacobsen, Alechinsky, Corneille and Dotremont. Their highly charged and dramatic paintings first came to the attention of the public in 1948. Produced in a spirit of rebellion against cultural norms, these are like dynamic projections, pure fountains of energy, Lyrical Abstraction given an Expressionist character. Popular art and folklore supplied the direct inspiration for the hallucinatory forms and violent colours of their type of spontaneous gestural painting.

Expressionism always retained its attraction for the northern European painters. With COBRA, the style gained a second wind, for this generation looked back beyond the Middle Ages that had been the inspiration for Die Brücke, to the art of the Irish and Viking peoples, where abstraction habitually appeared in totemic, or ideogramatic, guise. It was largely for this reason that the COBRA group rejected a commitment to modern abstraction; figuration and expression, gesture and language were for them intimately linked. All they adopted from modern painting was its liberation of gesture and colour, together with the notion that art could be created out of any element of reality that was at hand.

This total freedom of expression was something also demanded by Bernard Requichot, whose tragic disappearance in 1962 cut short a brilliant career, marked by a series of violent and chaotic works of a compelling originality. Arriving at non-figuration in 1954, Requichot soon found it as much of a restriction as any other recognized form or genre. For him, all the categories used to classify artists, and all the

1. Jorn:
   I'm Browned Off with the Sun,
   1961
2. Alechinsky:
   Swimming, 1955
3. Appel:
   La Nurse, 1950
4. Davie:
   The Martyrdom of St. Catherine,
   1956
5. Doucet:
   Time of Re-creation, 1948

different approaches these represented, were in the end simply irrelevant. His doubts, and his own approach to painting, are summed up in this one question: "What matter is there that is not aesthetic? What is aesthetically pleasing may be made unaesthetic... wooden logs, a mummified corpse, a picture, a statue, a mountain, which of these has the least appeal to the emotions? It is looking at a spectacle that creates the emotion. Out of the man who looks at logs, or the man who looks at mountains, or the man who looks at statues, which man sees the most? Surely no one can swear to those exact moments in which he looks at anything?" (*Cimaises,* March 1962)

There is a similar independent spirit in the work of the Englishman Alan Davie. Reliant, in his parallel career as a jazz musician, on improvisatory techniques, he explicitly drew the distinction between the certainty that comes with cerebral knowledge and the certainty of the artist, based on intuition.

Because it so rapidly acquired a fashionable status, Lyrical Abstraction or "art informel" became devalued by its imitators, and those qualities for which it had initially won acclaim became obscured. By the end of the sixties, Paris ceased to be the artistic capital of Europe; with the growth of the market and ever-rising prices, the ability seemed to have been lost to distinguish between pastiche and true originality. Umberto Eco sounded a warning note: "Meaning is referred back continually to the sign and becomes enriched by new resonances. Thus a veritable chain reaction is started, one that is characteristic of the field of aesthetic stimulus and of that organization of stimuli generally called form. In theory, this reaction is endless. In practice, it is interrupted when a form ceases to stimulate us; our withdrawal is obviously caused in part by a lessening of attention, a sort of habituation to the stimuli: on the one hand, the signs of which these consist have been perfected, there is a feeling of satiation, and their effects seem blunted; on the other hand, the associations that are sparked off in the course of perception, instead of remaining at the level of spontaneous associations, appear, through habituation, as well-rehearsed schemas... For a time the form is exhausted. For the sensibility to recover its freshness, a long period of quarantine is required." (*Op. cit.*)

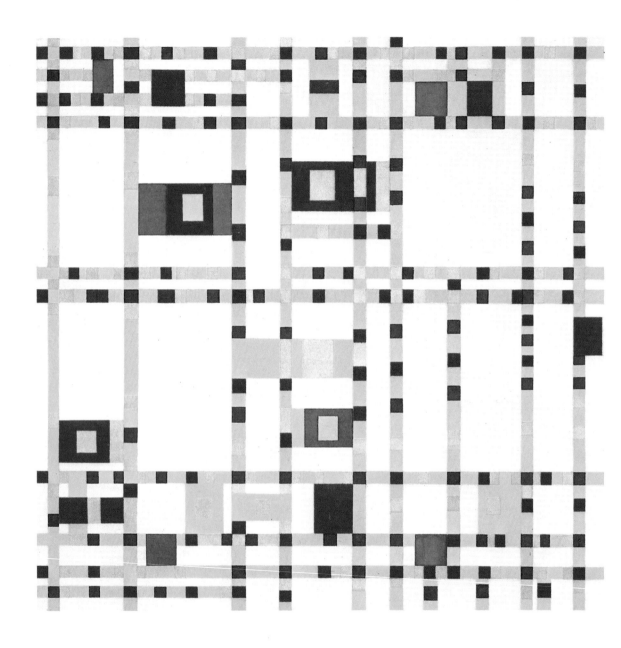

Mondrian: Broadway Boogie-Woogie, 1942-43

CHAPTER 11
KINETIC AND SPATIAL ART

From its beginnings, abstraction had oscillated between the two poles of reason and instinct, between construction and lyricism. Abstract Expressionism went from strength to strength after the thirties, as geometric abstraction seemed to founder for the want of new ideas. It was, among others, Mondrian who in his last period breathed fresh life into the geometric form and bent it to new purposes. In the years he spent as an exile in New York during the war, he became fascinated by the continual bustle of life in the metropolis. Without reneguing on his earlier work, reduced to the intersection of bars of colour against a white ground, in his last pictures he attempted to find a framework to express energy and movement, creating a depth of space out of their dynamic articulation; in *Broadway Boogie-Woogie,* a dance rhythm liberates the picture from the restraints of surface line, at the same time suggesting expansion outwards from the centre.

Shortly after this, in 1947, the Italian-based Argentinian Lucio Fontana invented *spazialismo,* or spatial art. "Art is dead," he declared, "but it is saved by gesture." Even as he reduced the picture to a monochrome surface, he at the same time endowed it with three-dimensionality, by means of ruptures and slashès in its surface. For Fontana, space was defined by the trajectory of gesture, recorded with a point or blade; everything lying outside this inscribed field was negative, void and inert. Space became real space, both in terms of the way the picture was created, and in its finished reality. Perforation and laceration are profoundly symbolic acts, directed against

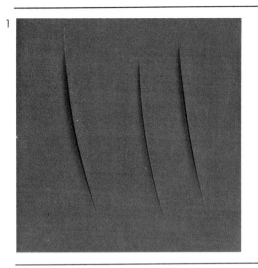

1. Fontana:
   Slashed Canvas, 1960
2. Pol Bury:
   Mobile Plane 2, 1954
3. Vasarely:
   Ilile-couple, 1952
4. Agam:
   Transformable Picture, 1954
5. Soto:
   Spiral, 1955

2

the surface. The sweep of the gesture does more than trace a sign, it actually attacks the painting or, more precisely, the idea of the painting. Movement is made figuration; the canvas bears the visible scar, uniting the space-time in which the action is performed with the space-time of the record of that act. Between Pollock's gestural action and the signs of the Europeans, a new area of exploration was opened up, destined to be the preserve of what came to be known as kinetic art, its concern precisely the exploration of that gulf between the material reality of painting and the psycho-sensual phenomena of perception. Few artists had previously ventured into this difficult territory. Marcel Duchamp, certainly, with his *Rotoreliefs* — virtual images produced by motion — also Gabo, Moholy-Nagy and Calder himself, although their works had more to do with sculpture than painting. It is a paradox that, by this route, painting was both to rediscover real space and at the same time be liberated from its materiality.

The Galerie Denise René, which opened in Paris in 1945, was to provide the focus of activity for the new generation of abstract painters who grappled with these concepts during the fifties. As both theorist and practitioner, seeking to recreate space or suggest movement by the use of a geometric morphology of forms, Vasarely was to impose himself as their undisputed leader. In 1955 an exhibition called "Mouvement" was staged at the Galerie Denise René, showing the works of Agam, Bury, Jacobsen, Soto, Tinguely and Vasarely alongside the productions of an older generation represented by Duchamp and Calder. The show was in effect a manifesto, calling for the reintroduction of a vitalizing force within geometric representation, achieved by means of real or apparent motion. "Optical effects," the critic Pierre Restany points out, "are called upon to play a central role in kinetic art, a role comparable to that played by gestural automatism in Lyrical Abstraction or Action Painting." (*Op. cit.*)

In the re-creation of movement by purely optical means, Vasarely had already made great strides. With all the idealism of a Malevich or a Mondrian, convinced that a new age was dawning, he devoted himself to the systematic exploration of an alternative vocabulary. He believed a new participatory relationship could be achieved between the work and its beholder, through the exploitation of the

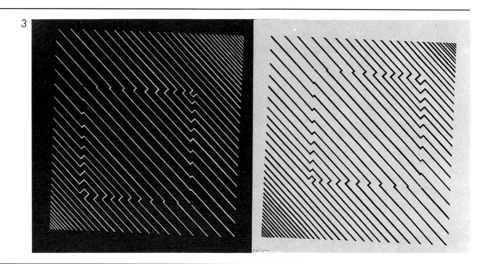

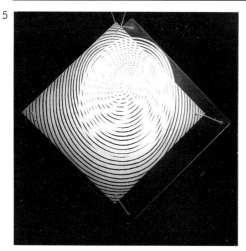

resources of contemporary technology. Struck by the impossibility of making a figure or colour remain within a single plane — which he defined as "the birth in a plane of a space that is still mysterious" — Vasarely set out systematically to analyse the phenomena of perception, and by this means discovered the dynamic qualities of optical illusions. Taking as his starting point the optical equality of positive and negative, he concluded that in a grid "inside" and "outside" are not separate but continuous. Gradually he arrived at more complex superimposed spaces, playing with oppositions of forms and colours, which he refused to regard as separate entities. In his *Yellow Manifesto,* he declared: "Form and colour are one. Form cannot exist until it is summoned by a quality of colour. Colour is not a quality until it has been delineated by form. Line (drawing, contour) is a fiction, deriving not from one but two form/colours at a time. It does not create form/colours, it is born out of their encounter. Two form/colours, necessarily contrasting, constitute plastic unity, that is, the unity of creation: the eternal duality of all things, recognized at last as inseparable. Unity is the abstract essence of Beauty, the primary form of sensibility." ("Mouvement" exhibition, *Notes pour un manifeste,* 1955)

Agam and Soto continued to experiment along the lines established by Vasarely, but they emphasized the physical participation of the spectator, who by adopting different viewpoints could read the work in a number of different ways, always in relief. Soto's first *Optical Repetitions* date from 1951; in these he obtained the effect of vibration by the repetition of

1. Morellet:
   Untitled, 1952
2. Cruz-Diez:
   Physichrome no. 1, 1959
3. Morellet:
   2 Lattices of Perpendicular Lines,
   1952

slightly protruding geometric units. Pursuing his investigations of three-dimensional perception, he went on to produce his famous "moiré" effects, in which a lined screen had metal rods suspended in front of it. As the rod moved or the spectator shifted his position, a new wave of optical activity was set up in the background, exploding the linear pattern.

Agam developed what he called "transformable" pictures: these consisted of a background on which were glued thin perpendicular strips or triangular sections; each set of facets constituted an independent composition, so that as the spectator moved he could see one picture transform itself into another. Soto and Agam frequently worked in real space, so that it is sometimes difficult to decide whether their works belong more particularly to sculpture or to painting. The same confusion exists with the subtly orchestrated *Physichromes* of Cruz-Diez or the works of Julio Le Parc, who, with his combinations of basic forms in movement and light, has described himself as the prototype of the artist-engineer. François Morellet is more severe, exploring different combinations and juxtapositions of fundamental structures and developing these into webs and lattices of an inspired complexity.

Kinetic art was taken up in England with particular effect by Bridget Riley, and also spread to Italy, where Milan became the focus of activity for a number of artists working in the region.

This second generation of geometric abstractionists were as convinced as their predecessors of the need to operate within society; frequently they worked in

3

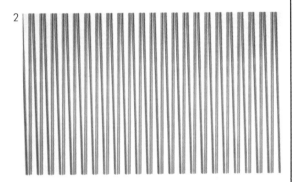

collaboration with architects or pursued dual careers as artists and designers.

The espousal of geometric idealism as a means of transforming human sensibility and intelligence before long became the hallmark of a new school of painting; its popular impact was considerable, in large measure because these artists inaugurated a new kind of art object, the "multiple", an original work of art mass-produced by machine. Vasarely had already advocated such a development in his 1955 manifesto: "As it is only the entities of the art of the past that are intelligible, as not everyone has the chance to make a profound study of contemporary art, we advocate its 'presence' in place of its 'understanding'. Sensibility being a distinctively human faculty, our messages will certainly reach the mass of the people by the natural route of their emotional response. The art of tomorrow will be a shared treasure or it will not be at all." Industrially mass-produced art fulfilled a social ideal, and it also transformed the work of art into a consumer object. With multiples, and through their collaboration on architectural projects, these artists came down from their ivory towers into the streets, and into people's houses, but the most important thing they did was remove the spectator from his passive role, by enlisting his cooperation.

With Max Bill, a former pupil of the Bauhaus, and Dewasne, geometricism took a new turn. Bill advocated the use of mathematical concepts, for which he found visual equivalents in his series or progressions, while Dewasne produced works of great monumen-

4

tality, intended to stress the expressive power of the painting surfaces made available by modern technology. Many painters were attracted to the idea of using the series to explore the relationship of colour and form, and this revival of interest in primary structures before long found a very different expression in Minimalism.

The growth and buoyancy of the art market, the proliferation of exhibitions and their coverage in the media, the spawning of a network of specialized magazines that kept an expanding public up to date with the latest developments, all these helped to transform art into a consumer activity. Movements became fashionable almost overnight, and the more meteoric their rise, the more quickly did they plunge to obscurity. In the new art world, the saturation of the market became a commonplace. Many trends were initially greeted with enthusiasm, but lost their appeal once the novelty had worn off. Never before had there been such a pressure on artists to produce always something new and original; only with a degree of hindsight is it possible to see that the artists who have survived and who have continued to produce work of quality are those who were content to be guided only by their own integrity and the logic of their internal development.

Often because of commercial rivalry, or simply because it provided good publicity, artistic squabbles tended to break out, exacerbating existing divisions and leading to a still greater fragmentation among the groups. At the very time when abstraction had won its battles internationally, it thus found itself under attack from a new generation. The sixties generally were a time of protest, and that was as true for art as in other spheres of life. There was a growing spirit of neo-Dadaism, a desire to sweep away all the excesses of gestural and lyrical painting; in the Anglo-Saxon world this tendency was expressed as Pop Art and in Europe as the New Realism. Both these movements set in train a return to figuration, even while retaining their distances from it; in part they were inspired by a sociological concern, in part by the exigencies of pictorial composition. In 1953, Rauschenberg produced his first combine-paintings, which exhibited a new type of figuration, uniting the sociological significance of the *objet trouvé* with the physical gesture of protest implicit in Action Painting. Influenced by Duchamp's ready-mades and Schwit-

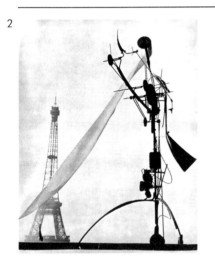

ters's collages, Rauschenberg found a way round "the significant impasse of gestural painting" by using collage to introduce into his work fragments of everyday reality; by this means he created a sort of narrative iconography that grew progressively more convoluted. At the same period, with his *Stars and Stripes* and targets, Jasper Johns effected a return to painting-as-painting, subverting the representative function of the object in his exploration of the relationship of form and substance. This generation rejected the notion that art and life were distinct; they drew on the manifestations of the contemporary world to give their work new urgency.

In Europe, the desire to look towards the real world was the underlying theme of the work of the New Realists. On 28 April 1958, Yves Klein created something of a sensation with his exhibition of "emptiness" at the Galerie Iris Clerc, where all that was exhibited in the space was the physical presence of the artist himself: "total space in all its freedom," wrote Pierre Restany, the movement's founder.

Shortly afterwards, the first Paris Biennale showed Hains's "décollages", paintings and posters torn into ribbons, one of Tinguely's "metamatics", a machine that produced abstract paintings, and the "monochromes" of Yves Klein. "It was then," said Restany, "that I recognized the common denominator of their approaches, a gesture: impregnation with pure colour on the part of Yves Klein, the mechanical animation of Tinguely, the selection of the torn poster by Hains. Each individual adventure develops its internal logic by starting from an extreme position, which constitutes the essence of the language, the mainspring of communication. That absolute gesture is a summons to the spectator whose participation is required. The imperative of expression linked to the act of appropriation reflects a fully developed moral stance. The moral autonomy of the gesture, already asserted in action painting, is taken to the absolute and tangible limits of its significance... In terms of their motivation, there is no difference between the gestural position adopted by the Lyrical Abstractionists or the action painters and that of the New Realists. The difference is merely quantitative; with Klein *all* the colour is blue, with Tinguely *all* the movement comes from the motor, with Hains *all* the images are in the poster." (*La Peinture Moderne*, T.V., 1982)

The objectivity of nature was presented with a dif-

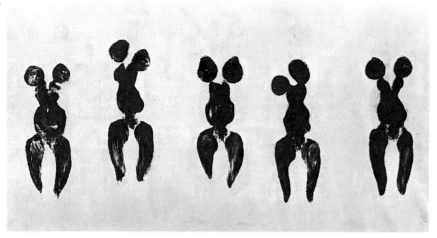

4

1. Jasper Johns:
   Flag, 1954-55
2. Tinguely:
   Metamatic, 1959
3. Hains:
   Untitled, 1961
4. Klein:
   Anthropometry from the Blue
   Period, 1960
5. Klein:
   Monochrome IKB, 1960

5

ferent slant by Arman in his exhibition "Le Plein" — when the Galerie Iris Clerc was filled with junk — and in his "accumulations", which fill up a space with many real elements, all the same; these assemblies were inspired by the repetitious nature of such mundane tasks as sealing or franking letters. From 1960, for the New Realists the means was synonymous with the end. As Yves Klein declared: "It is not enough to say or to write, I have gone beyond the concerns of art. You must have done it. For me, painting is no longer a function of the eye; it is a function of the only thing about ourselves that does not belong to us: our life." The *Anthropometries* (prints made from the bodies of women covered in blue paint) were the means of emphasizing the gulf between the work of art, in this case the monochrome, and life itself. Painting had become no more than the trace of an impregnation produced by a movement that was itself a function of the real world.

Once again, as before with Rodchenko, the limits of painting were transgressed. Restany concludes: "The erosion of the expressive power of gestural painting led to the act of appropriating reality and to various modalities of quantitative and assemblist language. Far from rejecting the contemporary world, the generation of 1960 wanted to become a part of it, and it proclaimed the expressive autonomy of the object, as product and symbol of industrial technology and the consumer society. But if the expressive adventure of the object created a developing awareness of the environment, it also stimulated the desire for neo-figuration." (*Op. cit.*)

Stella: Hyena Stamp, 1962

CHAPTER 12
RECENT DEVELOPMENTS

In the United States during the sixties, as Pop Art rehabilitated subject matter and the image, artists of the same generation continued to explore abstraction, and by returning to fundamentals, posing again the old Dada question "What is art?", they succeeded in bringing fresh life to the form. The common thread of their preoccupations was spectacularly revealed in an exhibition entitled "Post Painterly Abstraction", staged by the critic Clement Greenberg at the Los Angeles County Museum in 1964, which brought together the works of Sam Francis, Helen Frankenthaler, Kelly, Stella, Morris, Louis, Noland *et al.* All these artists insisted on the nature of painting as painting, and by exploiting uniquely and to the full its purely painterly qualities, they aimed to create art objects that were as real as the real world. Through the analysis of materials, the probing of the minimal relationship between surface, pigment and texture that justified a picture in laying claim to the status of work of art, they worked towards a definition of the *essence* of painting.

In the fifties, committed to achieving the recognition of a distinctively American school, Clement Greenberg summed up the situation facing these artists: "Though it may have started towards modernism earlier than the other arts, painting has turned out to have possessed a greater number of expendable conventions imbedded in it... It seems to be a law of modernism — thus one that applies to almost all art that remains truly alive in our time — that the conventions not essential to the viability of a medium be discarded as soon as they are recognized." ("American-

Type Painting", *Partisan Review,* 1955) Later he wrote: "Under the testing of this process more and more of the conventions of the art of painting have shown themselves to be dispensable, unessential. It has been established by now, it would seem, that the irreducibility of pictorial art consists in but two constitutive conventions or norms: flatness and the delimitation of flatness. In other words, the observance of merely these two norms is enough to create an object which can be experienced as a picture..." ("After Abstract Expressionism", *Art International,* 1962)

With the whole history of fundamental abstraction behind them, these Americans set out to explore the physical substance of painting, divorced from any subjective or idealist resonance. Their intention was to strip away everything not essential to the pictorial process. As Frank Stella declared, in 1964: "My painting is based on the principle that only what can be seen is there... What you see is what you see..."

Dubbed "hard edge" painting in 1958, and later subsumed within Post Painterly Abstraction, this reaction against Abstract Expressionism in fact had its roots within that movement. Gradually, as attention focused increasingly on flatness and the colour field, the scope of enquiry narrowed to concentrate on the actual physical make-up of the picture. Paradoxically, it was in the wake of Pollock that colour, as an independent entity, came to be regarded as the prime element of the picture, and the colour area or field replaced the sign. Where previously the emphasis had been on the various ways in which colour could be applied, now, in the wholesale exploration of pictoriality, it was surface properties that were highlighted. Crucial to this study was the recent invention of acrylic paint. Quite simply, painters found themselves liberated from the familiar impasto and transparent effects of oil paints. The new medium had compelling advantages: it dried quickly and had good penetration on any unprepared surface, it had a different colour saturation and it offered stability as well as a variety of glossy and matt effects.

In these early developments out of Abstract Expressionism, Helen Frankenthaler was one of the pioneers. In 1951 she visited Pollock's studio and was excited by his manner of working with the canvas on the floor. Two years later she experimented for herself with unprepared canvases laid out flat, to which she applied paint of very liquid consistency which

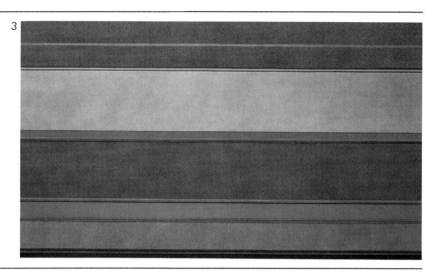

1. Frankenthaler:
   Mauve District, 1966
2. Frankenthaler:
   Blue Caterpillar, 1961
3. Noland:
   Navajo, 1971
4. Morris Louis:
   Beta Lambda, 1960

readily penetrated the surface, appearing not so much painted as stained. Her free and apparently unstructured pourings of coloured washes obtained novel effects; as the colour drew its own forms, it seemed the embodiment of that "drawing in colour" Matisse had practised in the big gouache cut-outs he produced at the end of his career. With the difference that in Frankenthaler's work, form and substance were one and the same. When Greenberg took them to visit her studio, Morris Louis and Noland at once recognized the possibilities of this approach. Noland said, "We were interested in Pollock, but could gain no lead to him. He was too personal. But Frankenthaler showed us a way — a way to think about and use colour." Her application of paint as a stain allowed for a greater surface unity without in any way denying the existence of the canvas.

Morris Louis's response was immediate. His *Veils* are washes of paint of different colours, allowed to run together and soak uniformly into the canvas. The canvas itself *is* the painting. In the subsequent series of *Unfurleds* and *Stripes,* Louis kept the rivulets of colour distinct; notionally, these appear to extend beyond the picture's edge, opening up space and carrying the eye outwards.

Not until 1959 with his *Concentric Rings* did Noland begin to explore the possibilities of staining revealed to him by Frankenthaler. The simple target form with its centrifugal rhythm enabled him to concentrate and contrast the resonances set up within the concentric bands of stained colour. Working with traditional paintbrushes and rollers, he

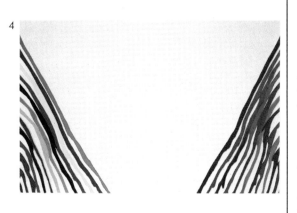

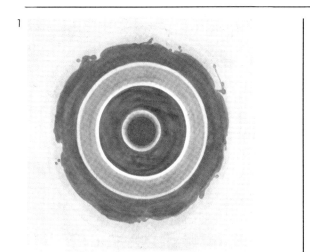

pursued his investigation of the pictorial form in a series of *Chevrons* (1964), opening up the picture diagonally, much as Louis had done before him. Eventually he painted a number of very long canvases of horizontal stripes, in which the repetition of the bands of colour seemed to call in question the fixed nature of the parallel framing-edge. In the earlier *Chevrons* too, the symmetry of the motif frequently echoed the shape of the frame, and seemed to push out beyond it. There is an obvious link with Mondrian's explorations of paintings extending beyond their boundaries...

Kelly is another painter who seems to exhibit the essentially Constructivist tendencies of hard-edge abstraction — although it must be said that these categorizations are to some extent a matter of judgement, except where the artist has made his position clear. Eliminating nuance in order to stress the opposition between the colour fields, his rigid lines of demarcation the very antithesis of gesturalist fluidity, Kelly's work defines the *sine qua non* of painting, its fundamental material and form.

In their efforts to relate the physical space of the canvas to the space of its environment, these artists looked above all to the example of Rothko and Newman. Both had concentrated their attention on the colour field — Newman increasing the size of his pictures until they themselves took on the character of an environment, and Rothko demonstrating that the goal of flatness was actually incompatible with the use of colour on a large scale — but what both asserted above all else was that the proper subject of paint-

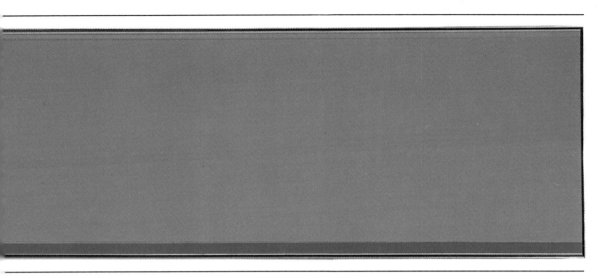

1. Noland:
   Untitled, 1960
2. Noland:
   Horizontal Stripes III-27, 1978
3. Noland:
   Erin, 1970
4. Kelly:
   Two Panels, Yellow and Black,
   1968

4

ing was painting itself. Henceforth the whole thrust of abstraction was to demonstrate the physical reality of the picture. In demanding that the picture should be allowed to reveal itself, these painters reversed the traditional position; if painting was formerly the means of the artist's self-expression, now it was the means of its own expression, with the painters acting as intermediaries... Some went so far as to eradicate all traces of personal handling or sensibility, so that the resulting work of art was identifiable only in terms of the concept that inspired it. Ryman's *White Mono-chromes* are the supreme example: the artist is present only in the initial choice of medium.

Around 1960, the shaped canvas made its appearance, this being a canvas that was either cut or stretched to an unusual configuration. It marked a new stage in the relationship of form to content, since now the form of the supporting surface was determined by the form of the painting. Noland arrived logically at this conclusion via the precise organization of his colour fields, and Kelly had gone a step further with works that consisted in the juxtaposition of two or more zones painted in all-over space, thus partially identifying external form with colour area. But the most radical interpretation of the shaped canvas was in the work of Frank Stella, who abandoned the traditional format altogether, allowing the final shape of the work to be dictated by the painting of which it consisted. Support was made subordinate to image. It was a fundamental reversal; no longer did the colour design exist in a more or less equal relationship to its background, it actually dictated its existence.

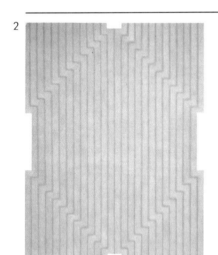

It was as a result of working on his *Black Paintings,* made up of black stripes alternating with stripes of bare canvas, that Stella developed his ideas about the subsidiary relationship of support to painting structure. "The problem that concerned me at that time was to find out if one could make abstract painting, how far you could go in the direction of flatness and in what degree that was viable, useful or beneficial. In short, what you could hope to gain from the practice of abstract painting in the plane; what were the positive aspects of working with flatness, how far it was practicable to go using the method, the advantages of doing so-called plane pictures or of using flattened space." (*Artistes,* no. 4, 1980; article published in French)

In these *Black Paintings,* where colour is renounced altogether in favour of black or metallic grey, Stella aimed to produce paintings that were easily read, non-referential objects, existing purely in their own right. In 1960 he presented his first shaped supports. Here the geometrical forms were allowed to develop logically from the artist's initial conception, and the canvas was then cut to echo their configuration, in such a way that the picture-edge itself encroached into the picture, echoing and interrupting the quasi-mechanical traces of the precisely delineated coloured stripes. From 1960 to 1966 the supports assumed ever more complex forms, appearing sometimes in the shape of an X, U, or S. Lacking an enclosing framework, these shaped canvases seemed to push their space out in all directions. They became structures, self-sufficient objects: "I'm not interested in know-

1. LeWitt:
   Pyramids, 1986
2. Stella:
   Marquis of Portago, 1960
3. Stella:
   Parczezew, 1971
4. Stella:
   Nogushi's Okinawa
   Woodpecker, 1978

4

ing if it's painting or sculpture or tap-dancing. One way or another, I've got to create art, in the way that works best for me. What matters to me is that the emphasis is on painting, the way it looks... I mean that although it has the character of a relief it is a painting you are looking at. I don't see it as a painted sculpture hung on a wall... it has to be art and it has to carry conviction. That's what matters." (Op. cit.)

In 1966 Stella began to explore colour and the spatial ambiguities it gave rise to, at first in irregular polygons where the forms disrupted the primary structures and transgressed their boundaries, then in a series of increasingly complex reliefs. By adopting a very fluent handling, Stella found a way to pursue his analysis of flatness and the colour area without falling into the trap of minimalist reductionism. In his *Brazilian Series* (1974), painted on aluminium and steel, he has more recently embarked on an idiom of brilliantly coloured scrawls and scribbles, which gives the work a sort of chaotic baroque intensity.

The series became for many of these artists a recognized mode within which to pursue their pictorial analysis; it had the advantage that it appeared to have an irrefutable logic of its own, supplying an objective confirmation of the work's progress. That objectivity was an important feature for Sol LeWitt, notably in the *Wall Drawings* in which he explored the effect of changing permutations within a series. LeWitt, however, like many of the artists grouped under the heading of Process Art, has concentrated principally on sculptural work, reflecting a preference for manipulating real elements in real space.

In the context of minimalist expression, apart from Ryman who since the late fifties has concentrated on methods of applying white paint to a variety of supports, we should mention James Bishop and Brice Marden, who look at painting in terms of its action on space, and Robert Mangold, whose particular interest is in boundaries and distortions. At the other extreme is Cy Twombly, whose neutral backgrounds are covered with graffiti-like gestural marks. While Pollock is a clear influence, Twombly gives the impression that even the most elementary exploration of picture properties is started always from scratch: with the colour that emerges fresh from its tube and is applied, stretched and spread in order to discover its consistency and transparency; the line that may be obtained from a new pencil, from those first tentative scribbles as you take it in your hand and test its responsiveness, to the thick scrawls that emerge as you begin to experiment and apply increasing pressure. Twombly "sees" by trying things out.

In Europe, during the same period, there was a similarly spirited rearguard action on the part of abstraction, exhibiting much of the same desire for radical solutions and redefinitions. In 1960, Simon Hantaï began to explore the legacy of Pollock through his "pliages": "It was necessary to interrogate gesture. The problem was: how to overcome the aesthetic privilege of talent, art, etc.? How to make the exceptional something ordinary? How to become 'exceptionally ordinary'? 'Pliage' was a way of resolving the problem. 'Pliage' involved no preconceptions, all you had to do was put yourself in the position of someone who had seen nothing; put yourself into the canvas." (in Geneviève Bonnefoi, *Hantaï,* 1973) The procedure consisted in folding or crumpling the canvas before it was painted, so that when it was opened out flat the colour was arbitrarily disposed. Hantaï was one of the first Europeans to experiment with the free canvas, that is, one not mounted on a stretcher. Central to his work is the relationship with the white of the background; previous to, and external to, the forms and colours, it supplies both the light and the physical context of the painting. Since 1960 Hantaï has followed the practice of titling his works according to the developing areas of his interest: *Materials, Studies, Whites, Tabulas,* etc.

Intimations of a new abstract painting began to be felt around 1966. The BMPT group, which derived its name from the initials of the painters concerned — Buren, Mosset, Parmentier and Toroni — gave to formal abstraction a new dimension of sociological and political significance. In their different ways they rejected all notion of the expression of feeling, insisting on a quasi-mechanical application of the form/colour to its support: Buren in canvases composed of vertical stripes; Mosset with white squares bearing the mark of a black ring; Parmentier with horizontal stripes; and Toroni by repetitions of the same brushstroke again and again at regular intervals. Buren, in addition, has written theoretical texts presenting a sociological analysis of the artistic phenomenon. "From the outset I tried to show as clearly as possible that actually a thing never exists in its own right, as a thing in itself. *A fortiori,* the whole direction of my

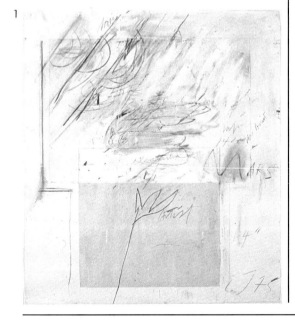

1

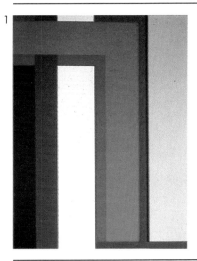

1. Devade:
   Untitled, 1971
2. Buren:
   Photo souvenir, 1968
3. Parmentier:
   Works of 1966, 1968, 1984
4. Cane:
   Untitled, 1974
5. Toroni:
   Untitled, 1970

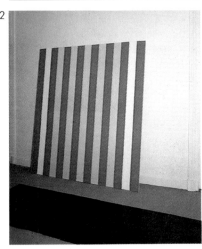

work. Nothing of what I show — starting with the material I employ — has existence except in relation to some other clearly defined thing. Anyone who directly experiences my work — provided, of course, he makes that minimum of effort it requires — will realize that its reduction is really about enlargement, an enlargement of the scope of vision. An enlargement that consists fairly and squarely in calling in direct question the whole of painting — no less — and the idea that it is a distillation or reduction of pure art. From that belief stem all those pronouncements (critical and art-historical) about the autonomy of the work of art. Pronouncements that are themselves inevitably reductionist, simplistic and a little too good to be true. If you re-examine the works and their contexts, you will see that their autonomy is a myth sustained only by such idealist pronouncements, and that not only are the pronouncements themselves questionable, but so to a very large extent are the works they defend, in other words the generality of art." (Interview in catalogue of "Buren" exhibition, Nouveau Musée, Lyon, 1980)

For the members of the Support-Surface group it was, however, the exploration of the literality of painting that dominated their work. Out of that narrow concentration on the material nature of painting, they were able to discover new possibilities of expression.

"Support-Surface" was the title of the manifesto exhibition held in 1970 at the Musée d'Art Moderne de la Ville de Paris, grouping together the works of Marc Devade, Vincent Bioulès, Patrick Saytour, Daniel Dezeuze, Claude Viallat and André Valensi —

4

5

soon to be joined by Jean-Pierre Pincemin, Louis Cane, Noël Dolla and Christian Jaccard. The group, whose theoretical position is stated in a publication called *Peinture Cahiers Théoriques* (1972), took as its starting point that credo of Post Painterly Abstraction: "Only what can be seen is there." Their analysis of the pictorial is however far more systematic than its American counterpart, and rooted firmly in an exploration of materials. Separating out the basic elements of colour and gesture, support and frame, and treating them as far as possible in isolation, they have arrived at a variety of impressively radical solutions. Of particular interest is their work on tool marks, the penetration of colour on unprepared surfaces, the canvas viewed as a screen, and the forms it may assume. Each painter has his particular area of concern: Viallat explores the relationship of system and randomness in surfaces stencilled with inclined ovoid forms; Cane cuts, folds and unfolds swatches of coloured canvas, in such a way as to mimic the effect of picture and frame; Dezeuze attacks the traditional concept of the stretcher by constructing it of pliant wood, so that it can be rolled and unrolled. In the past, as a protest against the gallery system, these painters staged exhibitions out of doors, a working environment that encouraged the practice of laying canvases out flat on the ground.

This radical, pragmatic approach to painting was before long supplemented by an interest in Freudianism on the part of many in the group — what Catherine Millet has described as "bringing out the unconscious sexual implications of painting and the analysis

1. Viallat:
   Untitled, 1969
2. Dezeuze:
   Cut Fragments of Tarlatan, 1972

of a symbolic dimension". In that altered context, colour came to be regarded as the primordial element, being of all the pictorial givens both the most irrational and the most ontologically pure. By a paradox, a Marxist determination to simplify formal structure, in order to assert the reality of things, actually encouraged the subjective utilization of colour — although this was not to happen before the support, hitherto regarded as a mere adjunct to painting, had acquired the status of art-object in its own right.

Although not all the group abandoned the traditional stretcher, it is symptomatic of their general approach that many of them saw the potential of the "free canvas" for all-over composition, or the extension of the work in space. Displaying the actual fabric of the painting as a mobile object (the first paintings they showed outdoors were hung in the air like flags), they would frequently exhibit both sides of a picture, back as well as front.

For all the group, it was important that the traces of the artist's work remained visible. Viallat said that his canvases "are no more than the image of the work that produced them". As a corollary, the group was concerned also to explore the effectiveness of the various tools of painting, often preferring to use more ordinary and anonymous implements in place of the artist's brush, items that were less liable to personalizing expression by reintroducing an element of sensibility. Gesture, they believed, should be reduced to its function as action. This restricted view of execution arose out of an explicit desire to desanctify the work of art — to make the labour of production more important than the finished work. Some of the group were content to create objects designed to be ephemeral, vulnerable to the workings of life and time. But the dimension of time, once reintroduced, brought with it additional complications. François Rouan, for example, started out painting intersecting stripes, and ended up amalgamating two images of different dates within a third such image.

The revival of abstraction brought about by the Support-Surface group helped to create a new interest in the work of an older generation of painters, and also influenced their direction. Degottex, for example, has extended the relationship of sign to environment by overlaying images with incised marks or peeling away parts of the picture. Similarly, Martin Barré's lyrical signs have assumed the form of a serial

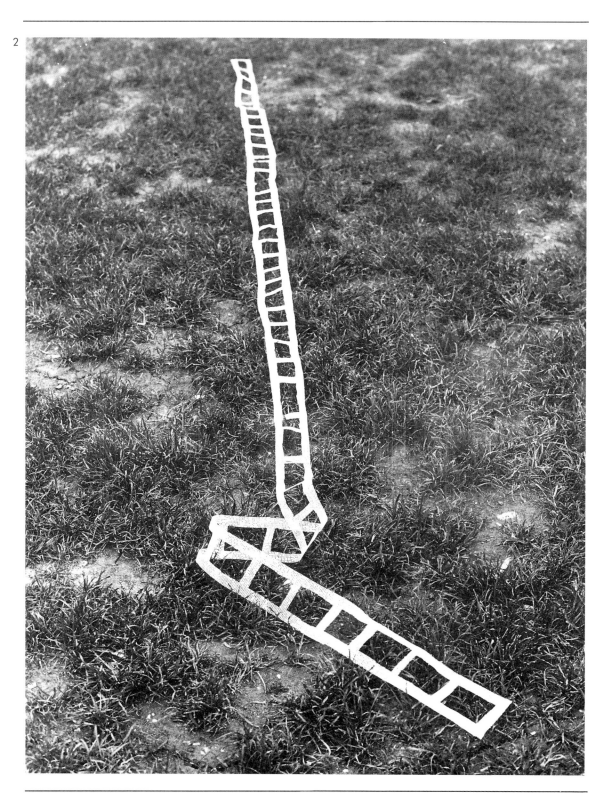

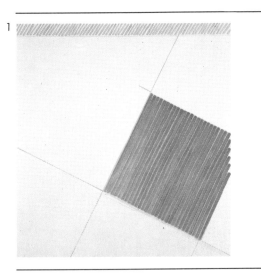

1. Barré:
   76-77-D-170-160, 1976-77
2. LeWitt:
   Wall-Relief, 1972

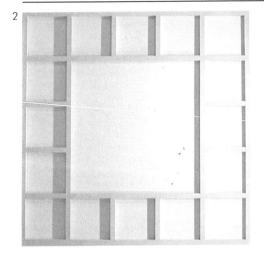

experimentation, laying bare the successive states of existence attached to the pictorial entity. "At a certain moment," he explains, "the painting emerges: it may emerge well or badly... As it emerges into the air, the light, something that is not fixed (hot-cold; light-dark), the picture should offer the contrast of its fixity, its moment of crystallization." (*Macula 2*, 1977)

In the seventies, Judith Reigl arrived in her work at a distinctive analysis of the painting process and the act of painting. Having initially used Surrealist automatic writing to produce anthropomorphic forms, she found new direction by concentrating on the painting support, and by scratching and incising the superimposed surfaces in such a way as to disrupt the relationship of "inside" and "outside" space.

The difference between the Europeans and the American adherents of Minimal Art was more a matter of the conclusions they drew than of basic attitudes. Both sought to emancipate art by making it referential only to the actual labour by which it was produced. But, once painting was reduced purely to an object in which colour and material defined form, the Americans — LeWitt, Robert Morris, Don Judd, Tony Smith and others — found their concerns shifting to the direct manipulation of space, more within the province of sculpture than painting. The relationship of form and colour, expressed in space, seemed to them to demand a different realization. Their objects are essentially the embodiments of concepts, and quite often the task of constructing them was left to technicians, since the idea itself was regarded as more important than any individual sensibility or manual skill. Art of this kind presents itself as a naked statement of itself — rejecting all significance beyond its apparent reality, isolated from all external influence, the stark expression of its own inner logic — so that, in some sense, we find ourselves in the seventies back again at the beginning. Abstraction has been taken to its very limits, through the analysis of all the constituent elements that go to make up painting, only to arrive back at the fundamental notion of the operation of form and colour. Beyond this point there is nowhere left to explore, except by turning towards a significant world; painting cannot endlessly confine itself to demonstrating the nature of its own processes without dwindling into repetition... There is a limit to how many times you can paint the first picture.

THE FUTURE

From Impressionism to Minimalism, via all the other art-historical "isms", abstraction has been a continuing strand in modern art.

Since the abandonment in the early years of this century of the system of representation inherited from the *quattrocento,* countless initiatives have been launched, countless new groups and movements formmed, culminating in the late seventies in a stifling formal reductionism. Many artists in many countries, and in Germany in particular, signalled their violent rejection of these closed formal systems by returning to figuration. But in a world dominated by the influence of the media, shifts in taste have accelerated. Thus, by 1985, the advance of this Neo-Expressionist trend was already halted, and abstraction made a reappearance. Whether in the wave of neo-geometric painters headed by the Swiss – Helmut Federlé, John Armleder, Olivier Mosset – or among Neo-Constructivists such as Bertrand Lavier, Imi Knoebel, Peter Halley and Gerhard Merz, this new abstraction is marked by its pervading spirit of parody and irony. What will be the dominant trend next year is impossible to predict; what is certain is that, over the whole spectrum of image-making, abstraction lingers in the air.

Whether it is espoused or rejected, whether it is the subject of parody or distortion, abstraction continues to influence form; that is why it is so important today to understand its history.

BIOGRAPHIES

The following biographies
were compiled by Diane Daval.
The list is selective :
where artists referred to in
the text (such as Matisse
and Picasso) are not included,
it is because abstraction was
not their central concern.

Left: Agam. Photo: André Morain.
Above: Alechinsky, 1982. Photo: Jean-Philippe Reverdot.

JOSEPH GIPSTEIN AGAM
born 1928 in Richon el Zion, Israel
Studies at Bezalel School of Art, Jerusalem. **1949** moves to Zurich to become a pupil of Itten and Max Bill. **1951** moves to Paris. Studies at Atelier d'Art Abstrait. Travels in Italy, Holland, Belgium, Switzerland. **1952** creates first transformable pictures, with moveable parts. **1955** contributes to "Le Mouvement", exhibition organized by Vasarely at the Galerie Denise René. With Soto, Tinguely and Pol Bury, is one of the pioneers of kinetic art. In the same year makes experimental abstract films. His "transformable" works demand the observer's participation in manipulating coloured shapes against a neutral background. The "polyphonic" pictures are made up of bevelled strips of wood, the facets painted so as to present the observer with a different picture as he changes viewpoint. In the so-called "polymorphic" works, the comparable transformation is effected purely within the picture. Concentrates subsequently on effects of light. From **1969** produces sculptures with moving parts, exploring the repetition of simple forms.

JOSEF ALBERS
Bottrop (Westphalia) 1888 - New Haven (Connecticut) 1976
1913-15 studies at the Academy of Fine Arts, Berlin, and later in Essen and Munich. **1920-23** attends the Bauhaus in Weimar. **1925-33** teaches at the Bauhaus in Dessau, running the stained-glass studio; **1928-33** in charge of the foundation studies course. **1933** moves to the United States. **1933-49** teaches at Black Mountain College, North Carolina. His early works are notably experimental in character, including investigations of opacity and transparency and other variations of colour and value within a defined structure. From **1948** concentrates on a single theme, that of overlapping squares arranged according to mathematical principles. Explores chromatic relationships and their ability to suggest either relief or movement – leading the kinetic artists to claim him as one of their own. **1950-60** teaches at Yale University, New Haven, and is appointed head of the department of painting and drawing. Author of numerous theoretical texts, among them *Interaction of Color* (1963). Extensive travels in the Southern states of the USA and in Mexico. Notable for the sheer variety of his rectilinear motifs.

PIERRE ALECHINSKY
born 1927 in Brussels
Studies at the École Supérieure d'Architecture et d'Arts Décoratifs in Brussels. Interest in the mechanics of book publication, graphics, typography and printing techniques. Subsequent concentration in his work on drawing, engraving and illustration. **1947** travels in Morocco and Yugoslavia. Becomes a member of the group "Jeune Peinture Belge". **1948** first trip to Paris. Joins the COBRA group, whose manifesto is written by the poet Christian Dotremont. Represents the group in Brussels. **1950** travels in Denmark and Sweden. **1951** moves to Paris. Works with S.W. Hayter at Atelier 17. Participates in numerous group exhibitions and as a result develops an interest in calligraphy. **1955** trip to Japan. During the fifties produces works based on fluid organic forms, the surfaces covered with abstract markings. In the sixties, paintings characterized by the inclusion of multitudes of tiny brightly-coloured monsters. Later adopts a distinctive compositional form somewhat reminiscent of the Gothic predella or altar-front painting: a number of small panels are grouped around a formally simplified central motif. Teacher at the École des Beaux-Arts in Paris.

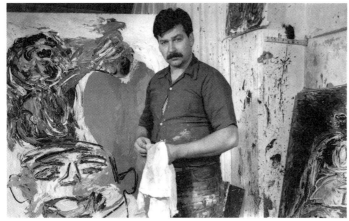

Above: Appel, 1960. Photo: Daniel Frasnay.
Right: Arman, 1986. Photo: Nicole Lejeune.

KAREL APPEL
born 1921 in Amsterdam

1940-43 studies at the Royal Academy, Amsterdam. His work rapidly assumes a character of violent figuration. From the outset reacts against the geometric academicism inherited from De Stijl. **1948** co-founder with Corneille and Constant of the "Experimental Group" and of the review *Reflex*, soon to be subsumed within the COBRA group. Their work is characterized by its concentration on colour and the use of heavy impasto. Motifs are the organic forms of human figures and explosively distorted landscapes. **1950** moves to Paris. At the full height of his powers. Works characterized by violent Expressionist gesture. **1961** investigates three-dimensional forms, shaping gnarled olive branches with an axe to accentuate the resemblance to convulsive human figures, painting the resulting sculptures in the aggressive colours of his pictures. Also numerous murals and stained-glass windows.

CARMELO ARDEN QUIN
born 1913 in Rivera, Uruguay

Until 1930 educated in Brazil at elementary and secondary schools run by Marist fathers. **1932** starts a law degree and begins to study painting and the history of art. **1935** meets Torres-García. **1936** first public showing of his pictures of polygonal forms at an anti-Fascist exhibition held in Montevideo in support of Republican Spain. **1938** studies philosophy and literature in Buenos Aires. Founds a studio collective and edits the review *Sinesis*. **1940** embarks on a study of the art of primitive peoples and from this evolves a theory of aesthetics which is based on materialist dialectic. In the early forties heads the Arturo group, centred on the Buenos Aires magazine of that name. **1944** paintings on polygonal supports and mobile sculptures. **1945** split in the Arturo group. **1946** launches the Madi movement (carMelo ArDen quIn), on a platform of freedom to use new materials and invent new forms capable of introducing movement into painting and sculpture. Publishes several manifestos. **1948** leaves South America and moves to Paris. Relaunches Madi and organizes a number of important exhibitions. **1950** co-founder of the Salle Espace at the Salon des Réalités Nouvelles, centre of activity for the new wave of geometric painters. **1953** the Madi group has a major show at the Sorbonne, and at the Salon des Réalités Nouvelles exhibits "optic-vibration" pictures and motor-driven sculptures. In the late fifties concentrates principally on cut-outs and collages. Publishes a variety of texts and exhibits regularly in France.

ARMAND FERNANDEZ (ARMAN)
born 1928 in Nice

Studies at the École des Arts Décoratifs, the Beaux-Arts and the Louvre. **1946** meets Yves Klein. Changes direction of his work, abandoning strict abstraction. **1956** first one-man exhibition at the Galerie du Haut Pavé in Paris. Shows his "cachets", executed not with brushes but with ink-pads or stamps that rapidly cover the surface of the canvas – his first use in painting of a "real" object. **1960** co-founder and signatory to the manifesto of the New Realism movement. Participates in the programme of artistic revival established during the sixties as a reaction against formalist abstraction. The same year stages the exhibition "Le Plein" in which he fills an art gallery from floor to ceiling with junk. Later creates *Accumulations* consisting of discarded items, all of the same sort, piled into glass vessels or encased in clear plastic. His *Colères* are works composed of fragments of objects, either on canvas or embedded in plastic. Also stages ritual burnings. **1967-69**, with the assistance of the Renault company, constructs assemblages

155

Left: Arp, 1954. Photo: Denise Colomb.
Above: Bazaine, 1975. Photo: Michel Nguyen, Galerie Lelong, Paris.

of mechanical parts. **1975** creates three-dimensional sculptures consisting usually of tools welded together, also monumental works.

HANS ARP
Strasbourg 1887 - Locarno 1966
1904 pupil at the School of Decorative Arts in Strasbourg. In Paris, first contact with modern art. **1905-06** attends the Weimar Academy. **1908** in Paris, studies at the Académie Julian. Returns to Weggis, Switzerland. **1909** meets Paul Klee. **1912** visits Kandinsky in Munich and exhibits with the Blaue Reiter group. **1913** in Berlin, contributes to the first Herbstsalon. **1914** in Paris and Switzerland. **1915** exhibits early abstract work in Paris. **1916** founder member of Dada group. **1917** first polychrome reliefs. Meets his future wife, Sophie Taeuber, and is influenced by the discipline and clarity of her work. **1918** collaborates with her on large geometric reliefs. **1920** in Cologne with Max Ernst: renewed Dada activity. **1923** meets Schwitters in Hanover and contributes to his review *Merz*. **1925** publishes with El Lissitzky *The Isms of Art*. **1926** moves to Meudon. Associated with Surrealism until 1930. Collaborates on decoration of L'Aubette in Strasbourg. **1930** member of the Circle and Square group. Creates works out of string and torn paper. First round-boss sculptures of organic forms. Increasing concentration on sculpture. **1940** in Grasse and Zurich. **1949-50** visits to the USA. Collected poems published. Occupies a distinctive position in the history of contemporary art, effectively bridging the gap between geometric abstraction and organic forms; a powerful influence because of his easy and humorous personality, and his ability to move freely between the various groups of the avant-garde.

JEAN ATLAN
Constantine 1913 - Paris 1960
1930 leaves Algeria to live permanently in Paris. Studies philosophy at the Sorbonne, without great enthusiasm. Develops an interest in African sorcery and Surrealist poetry. Enters teaching but is dismissed in **1941**. Becomes politically active and later joins the Resistance. **1942** arrested by the Germans and simulates madness under interrogation. Interned in a mental hospital, devotes himself to painting and drawing. **1944** first one-man exhibition. **1945** employed by Mourlot to produce black-and-white lithographic illustrations for Kafka's *Description of a Struggle*. **1949-55** lives in poverty. Moves from figuration to a forceful, rhythmic abstraction, marked by heavy black lines. His later work is more harmonious, the drawing less terse and the colours muted.

GIACOMO BALLA
Turin 1871 - Rome 1958
1895 settles in Rome. Early academic works praised by the critics. **1900** visit to Paris, where he discovers Impressionism and Divisionism. Becomes obsessed with problems of colour and light. In Rome, meets Boccioni and Severini. **1909** comes under the influence of Marinetti's Futurist dynamism. **1910** signatory of the *Manifesto of Futurist Painting and Sculpture*. **1912** paints *Dog on a Leash*, showing the successive stages of the animal's movements. Linear drawing is the dominant feature of his work but the emphasis shifts gradually from analysis to synthesis, echoing the development of Cubism. **1913-16** series of works inspired by observation of nature, which are nevertheless among the most abstract produced within the Futurist movement. Preference for broad scrolls and spirals. After **1918** the only one of the Futurists to persist with abstraction, apart from a period of descriptive figuration in the thirties. Much of his work has come to light only recently.

Left: Martin Barré.
Above: Bissière, 1958. Photo: Denise Colomb.

MARTIN BARRÉ
born 1924 in Nantes
Studies at the École des Beaux-Arts in Nantes. **1943** settles in Paris. **1950** adopts abstraction. Concerned from the outset with finding answers to one fundamental question: how can a painted line fill the white space of a canvas? From the fifties works directly with the tube of paint, in order that nothing intervenes between gesture and picture. **1955** first one-man exhibition at the Galerie La Roue, Paris. Contributions to the Salon des Réalités Nouvelles and the Menton Biennale. Around **1963** begins to use atomizers to spray paint on the canvas, the gesture in space being directly expressed as a black line on a white background. Systematic explorations of the technique: a period of *Zebras,* in which lines are distributed regularly across the surface, followed by *Arrows,* in which a stencil is applied to the canvas before spraying. **1972-73** reintroduces colour and develops new forms: superimposed, interlocking or overlapping grids composed of regular or random lines.

WILLI BAUMEISTER
Stuttgart 1889 - 1955
Studies under Adolf Hölzel at the Stuttgart Academy, where Oskar Schlemmer is a fellow pupil. At the same time works as an apprentice house-painter. **1912-14** in the course of trips to Paris, discovers Cubism, the influence of which is subsumed within an increasingly personal blend of Cubism and Constructivism. After a period devoted to compositions consisting exclusively of horizontals and verticals, in **1920** embarks on murals introducing curves and diagonals. Around **1928** begins the series *Painter with Palette.* Teaches at the Frankfurt School of Art. Sporting themes, transformed around **1933** into compositions composed of simple signs (anticipating the *Ideograms* of 1937-41). **1930** member of Circle and Square group. **1932** member of Abstraction-Creation. During the war dismissed from his teaching post and forbidden to exhibit. Scientific research on colour. Studies in prehistoric archeology. Series of paintings based on organic forms inspired by primitive culture. Ideogramatic reliefs in sand and pigment. **1946-47** marked return to formal severity and organization, lighter colours. Appointed professor at the Stuttgart Academy of Art. Publishes *Das Unbekannte in der Kunst.* **1953** series of large black paintings (*Montaru*), later white paintings (*Monturi*).

JEAN BAZAINE
born 1904 in Paris
Studies sculpture at the École des Beaux-Arts in Paris, while working for a humanities degree. Only later attracted to painting. **1932** first exhibition of pictures. In the forties discovers his direction, continuing to use the object as a starting point but stripping it of its normal appearance by a process of fragmentation, reducing it progressively to a series of geometric planes. Around **1947** objects cease to be identifiable. Having effectively abandoned figuration, nevertheless continues to derive inspiration from nature, expressing its characteristics in terms of colour and vigorous rhythms that ripple over the whole canvas. The compactly organized compositions seem to expand outwards beyond their frame. In the mid-fifties drawing ceases to define structure, being replaced by intricate arrangements of patches of colour. Also designs stained-glass windows (churches at Audincourt and Assy, Saint-Séverin in Paris), as well as mosaics (Audincourt and UNESCO building in Paris).

WILLIAM BAZIOTES
Pittsburgh (Pennsylvania) 1912 - New York 1963
Childhood in Reading (Pennsylvania). **1923** settles in New York.

Attends the National Academy of Design until 1936. **1936-38** teaches with the WPA Federal Art Project, set up to promote development in the arts. Moves gradually towards full-blown abstraction, which he achieves about **1940,** among the first of the American school to do so. **1942** takes part in the International Surrealist Exhibition in New York. Works of this period described as "abstract Surrealism". **1944** first one-man show at Peggy Guggenheim's Art of This Century Gallery. **1948** with Motherwell, Newman and Rothko starts an art school called "The Subjects of the Artist". Works at this time resemble the early Surrealist paintings of Robert Motherwell. **1955** features in Paris exhibition devoted to fifty years of American art. His paintings are strictly two-dimensional; often the backgrounds seem to evoke landscapes, against which are set simple forms frequently inspired by natural organisms, sometimes line-drawings, sometimes expressed as patches of colour. Certain stylistic similarities with Miró. Lives in New York and works as a university teacher.

MAX BILL
born 1908 in Winterthur
1925-27 studies at the Kunstgewerbeschule in Zurich. **1927-29** student at the Bauhaus. Its teaching profoundly influences the future course of his career. Acquires a good understanding of materials technology, and becomes convinced of the importance of architecture as the key to achieving a synthesis of all the arts, as well as bridging the gap between art and science. **1930** moves to Zurich to work as an architect. Extends activity to painting, sculpture and the applied arts. His paintings are highly disciplined constructions, based on straight lines and the rhythmic organization of geometric planes. The sculptures, combinations of multiple elements, have similar characteristics. From **1935** opposes the concept of "abstract art", favouring the more descriptive term "concrete art". **1935**

explores the problem of perpetual motion in his sculpture *Endless Torsion,* not completed until 1953. In his more recent painting abandons clearly demarcated surfaces in favour of interacting zones of colour in graduated shades. In architecture, designs for houses constructed of prefabricated parts. **1950-56** director of the Hochschule für Gestaltung in Ulm, of which he is both co-founder and architect. Organizer of several exhibitions and author of many books and articles on art.

VINCENT BIOULÈS
born 1938 in Montpellier
École des Beaux-Arts in Montpellier, under the direction of Camille Descossis. Second place in the Prix de Rome. Also has an arts degree and is an amateur musician. **1955** appointed as a teacher at the École des Beaux-Arts of Aix-en-Provence. In protest against the exaggerated values placed on works of art, paints pictures that are deliberately uncompromising, exhibiting them outside the usual circuit. Promotes artistic activity in the provinces, organizing street events and displays. **1966** "Impact" at the Musée de Céret. **1969-70** collaboration with the activities of the group ABC Production in Montpellier, Tours, Limoges, Perpignan, in conjunction with Alkéma, Azémard and Clément. **1970-72** active as a member of the Support-Surface group. There is a strong theoretical basis to all his work; his interest in painting is confined purely to the exploration of its material existence. Thus, in his monochrome pictures the emphasis is on format and colour, and the relationship of colour to form and texture.

JAMES BISHOP
born 1927 in Neosho (Missouri)
1957 onwards travels in Europe. Divides his time between studying art history and working as a painter. **1969** returns to the United States. From the start has reservations about developments in American

painting during the fifties. Initially influenced by Action Painting but later reacts against it. **1963** begins to define the canvas in terms of geometric zones, painted in two stages, at first keeping the colours (white and brown) distinct, then allowing them to overrun. His work has most in common with that of Ad Reinhardt. Like him he progressed finally to monochromes, paintings that are all white. His square canvases are subdivided into regular squares, which show through the paint like watermarks. Colour is exploited for its opposing qualities, such as opacity / transparency. The square is both figure and surface, emphasizing the role of the support. Other works explore the relationship of painted to unpainted space.

JULIUS BISSIER
Freiburg-im-Breisgau 1893 - Ancona 1965
Student at the University of Freiburg. Largely a self-taught painter but in **1913-14** attends the Karlsruhe School of Art for a short time. **1919** meets a sinologist named Ernst Grosse, who introduces him to Far Eastern art and culture. **1929-30** changes direction; abandons figuration to work on paintings containing a few simply expressed signs. Moves on to what he calls "psycho-grammes", calligraphic equivalents for particular states of feeling. Works exclusively in black and white. **1947** experiments with monotypes, introducing colour. **1956** embarks on a series of so-called miniatures, employing a type of oil-based tempera that produces work of a transparent delicacy. Use of this new technique coincides with an opening-up of his style and a return to a more figurative mode. His works are characterized by their understated restraint.

ROGER BISSIÈRE
Villeréal (Lot-et-Garonne) 1886 - Boissiérettes (Lot) 1964
Secondary school and École des Beaux-Arts in Bordeaux. **1910** moves to Paris but works in isola-

tion, no contacts with other painters. **1919** begins to exhibit at the Salon d'Automne and Salon des Indépendants. Small impressionistic drawings of landscapes. Joins the Esprit Nouveau group and publishes in the periodical of that name a series of articles on ancient and modern art. **1925-38** teaches at the Académie Ranson, meeting young painters whose subsequent careers are shaped by his influence. Attracted to Cubism; attempt to humanize the style and integrate it with the French tradition. Paintings of rigorous construction in subtle variations of colour. Several successful exhibitions. Nevertheless changes direction to experiment with new materials. A period of crisis in which he paints practically nothing. **1939** retires to live in provincial seclusion in the Lot. Eyesight problems during the war years. Stops painting. Works on large piecework tapestries in vivid colours. **1945** "Hommage à Bissière" at the first Salon de Mai. **1950-54** uses motifs from Polynesian art. Many paintings on wooden panels, of crude coloration. Increasingly fragmented compositions, more detailed brushwork. Other work includes stained-glass windows, etchings, lithographs and woodcuts.

CAMILLE BRYEN
Nantes 1907 - Paris 1977
1927 publication of first collection of poems *Opoponax*. Decides to concentrate on the plastic arts. Produces many automatic drawings, exhibited in **1934**. Active in the Saint-Germain-des-Prés and Montparnasse groups. Linked at times with the Surrealists, but closer to a Dadaist position. Creates objects assembled according to subconscious logic. **1937** holds a meeting at the Sorbonne to explain their "function". Meets Wols. Works in many different media. Takes part in the first three shows at the Salon des Réalités Nouvelles. Not until after the war does he work with stretched canvases. With Georges Mathieu

and Wols is an exponent of "psychic non-figuration", later Lyrical Abstraction. First public exhibition of the movement at the Galerie du Luxembourg in **1947**, including works by Atlan, Hartung, Riopelle, Ubac. A period of dramatic linear emphasis and violent colour is followed in **1955** by serene compositions in mosaics of colour, sometimes covered with a fine spray of paint.

DANIEL BUREN
born 1938 in Boulogne-Billancourt
Studies at École des Arts Appliqués and École des Beaux-Arts in Paris; fellow pupils are Parmentier, Viallat, Kermarec. Paints numerous large canvases consisting of alternate white and coloured stripes. Few opportunities for exhibition. Later, in **1967**, co-founds the BMPT group (Buren, Mosset, Parmentier, Toroni) whose expressed aim is to reduce painting to an infinitely repeated gesture. Wherever he can, even in the street, displays immensely long surfaces or posters consisting of vertical stripes twenty-seven millimetres in breadth, green or occasionally pink alternating with white. His radical and unvarying methods, coupled with the extent of his activities, make him a key figure in the art world of recent years. It is possible to view his *œuvre* as a portable system for "reading" space, applied to contexts that are increasingly monumental. His decoration of the courtyard of the Palais Royal (1986) aroused violent criticism.

ALBERTO BURRI
born 1915 in Città di Castello, Italy
1927 studies medicine in Città di Castello. Serves as a doctor in North Africa in Second World War. Taken prisoner by the Americans and interned in Texas. Starts painting in prison camp. **1945** settles in Rome. Gives up medicine to continue painting. **1949** first abstract works. Early critical success with series reflecting the spirit of his wartime experiences. Works consist of

assemblages or collages made from discarded raw materials, pieces of sacking, old metal, etc., sometimes picked out with black or red impasto. Strong concern for construction. Expressive use of material conveys a sense of anguish and decay.

POL BURY
born 1922 in Haine-Saint-Pierre, Belgium
1938 studies painting at the Académie des Beaux-Arts in Mons. From **1939** member of the Groupe de Recherches Surréalistes Rupture. Influenced at this time by Magritte and Tanguy. Founds with them the Groupe Surréaliste du Hainaut, and in Brussels the Phantomas group. Later works retain a Surrealist spirit, while exploring other techniques. **1945** takes part in the International Surrealist Exhibition. From **1947** contributes to exhibitions of the Jeune Peinture Belge group. Geometric works. **1949** founder member of the Art Abstrait group and active in COBRA, more out of friendship than artistic sympathy. Abandons painting. **1953** shows his first spatial constructions, geometric forms manipulated by the observer. Allied to the first wave of kinetic artists. Executes "concertina" paintings, with different compositions on the left and right facing panels. Sometimes the slats pivot on an axis. **1955** contributes to the exhibition "Mouvement" at the Galerie Denise René. **1957** onwards various experiments with light, beads of mercury, continuous discs and arhythmic movement. **1961** moves to Paris. **1964** returns to flat surfaces in his *Cinétisations*, cut-outs and montages of photographs.

ALEXANDER CALDER
Philadelphia 1898 - New York 1976
Completes course of study to qualify as an engineer. **1922** attends evening classes in drawing then studies painting at the Art Students' League. **1926** goes to Paris. First animations

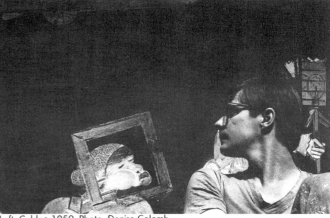

Left: Calder, 1950. Photo: Denise Colomb.
Above: Cane, 1982. Photo: Jean-Philippe Reverdot.

on circus themes. First wire sculptures, humorous interpretations of animals and human figures. **1928** first one-man show in New York. Experiments with wooden statues based on animal forms, also wire portraits. **1931** member of Abstraction-Creation group. Constructs first abstract sculptures and motor-driven moving assemblages. Goes on to eliminate mechanical propulsion with assemblies of objects suspended freely in space, to which Arp gives the name "mobiles". Later creates their counterpart, "stabiles". **1933** lives and works on a farm in Roxbury (Connecticut). After the war returns to France. Some of his metal constructions are painted in vivid colour, others are all black; always the colour is applied flat. Some works displayed outdoors, occasionally of colossal proportions. Also illustrates books, makes jewellery and does stage design.

LOUIS CANE
born 1943 in Beaulieu-sur-Mer (Alpes-Maritimes)
Commences studies at École des Arts Décoratifs in Nice. Moves to Paris and completes design training. Exhibitions from **1969** onwards. Rapidly assumes an independent position vis-à-vis other contemporary artists. While the trend generally is towards the creation of

objects, he concentrates on painting. Analytical investigation of the act of painting. With Viallat, Dezeuze, Bioulès, Dolla and Saytour, participates in the activities of the Support/Surface group which, although short-lived, is highly influential. Adopts large-scale formats, always employing free or unstretched canvases. His use of subtly modulated monochrome is designed to emphasize the materiality of colour. By cutting his huge surfaces of graduated tones to different shapes, folding and piling them on the ground, he explores the action of colour in space. In the latter half of the seventies his work reintroduces figurative references: initially by integrating architectural elements within monumental compositions, later by including human figures. Little vestige of abstraction remains, except in the distortion supplied by the pigment surface.

CORNELIS BEVERLOO (CORNEILLE)
born 1922 in Liège, Belgium
1940-43 lives in Amsterdam and studies at the Academy of Fine Art. **1948** with Appel and Constant founds the review *Reflex* and the Groupe Expérimental, forerunner of the COBRA movement. Co-founder in Paris of COBRA. **1949** first one-man exhibition in Paris. Settles in

Paris soon afterwards. Begins to establish a personal style. Many trips to Africa and America which influence the expressive content of his work, especially colour and brushwork. Concentration on the geological composition of landscape rather than simple description. Much of his inspiration derives from the popular imagination, legends and folk tales. Works predominantly linear, with black or coloured outlines. Spirited brushwork and vigorous graphism have been the principal legacy of the COBRA painters to contemporary painting.

CARLOS CRUZ-DIEZ
born 1923 in Caracas, Venezuela
1940-45 attends the School of Art in Caracas. **1946-51** manager of a large company dealing in artists' materials. Also illustrator for the *El National* newspaper in Caracas. Concerned principally with the interaction of colours, explored through systematic variations of simple forms. **1956-59** makes use of the phenomenon whereby an image remains for a time imprinted on the retina, altering perception. **1957** founds the Estudio de Artes Visuales, a centre for studies in graphic and industrial design. **1958-60** vice-principal and teacher at the Caracas School of Art. **1959** onwards creates reliefs assembled concer-

Left: Davie, 1967. Photo: Daniel Frasnay.
Above: Debré, 1984. Photo: Nicole Lejeune.

tina-fashion from narrow strips of cardboard, metal, painted wood and other materials; different figures are painted on the left and right sides so that the observer sees a different picture as he changes viewpoint. Entitles these works *Physichromes* and *Chromo-interferences*. Also reliefs where the observer is invited to manipulate moving parts; concerns related to those of the kinetic artists. Creates chromatic environments (in Dortmund, Grenoble, Villetaneuse, etc.). **1960** onwards lives in Paris.

ALAN DAVIE
born 1920 in Grangemouth, Scotland
Son of a painter and engraver. **1937-40** educated at Edinburgh College of Art. **1940-46** national service in the Royal Artillery. **1946** teaches painting to schoolchildren. First one-man exhibition in Edinburgh. **1947** professional jazz musician. Marries the potter Janet Gaul. **1947-49** travels extensively in Europe. **1948** one-man shows in Florence and Venice. **1949-53** earns his living making jewellery. From **1950** numerous exhibitions in London. **1953-56** teaches painting to secondary-school children. **1956** onwards exhibitions in the United States. **1956-58** works in broadcasting. **1959-60** teaches at the Central

School of Art in London. Numerous one-man shows and participation in group exhibitions. Pursues activity as jazz musician. Regards painting as a means of achieving spiritual enlightenment. Interested in Zen Buddhism. Work in general a blend of primitive influences with symbols of personal and magical significance.

OLIVIER DEBRÉ
born 1920 in Paris
Studies architecture at the École des Beaux-Arts but concentrates increasingly on painting, which from 1940 becomes his exclusive concern. **1939** study trip to England. Early works influenced by Expressionism. Contributions to the Salon des Surindépendants and Salon de Mai. **1943** abandons figuration. Abstraction founded in study of materials and pigment. Muted colours with predominant tones of ochre and earth-browns. In late fifties elements of a distinctive style emerge, with the introduction of a palette of blues and greens. **1962** change of direction. Abandons investigations of matter and heavily impastoed surfaces, but continues to work largely in monochrome. Turns to large formats, surfaces covered with stretches of fluid colour, pushing outwards in a series of indentations towards the canvas edge. Serene yet intense lyricism.

JEAN DEGOTTEX
born 1918 in Sathoney (Ain)
No formal art training. **1933** settles in Paris. **1938** starts painting. Early works of Fauvist inspiration. Some ten years later moves in the direction of abstraction; works in the style of Lyrical Abstraction then dominant in France. Studies Oriental painting and Zen Buddhist philosophy. Influenced both by Eastern calligraphy and the automatic writing practised by the Surrealists. **1955** Breton writes the preface to one of his exhibition catalogues. Paintings of restrained simplicity, often contrasts of grey or black signs against a white background. Rapid gesturalism. Unlike other artists working in this area does not attempt to fill his surfaces. Characteristically uses a single sign set against a neutral ground. **1970** utilizes sheets of neutral-coloured plastic as supports. Later uses black surfaces outlined in black (*Media* series of 1973-75). More recently, experiments with incised designs (series of *Painted Papers* of 1975-76).

ROBERT DELAUNAY
Paris 1885 - Montpellier 1941
Leaves school to train in a theatre design studio in Belleville. **1904** becomes a full-time artist. Influenced by Gauguin, and later by the Neo-Impressionists and the colour

Above: Degottex, 1982. Photo: Jean-Philippe Reverdot.
Right: Sonia Delaunay, 1920.

theories of Chevreul. **1908-09** increased emphasis on construction following exposure to Cubism. Softening of the rigid forms of Cubism. Decomposition of light into the colours of the spectrum. **1911-12** takes part in the two exhibitions of the Blaue Reiter group. **1912** embarks on a so-called "constructivist" period of soft geometric shapes (series of *Windows*), a style to which Apollinaire gives the name Orphism. Dynamic non-naturalistic treatment of light and colour. Goes on to eliminate subject matter altogether. Juxtaposition of coloured circles (*Simultaneous Discs* and *Circular Forms*). Later sporting themes. **1918** works with the Ballets Russes. **1925** decorates the Pavillon Mallet-Stevens at the International Exhibition in Paris. **1930** reverts to abstraction. First plaster reliefs. Monumental bas-reliefs in colour for the International Exhibition of 1937. **1939** organises the first exhibition of the Salon des Réalités Nouvelles, devoted to abstract art.

SONIA DELAUNAY
Gradiesk (Ukraine) 1885 - Paris 1979
Childhood in St. Petersburg. Studies in Germany, in Karlsruhe, then in Paris at the Académie de la Palette. Initially influenced by the violent colour of van Gogh and Gauguin.

First marriage to the critic William Uhde. Meets Robert Delaunay in **1907** and marries him in **1910**. Close artistic collaboration. Works of this period echo developments in Cubism and Orphism. Increasingly adapts the principles of "simultaneous painting" to a personal style, apparent **1913** onwards in such works as *Electric Prisms* and *Le Bal Bullier*. In that year exhibits in Berlin the first "simultaneous" book, an illustrated edition of Blaise Cendrars's *Prose du Transsibérien.* **1915-20** long periods in Spain and Portugal. Reverts to a more figurative style. **1918** set designs for Diaghilev's ballet *Cleopatra.* Back in France turns to the applied arts: avant-garde fashion designs, innovative textile design and bookbinding. In the thirties returns to painting. Active participation in many abstract groups, including Abstraction-Creation. **1937** works with Robert Delaunay on large murals for the International Exhibition in Paris. **1941** in Grasse with Magnelli, Arp and Sophie Taeuber. New period of work, featuring simple stripped-down forms. After the war returns to Paris and takes an active role in artistic affairs, collaborating in the establishment of the Salon des Réalités Nouvelles.

MARC DEVADE
Paris 1943 - 1983
As important for his theoretical writings as for his works as an artist. Member of the editorial boards of *Tel Quel* and *Peinture-Cahiers Théoriques.* Initially his painting resembles that of the American school of hard-edge abstraction. Later develops an interest in chromatic variations. Co-founder of Support-Surface group influential in France during the seventies, encouraging a revival of interest in painting at a time when Pop Art and associated movements appear to place the emphasis on the object. His work questions the fundamental purposes and practice of painting, concentrating on materials and eliminating all non-visual reference. Rigorous examination of the pictorial elements, support, colour, surface, etc. His austere monochrome canvases, composed of understated graduations of colour, may thus be seen as stages in a systematic analysis of the act of painting.

JEAN DEWASNE
born 1921 in Lille
1938-39 first two years of architectural studies at the École des Beaux-Arts in Paris. **1949** paints his first abstract picture. After the war opts definitively for abstraction (with Hartung, de Staël, Poliakoff). Col-

Nelly and Theo van Doesburg, 1925. Above: with the dancer
Kamarès. Right: with Schwitters and Vordemberge-Gildewart.

laborates with Arp, Pevsner and Sonia Delaunay in founding the Salon des Réalités Nouvelles. **1946** winner of the Kandinsky Prize. **1950** with Edgard Pillet founds the Atelier d'Art Abstrait. Teaches various courses including one on the technical aspects of painting, covering the chemical composition of pigments, theories of vision, colorometry and related problems of plasticity. In his own work abandons the traditional painting mediums in favour of ripolin and a variety of lacquers and enamels, his purpose being to produce items of a technical perfection comparable with that achieved by industrial processes. Dynamic compositions of uncompromising severity, using precise geometric forms. Develops an interest in the use of curved space and surfaces; in **1951** decorates the body of a car with pictorial motifs. Several other applications of the principle to industrial processes. A number of large murals, including one for the University of Lille, in **1968-69.**

DANIEL DEZEUZE
born 1942 in Alès (Gard)
Co-founder of the review *Peinture - Cahiers Théoriques,* with Cane, Devade and Bioulès. Belongs to the Support/Surface group, but ceases to be a member in 1972. Adopts a materialist approach to painting,

which he regards purely as a field of analytical study. Investigations centring on the canvas stretcher. Initially presents the stretcher itself as the art object, either bare or covered with transparent plastic sheeting. Later variations on the theme: long struts of pliable wood, at first left bare and later painted, allowed to unroll along the ground. By this means seeks to define the role of the stretcher and at the same time to demonstrate the existence of an area that is "out of frame", in just the way something in a film can be "out of shot". Regular exhibitions in Paris. Pursues a parallel career as a teacher. Lives in Nice.

THEO VAN DOESBURG
Utrecht 1883 - Davos 1931
Paints from an early age but also writes fables, plays and articles. **1913** first speculations on the integration of painting and architecture. **1915** publishes an article in praise of Mondrian, whom he later meets. Begins to experiment with abstraction. **1916-17** increasingly abstract pictures based on transformations of motifs that include cows, still lifes and card-players. **1917** with Mondrian founds the review *De Stijl.* Collaboration with the architects Oud and Wils. **1921** major lecture tour of central European countries. Friendship with Schwitters. **1922**

contributions to the Dada review *Mecano.* Introduces Dada to Holland. **1923** moves away from Mondrian's strict Constructivist principles and develops what he calls "elementarism". Introduces diagonal lines. **1925** publishes the elementarist manifesto. **1927** works on the decoration for the Strasbourg café-cinema L'Aubette, now destroyed. **1929** moves to Paris. **1930** contributes to the sole issue published of the review *Art Concret.* Work also includes sculpture.

NOËL DOLLA
born 1945 in Nice
1962-65 studies at the École des Arts Décoratifs in Nice. Associates with the artists who form the so-called École de Nice, founded by Raysse and Arman. Two of the group soon move beyond the ideas of New Realism: Ben, who stages the first exhibition of Dolla's work; and Viallat who with Dolla, Saytour, and Pagès is a founder member of the Support/Surface group. From the outset Dolla's work is integrated with the general concerns of the second wave of painters of the Nice School. Around **1970** produces works in which the surface of the support (wood, canvas, etc.) is perforated or stippled with holes; his intention is to point to the arbitrary nature of the limitation imposed on

the space. Emphasis on the materials of painting leads him to join the Support/Surface group. Contributes to many of their collective exhibitions, notably in provincial centres. **1972** invited to show his work at the "62/72" exhibition held at the Grand Palais, a major retrospective of artistic activity in France during the previous ten years. Subsequent revival of interest in painting, centring on problems of colour and format. Renewed exhibition activity after 1972.

CESAR DOMELA
born 1900 in Amsterdam
1914 during a trip to Paris is impressed by a visit to Henri Laurens's studio. **1919-22** largely untrained, starts to paint works in a style reminiscent of Synthetic Cubism: landscapes and still lifes reduced to geometric forms. **1923** first works in a Constructivist style of abstraction. Contributes to the exhibition of the Novembergruppe in Berlin. **1924** in Paris meets Mondrian and van Doesburg. Becomes a member of De Stijl and adopts the principles of Neo-Plasticism. Soon feels the need to abandon the restricted formalism of this approach. **1925** introduces diagonals into his work. **1927** moves to Berlin. Earns his living as an interior designer and commercial artist. **1929** first reliefs, utilizing

ever more various materials but still constructed on Neo-Plastic principles. **1932** introduces curved lines into his paintings; first use of metal grids in the reliefs. **1933** moves to Paris. Member of Abstraction-Creation. **1934** sets up a silk-screen workshop. **1935** introduces plastic materials into his reliefs. **1937** with Sophie Taeuber founds the review *Plastique.* **1941** creates a series of jewellery designs. First use of animal matter in his work. **1946** founds the Centre de Recherches group, which stages exhibitions of abstract art. Collaborates on the establishment of the Salon des Réalités Nouvelles. His work from **1940** onwards has, with reason, been characterized as "baroque geometry", both because of the diversity of the materials he employs and because of his dynamic use of flowing curves.

CHRISTIAN DOTREMONT
Tervuren, Belgium 1922-1979
1937 attends drawing classes at the Louvain Academy. **1930** publication of long poem entitled *Ancienne Eternité.* Influenced both by Surrealism and Far Eastern calligraphy. November **1948** attends launching of COBRA group in Paris. Subsequent writings and drawings much influenced by the experimental approach of the group. **1949** first paintings in a highly personal style,

but principal interest remains the graphic representation of calligraphic signs. **1956** first of many visits to Lapland. **1963** onwards executes "logograms", picture-poems that combine lyrical expression with graphic invention. Initially small figures in pastel or ink; later begins doing large, fluent ideograms. **1971** publication of anthology entitled *Typographisme.*

JEAN DUBUFFET
Le Havre 1901 - Paris 1985
1916 settles in Paris. Attends the Académie Jullian for two years. Starts painting while working in his father's business in the wine trade. Executes masks and puppets. Not until **1942** does he devote himself full-time to painting. The distinguishing feature of his work is a readiness to experiment with new materials. Starts by painting views of Paris in vivid colour. Series of "hautes pâtes", figures incised in monochrome impasto, the pigment often mixed with sand, gravel or tar. **1947** trip to the Sahara. Subsequent exhibitions of his collections of Art Brut, which he prefers to "civilized" art. Two further visits to the Sahara. **1949** Expressionist images displaying the textures of the human, animal and vegetable worlds. In the early fifties large opaque reliefs, then pen-and-ink drawings. **1954**

Opposite, from left to right: Doucet, Constant, Dotremont, D. and J. M. Atlan, Corneille, Appel. Above: Domela, 1987. Photo: Lejeune. Right: Estève.

onwards sculptures made from scraps of mineral-based or organic materials such as plaster, sponge, papier mâché and silver paper. Pursues the dialogue between figures and material in several meticulously catalogued series, which include not only graphic works and paintings but also sculptures, often on a monumental scale. His last two series (*Mires* and *Non-lieux*) may be read both as the culmination of his life's work and as surfaces of a totally pure abstraction. Also author of many polemical and theoretical texts, a selection of which are collected under the title *Prospectus et tous écrits suivants*.

VIKING EGGELING
Lund (Sweden) 1880 - Berlin 1925
1900-08 periods of study in Switzerland and Italy. **1911** goes to Paris. Association with Modigliani and Hans Arp. Influenced by the Cubists and André Derain. **1915** returns to Switzerland. **1916** in Zurich. Meets Tristan Tzara. **1917** rapid movement in his work from a personal interpretation of Cubism towards non-figuration. Executes abstract drawings. Activities associated with the Zurich Dada group. **1918** friendship with Hans Richter, who invites him to stay at the Schloss Klein-Koelzig in Germany. Together they explore the development of geometric form in space. Applying these ideas, inspired by the musical system of counterpoint, composes in Berlin in **1919** a "scroll picture" entitled *Horizontal-Vertikal-Messe*, and in **1920** the *Diagonal-Symphonie*. In **1921** turns the second scroll into a film, one of the first abstract works produced for the cinema.

MAURICE ESTÈVE
born 1904 in Culan (Cher)
1918 settles in Paris. Attends the free studios of Montparnasse but is largely self-taught. Studies the great painters of the past. **1923** period in Spain. For a time runs the design studio of a textile manufacturing firm in Barcelona. **1924-29** influenced in particular by Cézanne, van Gogh and the Surrealists. Subsequent interest in Léger: precise simplified forms, flat areas of colour. Around **1935** moves away from the principles of naturalism. Light effects, expressed in subtle graduations of colour. **1937** works with Robert Delaunay on the decoration of the Pavillon de l'Aviation and Pavillon des Chemins de Fer at the International Exhibition in Paris. Up to **1938** exhibits at the Salon des Surindépendants. From **1938** works with his own very distinctive repertoire of forms and colours. Human figures and objects appear as elements in strongly constructed ensembles. Around **1944** forms become more supple and palette is intensified. From **1948** moves away from the representation of outward appearances. Compositions constructed of solidly articulated forms. **1956-73** collages assembled with wit and humour. Fluid, transparent watercolours.

ALEXANDRA EXTER
Belestok (near Kiev) 1882 - Paris 1949
Until **1906** formal art training in Kiev. Visits to the major European cities. In Paris attends the Académie de la Grande Chaumière, where she rents a studio in **1909**. Meets Picasso, Braque, Marinetti, Papini. **1912** settles in St. Petersburg but continues to travel, maintaining contacts with avant-garde groups in Russia and throughout Western Europe. Works shown at most of the major exhibitions of Russian contemporary art. **1915** takes part in "Tramway V". Stage designs for the director Alexander Tairov. **1918** founds a design studio in Kiev where she teaches the principles of Suprematism; a number of her pupils go on to become influential members of the movement. **1920-22** teaches in the state workshops. **1921** shows work at the exhibition "5 × 5 = 25". First experiments with textile design. Continues to work in

the theatre. **1923** sets and costumes for the film *Aelita*. With Nijinsky designs the decors for the first Exhibition of Agriculture, Crafts and Industry, held in Moscow. **1924** emigrates to Paris. Activity as a theatre designer and interior decorator. Also fashion drawing and illustration.

JEAN FAUTRIER
Paris 1898 - Châtenay-Malabry 1964
Brought up in England. **1912** studies at the Royal Academy. **1914** returns to France. Serves at the front for three years, is wounded and gassed. Around **1923** meets Jeanne Chastel who becomes his patron and stages an exhibition of his work in a garage in Paris. Around **1926** begins to be noticed by dealers such as Paul Guillaume. Initially realistic figuration, later a more allusive style. Landscapes and still lifes. **1928** series of lithographs illustrating Dante's *Inferno,* commissioned by Gallimard and André Malraux. Change of direction; beginnings of "informel" style. Around **1929** abandons oil painting in favour of pastel and tempera: increased surface animation. **1935-39** forced by the economic crisis to work as a hotel-keeper and ski-instructor in the Alps. At the outbreak of war again employs oil paints, but on

paper. Prepares surfaces by applying a thick textured ground, working this into a relief before colour is introduced. Restricted palette of muted tones of colour, mostly grey. Meticulous technique. **1945** exhibition at the Galerie René Drouin of the famous series of *Hostages.* Images of extreme conciseness. Complete identification of pictorial matter with expressive content.

LYONEL FEININGER
New York 1871 - 1956
Parents are musicians. **1887** goes to Germany. Gives up music in favour of painting. Trains as a decorative artist in Hamburg, later lives in Liège and Berlin, where he settles in 1893. **1892-93** visit to Paris. Attends the Académie Colarossi. Around **1912** under the influence of Cubism discovers his personal style. After **1912** works based on the principles of the Golden Section group of Cubist painters. Organizations of simple planes in a pattern of facets, marked out in straight lines. Even, angular drawing. Later works of increasing complexity. **1915-19** close to non-figuration. **1919** one of the first artists approached by Gropius to join the teaching staff at the Bauhaus in Weimar. Remains associated with the Bauhaus until its closure by the Nazis in 1933. After 1919, influenced by the bias of

teaching at the school, greater clarity in the organization of planes, which visibly reflect the architecture of buildings. Fluid, transparent colours. **1933** one of the Blue Four. **1937** moves back to New York. Always a significant feature of his work, watercolour becomes a major part of his activity following the return to the United States. More concise expression: fine, rapid line-drawing, opaque colour, distinctive chromatic combinations. Themes taken from Manhattan architecture and views of the ocean.

LUCIO FONTANA
Santa Fe 1899 - Varese 1968
Born in Argentina. Aged six, accompanies his family to Italy. **1927-28** studies at the Brera Academy in Milan; academic bias of teaching finds no reflection in his work. Immediately moves on to explore abstraction. **1934** brief visit to Paris. Member of Abstraction-Creation group, although not exclusively committed to geometric formalism. **1939-46** returns to live in the Argentine. **1946** publishes the *Manifesto Blanco* outlining his philosophy of "spazialismo", set out in greater detail in the later *Technical Manifesto of Spatial Art.* Seeks a synthesis of all the physical elements, with the intention of uniting the different art forms and abolish-

Opposite: group of Bauhaus teachers, Dessau, 1926. Above: Gottlieb, 1966.
Photo: Frasnay. Right: Goncharova, 1952. Photo: Colomb.

ing the distinction between art and nature. **1949** transforms the Galleria del Naviglio in Milan into an experimental space in which abstract forms are suspended. **1949-51** period of experiment with perforated canvases as a means of redefining the relationship of pictorial to actual space. Series of mostly monochrome paintings with apparently random patterns of holes punched in the surface. Subsequent enlargement of this theme in series of canvases slashed with a razor blade. The radicalism of his approach is allied to a strong aesthetic sense.

SAM FRANCIS
born 1923 in San Mateo (California)
1941-43 studies medicine and psychology at the University of California, Berkeley. Serves in the American Air Force in World War II. Gravely wounded and hospitalized in Denver. **1944** starts painting during convalescence and goes on to become a full-time painter. Studies in art at the California School of Fine Arts, San Francisco. **1947** first abstract canvases. Manner close to that of Rothko or Still. Works in all-over space, the whole field of the canvas being covered with a multitude of biomorphic forms. **1950** settles in Paris. For a brief period a

pupil of Fernand Léger. Association with Riopelle, Joan Mitchell, Ruth Francken. Meets Giacometti and Bram van Velde. Abandons use of colour, until 1951. **1953** series of monochromes. **1957** and **1959** visits to Japan. Marked influence of Far-Eastern art. Works with ovoid forms set in isolation against white fields. **1961** moves to Santa Monica, California. Experiments with lithography and the role of colour as an element in structuring space. **1968** returns to painting, in predominantly white canvases. Among the first to concentrate on the paint surface as a medium of lyrical expression.

HELEN FRANKENTHALER
born 1928 in New York
Studies at Bennington College, Vermont. Pupil of the Mexican painter Rufino Tomayo, and in **1946** of Paul Feeley, from whom she absorbs the lessons of Cubism. **1950** first presentation of paintings in a group exhibition held at the Kootz Gallery in New York. **1951** visits Jackson Pollock in his studio. The experience is decisive. Is influenced in particular by his practice of laying the unprepared canvas out flat on the floor and then dripping paint. In her own work uses very thin fluid pigment which spreads freely over the surface. Juxtaposes and superimposes the transparent coloured stains,

varying the penetration of the canvas by the painting medium. Pioneer of the technique taken up by Kenneth Noland and Morris Louis. **1962** onwards uses acrylic paint. Its slower drying capability imposes more structured compositions, which continue to be made up of juxtaposed blotches of colour. Titles reflecting a degree of naturalistic reference. One of the pioneers of improvisatory painting.

NAUM GABO
Briansk, Russia 1890 - Connecticut 1978
Pseudonym of Naum Pevsner. Brother of the sculptor, Antoine Pevsner. Studies physics and mathematics in Munich. **1912-14** visits to Italy and Paris, where he meets members of the avant-garde. **1914** goes to Stockholm. **1915** first Cubist sculptures, constructed of planes of metal and other materials. **1917** settles in Moscow. Associates with Malevich, Tatlin, Rodchenko. **1920** produces with his brother a *Realist Manifesto*, setting out the fundamental notions of Constructivism. First kinetic sculpture. Reliefs in transparent plastic. **1922** leaves Russia for Germany, where he lives for ten years, spreading Constructivist ideas. Contacts with Mies van der Rohe, Kandinsky, Klee, Walter

Gropius. **1927** costumes and stage sets in steel and transparent plastic for the Ballets Russes. **1932** settles in Paris and becomes active in the Abstraction-Creation group. **1935** goes to England. Emphasis on curved surfaces of increasing complexity. In **1946** emigrates to the United States. Constructions on a monumental scale.

NATALIA GONCHAROVA
Lajino (Toula) 1881 - Paris 1962
Draws from an early age. Starts a history degree but abandons studies. **1898** enrols at College of Painting, Sculpture and Architecture, Moscow. Diploma in sculpture. Travel in Europe. **1900** meets Larionov, whose companion she becomes. First exhibitions. From **1904** abandons sculpture in favour of painting. In her work integrates influences absorbed from Impressionism, and later Fauvism, into the tradition of Russian folk art and icon-painting. Pictures in a primitivist style. **1908** arrives at a type of Cubism using the colours of the spectrum. **1910** with Larionov invents Rayonism. Association with Malevich and Tatlin. Works uniting the inspirations of Cubism and Futurism. **1912** contributes to the second Blaue Reiter exhibition. Illustrates Futurist pamphlets. **1913** signatory of the Rayonist Manifesto. **1914** meets Diaghilev, who commissions sets and costumes for his productions. Subsequently numerous designs for the Ballets Russes. Around **1955** reverts to Rayonism in works of a less abstract type.

JEAN GORIN
Saint-Emilion-Blain (Loire-Atlantique) 1899 - Paris 1981
Attends the Académie de la Grande Chaumière in Paris. **1919-22** studies at the École des Beaux-Arts, Nantes. Pursues an independent line, influenced successively by Cézanne, van Gogh, Matisse, later Gleizes and the "purism" of Ozenfant. **1926** reads an article on Mondrian and becomes the first exponent in France of Neo-Plasticism. **1927** start of a long association with

Mondrian. Develops a personal style founded in an extension of his plastic principles. Flat wooden reliefs, delicately modulated. Introduction of diagonals and circles. **1930** member of Circle and Square group. **1932** activity in association with Abstraction-Creation group. Works largely in isolation. **1946** founder member of Salon des Réalités Nouvelles. **1953** signatory of manifesto issued by the group Espace. Interest in the spatial organization of colours: wooden reliefs and constructions commissioned as decorations for interiors, as in **1968** for the Institut Universitaire Technologique, Nantes.

ARSHILE GORKY
Hajotz Bzore (Turkish Armenia) 1904 - Sherman (Connecticut) 1948
Born Vosdanig Adoian. Lives in Armenia until **1914**. Emigrates to Russia. **1916-18** studies at the Polytechnic Institute, Tiflis. **1920** exile in the United States. Adopts the name Arshile Gorky. Studies engineering in New York. Paints in his spare time. Visits museums and galleries. Largely self-taught but brief periods of art training at Rhode Island School of Design, the New School of Design, Boston (1923-24) and the National Academy of Design in New York (1925). **1926-31** teaches first at the New York School of Design, then at the Grand Central School of Art. During the Depression works for the WPA Federal Art Project. First exhibitions and growing reputation. Executes large frescoes and murals for public buildings. **1936** continuing influence of Picasso's pre-Cubist works. Later inspired by the lyricism of Kandinsky's first abstract paintings. Meets the Surrealists in New York, in particular Matta in **1939**. Incorporates these various influences within a distinctive style, intense and tragic in tone. Draws inspiration from themes in nature, although his works are non-descriptive. A key figure in the early evolution of Abstract Expressionism in New York. Suicide in 1948.

ADOLPH GOTTLIEB
New York 1903 - 1974
Pupil at the Art Students' League, New York; taught by Robert Henri and John Sloan. **1921-22** two years travelling in Europe. While in Paris attends the Académie de la Grande Chaumière. **1935** with Rothko and Bolotowsky founds the group "The Ten". During the Depression undertakes major works within the context of the WPA Federal Art Project. From **1942** paintings are regularly exhibited at Peggy Guggenheims's Art of This Century Gallery. Contacts during the war years with the Surrealist émigrés in New York. Their influence, together with an interest in Jungian theories of psychoanalysis, leads him towards the biomorphic forms characteristic of Miró or Arp. Concentration on images drawn from the unconscious. **1944-45** president of the Federation of Modern Painters and Sculptors. Interest in American Indian art, which inspires the series of *Pictographs* executed from 1941 to 1951. Subsequently moves towards simplified forms and bright colours : abstract symbols suspended against large monochrome surfaces.

SIMON HANTAÏ
born 1922 in Bia (Hungary)
Art training in Budapest. **1948** leaves Hungary. Travels in Europe, notably in Italy. **1949** settles in Paris. **1952** contacts with the Surrealist group. **1953** first exhibitions at the Galerie de l'Etoile Scellée in Paris. Preface to exhibition catalogue written by André Breton. Works inspired by the traditions and spirit of Surrealism. Experiments with a variety of techniques: pliage, collage, frottage, multi-media, etc. A bias towards technical experiment is a continuing feature of his work. Around **1954** discovers Mathieu's Lyrical Abstraction and Pollock's Action Painting. Concludes that techniques of automatic writing find full expression only within abstraction, where a total spontaneity of gesture permits the direct translation of unconscious

"The Irascibles", 1950. From left to right, back row: de Kooning, Gottlieb, Reinhardt, Ida Sterne;
middle row: Pousette-Dart, Baziotes, Pollock, Still, Motherwell, Tomlin; front row: Stamos, Jimmy Ernst, Newman, Brooks,
Rothko. Photo: Nina Leen, Time Life Inc., 1951.

Above: Hantaï. Photo: Edouard Boubat.
Right: Hélion, 1985. Photo: Nicole Lejeune.

impulses into painting. Begins to work on very large formats. **1960** reverts to pliage, exploring the potential of the technique in series entitled *Mariales* (1960); *Catamurons* (1964); *Menus* (1967), etc. Uses large un-stretched canvases which are folded or crumpled before the pigment is applied. In the resultant all-over compositions random colour patterns emerge, created by the initial folding of the canvas. At first contrasts of two colours only, later the introduction of a more varied palette.

HANS HARTUNG
born 1904 in Leipzig
1912-14 in Basel, then Dresden. Starts painting at a young age. Early works inspired by Nolde, Kokoschka, Marc. First non-figurative works in 1921-22: pen-and-ink or crayon drawings and water-colours. **1924-28** studies philosophy and the history of art. Over the same period extends his knowledge of the technical aspects of painting by attending classes at schools in Leipzig, Dresden and Munich. Figurative works. Study trips to Italy, Holland, Belgium and France, visiting museums and copying old masters. **1935** moves to Paris to escape persecution under the Nazis. First major works, in a style of abstraction unrelated to his earlier manner. Energy of line, blotches of ink,

coloured planes set against a neutral ground. Variety of motifs. **1935-38** works shown at the Salon des Indépendants. Serves during the war in the Foreign Legion. **1943** gravely wounded; his leg is amputated. **1945** returns to Paris and takes up painting again. Development of a typical sunburst motif of radiating lines. Various intensities of black standing out violently against backgrounds of luminescent colour. Spontaneity of gesture allied to meticulous technique. One of the foremost representatives of the school of Lyrical Abstraction. Highly influential both in Germany and France.

STANLEY WILLIAM HAYTER
born 1901 in London
Son of a painter. **1915** first pictures in an Impressionist style. **1917** studies chemistry at Kings' College, London. **1921** awarded an honours degree. Early experiments with engraving techniques. Joins the Anglo-Iranian Oil Company and works in Abadan until 1925. In his spare time pursues his artistic interests. **1925** returns to London and exhibits works executed while abroad. Decides to work full-time as an artist. **1926** settles in Paris. First dry-point engravings, aquatints and woodcuts. **1927** founds a studio workshop which becomes famous

under the name Atelier 17. Soon enjoys a worldwide reputation. Works with Miró, Arp and Tanguy. Experiments with forms of linear construction against backgrounds of plain colour. **1933** first exhibition with the Surrealist group. Engravings in a style of graphic automatism verging on abstraction. **1934** first exhibition of Atelier 17, in Paris and London. **1939** marries the American sculptor Helen Philips. **1940** emigrates to the United States and teaches at the California School of Fine Arts in San Francisco. First etching in simultaneous colour. **1946** returns to Paris and finally settles there in **1950**. Relaunch of Atelier 17. Numerous one-man shows and collective exhibitions. **1963** fluorescent paintings based on curvilinear patterns. In both engravings and paintings is concerned to create an image suggestive of movement. Throughout his career has maintained his activities as a teacher.

JEAN HÉLION
Couterne 1904 - Paris 1987
Moves to Paris in **1921**. Architectural studies. Develops an enthusiasm for painting and the old masters. No formal fine art training. **1926** meets Torres-García, who introduces him to Cubist painting. Rapid evolution in his work towards

Left: Hartung, 1954. Photo: Denise Colomb.
Above: Hayter, 1981. Photo: Jean-Philippe Reverdot.

abstraction. **1929** exhibition of first abstract pictures. **1930** with Theo van Doesburg founds the Art Concret group. **1931-34** associated with the new Abstraction-Creation group. Up to the outbreak of war paints large harmonious compositions in a style derived from Neo-Plasticism. Adaptation of these principles to include circular forms, suggestive of movement. **1935-39** lives in the United States. **1939** returns to France. Joins the armed forces. **1940-42** held as a prisoner of war in Germany. While interned becomes obsessed with the forms of the real world. Late **1942** escapes to the United States. Abandons pure abstraction and begins to introduce elements of figuration. Scenes of everyday life: hieratic figures in rigorously constructed environments. **1946** onwards settles in Paris. From **1952** puts increasing emphasis on figuration, within compositions whose organization of pictorial mass and structured representation betray a long experience of abstraction.

ANTHONY HILL
born 1930 in London
Son of an academic painter. Initially attracted to a career in science. Pupil at the Central School of Arts and Crafts and St. Martin's School of Art, but largely self-taught. **1951**

contributes to the first exhibition of abstract art held in England since the war. Early reputation based on abstract pictures in a rigorous style of bare geometric formalism. Several visits to Paris, in the course of which he associates with Vantongerloo, Sonia Delaunay, Picabia and Seuphor. Through them absorbs the lessons of Constructivism, which he applies in modified form to his own compositions in shallow relief. In these works combines a variety of materials such as aluminium sheeting, vinyl, etc. Retention of the picture plane, which serves as the support for three-dimensional structures. Lives in London.

HANS HOFMANN
Weissenberg (Bavaria) 1880 - New York 1966
Studies in physics and mathematics. **1904-14** with the help of his patron, the Berlin collector Philip Freudenberg, establishes himself in Paris. Influenced by Cézanne, the Fauves and later Cubism. Friendship with Robert Delaunay. **1915** opens an art school in Munich. In the attempt to rid himself of Cubist influence, paints very little at this time. Concentrates on drawing. During the twenties spends summers with his pupils in Raguse, Capri and Saint-Tropez. **1930** teaches in summer school at the University of Cali-

fornia. **1932** emigrates to the United States. Teaches at the Art Students' League, New York. **1934** founds in New York a school bearing his name. Around **1936** returns to painting. **1957** closes down the art schools under his direction. Initially known for his activities as a teacher. A crucial influence in the early development of Abstract Expressionism because of his contacts with young American painters, to whom he passed on personal knowledge of the great European painters and their working methods. His own work reflects the emphasis of his teaching. In the later paintings structured composition has almost entirely given way to the juxtaposition of fields of colour occupying space of varying depth.

JOHANNES ITTEN
Süderen-Linden (Switzerland) 1888 - Zurich 1967
Studies at Bern University and the Geneva École des Beaux-Arts. Concentrates on painting. **1912** makes contact with the Sonderbund in Cologne. **1913-16** becomes a pupil of Hölzel at the Stuttgart Academy. Under his influence paints his first abstract pictures. From **1916** teaches drawing at an art school in Vienna. **1919-23** takes charge of the foundation course at the Bauhaus in Weimar. **1923** sets up a

Above: Jaccard, 1982. Photo: Jean-Philippe Reverdot.
Right: Jawlensky.

weaving workshop in Switzerland. **1926-34** runs his own art school in Berlin. **1932-38** runs the School of Textiles in Krefeld. **1938-54** director of the Kunstgewerbeschule and the Musée des Arts et Métiers, Zurich. Author of many articles and publications presenting his artistic and pedagogical philosophy ("The Art of Colours", 1961; "My Foundation Course at the Bauhaus", 1963). His earliest abstract compositions are in a broadly Cubist manner, their most notable departure being the use of variations based on curvilinear designs. Later experiments with colour values, within a grid of horizontal and vertical lines.

CHRISTIAN JACCARD
born 1939 at Fontenay-sous-Bois
1962 first exhibition at the Cabinet des Estampes, Geneva. **1963** onwards participates in group exhibitions. Main area of interest is the investigation of the canvas and its properties. Generally adopts a procedure in two stages: the transformation of the untreated canvas into a sort of tarpaulin, by inserting eyelets at regular intervals and sewing seams along the edges; then, the application to the canvas surface of a type of matrix, this being created by means of cords dyed in various colours and pressed against the canvas to leave a mark. The explicit

aim is to desanctify the picture field, by giving it a functional appearance. The canvas ceases to be the bearer of illusions and becomes instead an object of experiment. Two systems are superimposed — one actual (the support), the other virtual (the imprint) — and in their interaction they comment on the various significances and qualities of the material. In this way, exploiting craft methods, it is possible to make an exhaustive assessment of the textile in terms of its attributes and potential. The various textures produced on the surface create effects of transparency. More recently, fire is used as the element providing structure, the canvas bearing the marks of scorching and burning at regular intervals.

EGILL JACOBSEN
born 1910 in Copenhagen
1932-33 studies at the Royal Academy in Copenhagen. **1933** the painter Wilhelm Bjerke-Petersen and sculptor Ejler Bille stage the first exhibition in Denmark of abstract works. In response the review *Linien* is founded, which becomes the focus for the activity of a number of young painters, Jacobsen among them. During the war the name is changed to *Helhesten,* then the group joins with the Belgians and Dutch to become part of COBRA.

1934 first visit to Paris. Admires Picasso but rejects his close reliance on the forms of the real world. Early interest in spontaneous gesture and investigations of painting materials. Back in Denmark, more authorative and rhythmic use of line. Increasingly departs from naturalistic themes. Use of mask motifs. **1937** executes a painting by bombarding a canvas with colour, without exerting any conscious control. Subsequently, paintings of violent rhythm, accentuated by the positioning of geometric forms inhabited by organisms of plant and animal origin. Brilliant colour. Active in COBRA group. **1959** first abstract painter to be appointed to the staff of the Royal Academy in Copenhagen.

ALEXEJ VON JAWLENSKY
Suvlovo 1864 - Wiesbaden 1941
Originally an officer in the Imperial Guard before taking up painting as a career. From **1889** studies at the Academy in St. Petersburg and under Repin; from **1886** studies in Munich at the school run by Anton Ažbè, where Kandinsky is a fellow pupil. Influence of Cézanne and van Gogh. **1905** visits to Brittany and Provence, which awaken his gifts as a colorist. Meets Matisse, who exerts a major influence on the course of his work. **1909** founder member in Munich of the Neue

Left: Jorn, 1982. Photo: Alechinsky.
Above: Kandinsky, 1936.

Künstlervereinigung. Broad expanses of flat colour. Brilliant palette. Stylistic similarities with the Fauves and the Blaue Reiter group, but does not exhibit with them. **1911-14** introduction of simpler and more monumental forms, increasing geometricization. Influence of Cubism. **1914-21** lives in Switzerland. Paints landscapes and heads. **1921** settles in Wiesbaden. **1924** joins with Kandinsky, Klee and Feininger in the Blue Four group. Paints nothing except the human face. **1935** compositions darker in tone and less reliant on geometric form.

ASGER JORN
Vejrum (Denmark) 1914 - Aarlius 1973
During the war years, member with Ejler Bille and Egill Jabobsen of the "Danish Abstract Surrealist" group. During this period figurative paintings of convulsive forms, motifs taken from Viking mythology. Interest in prehistoric culture and folk art. **1948-51** belongs to the COBRA movement; today is seen as its most gifted and consistent representative. **1955** settles in Paris. Founds the "Mouvement pour un Bauhaus imaginiste" and is active in the embryonic Situationist International. Paintings of a violently Expressionist character. Exhibitions in **1959** and **1962** of his *Disfigurations,* old colour reproductions defaced with strange marks and signs. Dramatic brutalist style. Spontaneity of gestural expression.

DONALD JUDD
born 1928 in Excelsior Springs (Missouri)
1946-47 military service in Korea. **1948-49** pupil at the College of William and Mary, Williamsburg (Virginia). **1949-53** studies at Columbia University, New York. Also attends the Art Students' League. **1957** first one-man show of paintings at Panoramas Gallery, New York. No further exhibitions until **1962**, when he shows sculptures which he describes as "specific objects". Returns to Columbia University to study art history. **1959-65** art critic for *Art News* and later *Arts Magazine.* **1962-64** teacher at the Brooklyn Institute of Arts and Sciences. **1965** trips to Sweden and to Paris. **1967** runs a sculpture course at Yale University. From **1968** designs structures in stainless steel and concrete for specified open-air sites. Later mural sculptures usually comprising repetitions of simple elements, very much in the spirit of Minimal Art. These strict geometrical works are assembled according to mathematical principles using industrial techniques. A typical example is a piece constructed of rectangular parallelepipeds mounted vertically on a wall at fixed intervals. In some of his structures he exploits the contrasts of materials used in combination.

WASSILY KANDINSKY
Moscow 1866 - Neuilly-sur-Seine 1944
Early studies in Odessa. From **1886** studies law and political economy in Moscow. **1889** conducts an ethnographic survey in northern Russia, in the course of which he discovers the brilliant colours of Russian folk art. **1895** at an exhibition of Impressionism discovers Monet. **1896** gives up legal studies in order to concentrate on painting. Goes to Munich. Pupil of Anton Ažbè. **1900** attends the Munich Academy and is taught by Franz Stuck. **1901** founds the Phalanx group and opens his own school. Travels extensively and in **1906** settles in Sèvres, near Paris. Impressionist and Fauve periods. **1907** returns to Munich. In Dresden exhibits with Die Brücke. **1909** founds the Neue Künstlervereinigung. **1910** first abstract watercolour. Publication of *Concerning the Spiritual in Art.* Meets Marc, Macke and Klee. Edits the Blaue Reiter Almanach. **1911-12** two Blaue Reiter exhibitions. **1910-20** so-called "tragic" period. Violent line and colour, intense lyricism. After the

Revolution holds various official positions in Moscow. **1921** returns to Germany. **1922** teaches at the Bauhaus in Weimar. **1920-24** so-called "architectural" period. Geometric forms. **1924** one of the Blue Four. **1925** moves with the Bauhaus to Dessau. **1926** publication of *Point and Line to Plane*. **1925-28** so-called "circle" period. **1933** the Bauhaus in Berlin is closed down by the Nazis. Kandinsky's canvases are confiscated. Exile in Paris. Abandons strict geometric forms in favour of arrangements of signs in compositions of marvellous equilibrium.

ELLSWORTH KELLY
born 1923 in Newburgh, New York
Early studies in Englewood (New Jersey) and Brooklyn. Two years art training in Boston under Carl Zerbe. **1948** goes to Paris and remains there until **1954**. French painting is a formative influence on his work. Studies Byzantine art. Attends the École des Beaux-Arts. Association with Michel Seuphor, Vasarely, Arp, Vantongerloo. Orientation towards geometric abstraction. **1950-51** contributions to the Salon des Réalités Nouvelles. Influence of Op Art. **1954** returns to the United States. Lives in New York. Develops a style using broad expanses of flat colour organized in geometric patterns. From the late fifties reduction of these coloured forms to systems of squares and rectangles, obedient to the principles of Neo-Plasticism. Later experiments with monochrome canvases designed to be viewed together as a single composition, a variant on the concept of the shaped canvas, where painting and support are synonymous. One of the most innovative examinations of the act and materials of painting.

PAUL KLEE
Munchenbuchsee, near Bern 1879 - Muralto-Locarno 1940
Initially attracted to a musical career but opts for painting. **1898-1901** goes to Munich and trains under Knirr, then at the Academy under Stuck. **1902** returns to Bern. Until **1906** concentrates largely on engraving, motifs in a style of distorted naturalism. Visits to Paris and Italy. **1906** returns to Munich. **1908** exhibits at the Munich Secession. **1909** inspired by the discovery of Cézanne, van Gogh, Matisse. **1911** meets Kandinsky, Macke and Marc. Participates in the Blaue Reiter exhibitions. Visit to Paris, where he meets Delaunay and discovers Cubism. **1914** trip to Tunisia. Revelation of colour: watercolours with rectangular zones of juxtaposed colour; everything in the surface plane. **1916-18** period of ideograms. From **1920** a teacher at the Bauhaus, first in Weimar, then Dessau. Alternate emphasis on line and colour. **1928** visit to Egypt. **1931** resigns from the Bauhaus to teach at the Düsseldorf Academy. **1933** leaves Hilter's Germany to live in Bern. Enlarged formats, lighter colours. **1937** visited by Braque and Picasso. Late works in an increasingly elliptical style.

YVES KLEIN
Nice 1928 - Paris 1962
Born into a family of painters. Self-taught. **1956** executes monochrome paintings, panels in uniform plain colours. Around **1957** concentrates exclusively on surfaces painted blue, the colour which symbolizes for him the infinite extent of the universe. **1958** at the Galerie Iris Clerc stages an exhibition entitled "Le Vide" in which the walls are left entirely blank. **1957-58** for the opera house at Gelsenkirchen creates stage sets in blue monochrome, with reliefs in natural sponge and polyester. **1958-60** creates his *Anthropometries*, impressions made by nude models and blue paint on canvas. **1960** *Cosmogenies*, works composed with the aid of natural elements such as wind and rain. **1961** *Fire Paintings*, created by using burning gas jets on asbestos sheeting. **1962** experiments with casts taken from living human bodies. Profoundly influential within his generation, both for the iconoclasm of his work and for his theoretical texts. Like Duchamp, Fontana or Beuys has the ability to make his gestures, and indeed his life, take on a significance that surpasses the strict concerns of art.

FRANZ KLINE
Wilkes-Barre (Pennsylvania) 1910 - New York 1962
Studies at Girard College, Philadelphia, then at the School of Fine Arts, Boston, and Heatherley's Art School, London. **1939** moves to New York. Paints landscapes, studio interiors, street scenes, portraits. **1940-45** earns his living drawing humorous sketches and as a decorator of bars and nightclubs. Expressionist use of colour already evident. Paintings and drawings of this period are frequently studies of his wife's face. **1945-50** moves away from anecdotal subject matter. Forms are increasingly simplified, as though viewed through a magnifying glass. **1948** reverts briefly to scenes of urban life. Concentration on drawings executed with brush and ink: hieroglyphs in broad black lines, flowing energetic brushwork. Later introduces such calligraphic signs into his paintings. Abandons representation. Influenced by his friends Pollock and de Kooning. Adopts larger formats. Broad expansive gesturalism. Collages assembled of torn and crumpled paper. Around **1957** reintroduces colour into his work.

IVAN KLIUN
Bolshie Gorki 1873 - Moscow 1943
Trains as an artist in Warsaw and Kiev. **1910** makes contact with the Futurist group in St. Petersburg, the "Union of Youth", and participates in the last of their exibitions, in 1912-13. **1912** links with Malevich. Works in a manner influenced by Synthetic Cubism. **1913** first experiments with reliefs and sculptures. **1915-16** adopts Malevich's philosophy of non-objective art. Co-signatory of the Suprematist manifesto distributed at the opening of the last Futurist exhibition "0.10".

Participates in most of the major avant-garde exhibitions held in St. Petersburg and Moscow. **1915-17** exclusively concerned with the exploration of rectangular and circular plane surfaces. **1917** director of the exhibitions network of the NKP (Commissariat for Education). **1918** in November works on decorations for the streets of Moscow, for the celebrations marking the anniversary of the Revolution. From this date compositions exploring the effects of light. His painting becomes an Impressionist interpretation of non-objective themes: simple forms bathed in light and setting up coloured vibrations. **1918-21** teaches painting in the Vkhutemas, or free art studios. **1921** teaching post with INKHUK. Participates in the first Russian exhibition in Berlin, also numerous exhibitions in Russia, up to 1930. **1921** ceases to work for Vkhutemas and INKHUK. After **1925** abandons abstraction and adopts a more representational style. Evolves towards a type of Post-Cubist lyricism, and later comes under the influence of Purism.

KATARZYNA KOBRO
Riga 1898 - Lódź 1951
Member of various avant-garde movements in Russia. **1922** settles in Poland with her husband, the painter and theoretician Wladislaw Strzeminski. Belongs to groups such as BLOC (1924), Praesens (1926), "a.r." (Revolutionary Artists; 1930). Works showing a strong influence of Suprematism: strict geometric compositions. Early investigations of three-dimensional constructions, of which few survive: studies of polar forces and tensions operating within fixed formal systems. In the late twenties concentration on spatial compositions of geometric forms, based on precise calculations and fixed mathematical relationships of modules. Also sculptures of a figurative type, influenced by Cubism. **1931** publication of *Composition of Space* setting out the theoretical basis of her work.

From **1935** an entirely new strand of "biological" compositions. Works shown in numerous exhibitions of abstract art in Europe and the United States.

WILLEM DE KOONING
born 1904 in Rotterdam
1916 leaves school to take up an apprenticeship with a decorating firm. At the same time attends evening classes in painting at the Rotterdam Academy. **1920** first encounter with modern art and the painters of De Stijl. **1924** lives for a year in Belgium. Contacts with Flemish Expressionism, significant for the later development of his work. **1926** settles in the United States. Up to now, works founded on elements of reality. Increasing dimension of symbolism, accentuated after meeting Arshile Gorky in **1928**. Simplification of forms. **1934** onwards abstract works. **1935-36** large abstract compositions for the WPA Federal Art Project. From **1938**, in parallel with his abstract studies reverts on occasion to a type of figuration, until **1944**. Incisive linear emphasis is translated into a dynamic gesturalism. From **1945** paints exclusively works of great violence with reference in human anatomy; series of paintings of monumental women. From **1955** abstract compositions: expressive use of texture and colour, vehement gesture. One of the first of the Abstract Expressionists.

FRANZ KUPKA
Opocno (Bohemia) 1871 - Puteaux 1957
1888 studies at the Prague School of Art. **1892** art training in Vienna. Revelation of Impressionism. **1894** settles in Paris. Admires Rodin and Toulouse-Lautrec. Studies from nature. Activity as an illustrator. **1906** radical departure in his work as he embarks on a progressive distortion of forms, using cold or bright colour that is independent of subject matter. **1909** affirmation of a new stylistic approach in the *Large Nude*, where the body is fragmented into luminous chromatic zones.

Cubist geometry is combined with brilliant Fauve colour. First attempt to express movement by representing its different stages. Images buried in complex organizations of facets and planes. Active in the Golden Section group. **1914** enlists in the armed forces. After the war resumes painting, in increasingly rigorous compositions. Studies of the modulation of colour and structure. After **1928** concentration on strict geometric forms. **1931** member of Abstraction-Creation group. Unrecognized until after World War II.

CHARLES LAPIQUE
born 1898 in Theizé (Rhône)
Scientific education at the École Centrale. **1920** starts painting. **1922-28** works as an engineer. Appointment as a laboratory technician in the Science Faculty of the Sorbonne. Uses the opportunity to carry out research on colour perception. **1925** first one-man exhibition. **1938** completes a doctoral thesis on optics entitled "Optique de l'Œil et la vision des contours". For a short period embraces Cubism. Association with young abstract painters such as Bazaine and Estève. Although he produces a number of successful abstract paintings, emerges from the experience a convinced supporter of figuration. **1943** onwards works full-time as a painter. Variety of subject matter, characterized both by a meticulous concern for realism and the interpolation of entirely imaginary dream images. Spaces with multiple perspectives which defy the traditional keeping of colour values: for example, uses warm colour for backgrounds and blue for foregrounds. Pigment is applied to the canvas with an impulsive gesturalism somewhat reminiscent of Tachisme or Lyrical Abstraction. **1956** publication of his *Essais sur l'espace, l'art et la destinée*.

Above: de Kooning. Photo: Daniel Frasnay.
Right: Lapique, 1985. Photo: Nicole Lejeune.

MIKHAAIL LARIONOV

Tiraspol (near Odessa) 1881 - Fontenay-aux-Roses 1964

1898 embarks on studies at the College of Painting, Sculpture and Architecture, Moscow. **1902-06** adopts an Impressionist manner. **1906** visit to Paris for the exhibition of Russian art staged by Diaghilev; absorbs the latest influences in French painting. Develops a distinctive "neo-primitivist" style inspired by folk art. Involved as organizer or contributor with all the major Russian avant-garde exhibitions. Friendship with Malevich. Tatlin's teacher. **1909** exhibits a canvas in Cubist style that is among the first works verging on non-figuration. **1910** exhibition at the Kraft studio with his companion Natalia Goncharova; speaks for the first time of Rayonism. **1911** co-organizer of the "Jack of Diamonds" exhibition. **1912** exhibits paintings in Munich with the Blaue Reiter group. Helps organize the "Donkey's Tail" exhibition. **1912** writes a manifesto of Rayonism, published in Moscow in 1913. With its emphasis on rays of light of pure colour, the movement is one of the earliest manifestations of abstraction. **1913** reverts to a mode of realist expression based on popular art. **1914** settles in Paris. **1915** association with Diaghilev. All but abandons painting to work with the Ballets Russes, as stage designer and choreographer. Partial paralysis. Starts painting again one year before his death.

BART VAN DER LECK

Utrecht 1876 - Blaricum (Holland) 1958

Studies at Amsterdam Academy, under A. J. Kindere. Early works in a realist style, mostly landscapes and portraits. Influenced by the Symbolism of Toorop. Around **1908** influence of van Gogh. **1910** elements of personal style emerge. Scenes of everyday life, using amplified forms and flat expanses of colour. Association with architects such as Berlage. Designs for stained glass. Increasingly geometricized forms, use of pure colours. Meets Mondrian, who is influenced by the precision of his technique. **1917** joins the De Stijl group. Period of abstraction. Subsequently moves away from Neo-Plasticism and pursues a course midway between figuration and abstraction. Retains his palette of primary colours and the method of building up a composition out of small lines or motifs set against a white ground. Later concentration on mural paintings. Also designs for tapestries and ceramics.

EDOUARD JEANNERET (LE CORBUSIER)

La Chaux-de-Fonds 1887 - Roquebrune-Cap-Martin 1965

1900-05 studies engraving at the École des Beaux-Arts, La Chaux-de-Fonds. Pupil of L'Epplatenier. **1905** trains as an architect, while pursuing his interest in graphic techniques. Meets many architects (among them Joseph Hoffmann, Tony Garnier, Auguste Perret, Peter Behrens). **1911-12** in Hellerau studies the problems of industrial design with the Deutscher Werkbund. **1917** settles in Paris. Interest in the early Cubist experiments. **1918-19** paintings and drawings based on geometric structures. **1920** with Amédée Ozenfant founds *L'Esprit Nouveau*, which is published until 1925; the review provides a platform for their philosophy of Purism. Author of a number of texts, including *Vers une architecture*, published in 1923. Revolutionary architectural designs which eliminate all reference to the outmoded forms of the past. Concern to adapt architecture to meet the demands of modern society, and to produce buildings that stand as plastic works of art in their own right. Envisages a type of painting that is entirely subsidiary to its architectural context. From **1929** introduces human figures into his paintings, hitherto restricted to still lifes.

Left: Kupka. Photo: Liberman.
Above: Le Corbusier, 1962. Photo: Denise Colomb.

Style of restrained dynamism, no extravagant curves or audacious volumes. **1930** establishes his "modulor", a unit of measurement related to the scale of the human body. **1936** tapestry designs for the Aubusson works.

FERNAND LÉGER
Argentan, Normandy 1881 - Gif-sur-Yvette 1955
1897 apprenticed to an architect in Caen. **1900** goes to Paris. Studies at the École des Arts Décoratifs. **1908** occupies a studio at La Ruche. Influenced by Impressionism and later Cézanne. **1910** meets Picasso and Braque. Attends the sessions held at the home of Jacques Villon in Puteaux, which lead in 1912 to the foundation of the Section d'Or group. **1912-14** paintings of objects fragmented into geometric designs. **1914** called up to serve in the army. Drawings of soldiers and the machines of war. **1916** discharged. **1917** embarks on "mechanical" or "tubist" period. Finds inspiration in industrially produced items and modern engineering. Large compositions of shapes lying flat on the canvas. From **1920** the dominant theme is the human figure, presented as an automaton. Up to **1924** monumental works in a more static idiom. Alternate periods of abstraction and figuration. **1924** film *Ballet*

mécanique. Abstract mural compositions. **1925** paintings shown in the Pavillon de l'Esprit Nouveau at International Exhibition of Decorative Arts in Paris. Concerned with the problem of using colour to create space. **1940** lives in Marseilles and then moves to the United States. Influenced in his subject matter by American society. **1945** returns to France. Immobile figures in classically composed canvases. Other spheres of activity include stage design, mosaics, stained glass, tapestry and sculpture in polychrome ceramic.

JEAN LE MOAL
born 1909 in Authon-du-Perche (Eure-et-Loir)
Studies at the École des Beaux-Arts in Lyons. Settles in Paris. Works at the École des Arts Décoratifs, then at the Académie Ranson, where he meets Bissière in 1934. **1935** begins to discover a personal style, deriving from Fauvism and Cubism. Simplification of forms. In the early fifties paints landscapes, interiors, still lifes: assured structure, soft light, muted colours. Objects reduced to their bare frameworks. Around **1955** objects disappear but the pictures continue to evoke the external world. Principal inspiration is landscape, less in terms of its material reality than in the play of light over

its forms, expressed in fluid colour. Progressive elimination of line in favour of juxtapositions of vibrant coloured masses. Predominance of verticals. Gradually the patches of colour expand into broader rhythms and take on more varied tonalities. Responsible also for many murals, stage sets and costumes and stained-glass windows (churches of Saint-Martin in Brest and Audincourt, cathedral of Saint-Vincent at Saint-Malo, etc.).

JULIO LE PARC
born 1928 in Mendoza, Argentina
1943 studies at Buenos Aires Academy. Immediate interest in avant-garde groups and ideas. Graduates with a teaching diploma in drawing and painting. **1958** settles in Paris, with the aid of a bursary from the French government. **1960** founder member of the "Groupe de Recherche d'Art Visuel". **1966** first one-man exhibition in Paris. In the same year participates in the exhibition "Kunst-Licht-Kunst" in Eindhoven: the first major international exhibition devoted to the use of artificial light as a form of artistic expression. Throughout his career concentrates exclusively on optical phenomena, exploring a range of effects obtained by the use of moving parts, or with artificial lighting, by exploiting transparency, or by involving the

Left: Manessier, 1984. Photo: Nicole Lejeune. Above: Magnelli, 1966. Photo: Frasnay. Opposite: Malevich (centre), 1913.

physical participation or movement of the spectator. Makes extensive use of black and white on metal or transparent materials. Disregards aesthetic considerations in his work, concentrating on mechanisms and psychological effect. Also participation in collective paintings of a political motivation.

PERCY WYNDHAM LEWIS
Amherst, Nova Scotia 1882 - London 1957
Painter, novelist, critic and political commentator. **1893** parents are separated. Lives in London with his mother. **1898-1901** studies at the Slade School of Art. **1902-08** period of travel and study in Europe, where he encounters writers of anti-Romantic views. **1909** returns to England. Publication of first stories. **1911-12** contributes to the Neo-Realist Camden Town Group exhibitions and those held by the Allied Artists Association. From **1913** moves towards abstraction. Soon leaves above groups and also Roger Fry's Omega Workshops, with which he is briefly associated. **1913** sets up the Rebel Art Centre. **1914** founds the Vorticist movement, a synthesis of Cubism and Futurism, which however rejects the Futurist emphasis on movement in favour of a highly structured static expression, usually based on vertical lines. The principal English avant-garde movement. Collaboration on major decorative works. **1915** founder member of London Group. War artist until 1917; adapts his style to the subject matter of war. **1920** activity in association with the Ten Group, coinciding with a return to figuration, portraits and self-portraits. Deserts painting for political and literary activities, apart from illustrations for his own books. **1954** publication of his last essay *The Demon of Progress in Art.*

SOL LEWITT
born 1928 in Hartford (Connecticut)
Studies at Syracuse University, New York. **1965** first one-man exhibition. Before defining his position as a Conceptual artist, is associated with the Minimalist movement. Simple permutations of primary units, very much in the manner of his later works. Conceptual art implies the presentation above all else of an idea; in its stark and disciplined regularity LeWitt's work takes on the character of illustration of a formula; within it all the art forms — sculpture, drawing, mural painting — are subjugated to form a distinctive synthesis. His method is to present variations of basic units, usually parallelepipeds reduced to their bare framework, their alignment dictated by a fixed order of permutation. It is the concept that matters. The execution is no more than a statement of that concept. Carried to its logical conclusion, such an approach leads inevitably to the creation of works of art designed to be ephemeral: a mural which is marked out on a wall, making its imprint on space, and which is then obliterated.

EL LISSITZKY
Poshinok, near Smolensk 1890 - Moscow 1941
1909-14 studies in engineering at the Darmstadt Polytechnic, followed by architectural studies in Moscow. **1911** visits Paris. Contacts with contemporary painters. **1918** invited by Chagall to teach at the Vitebsk Academy. Influenced by Malevich and the Constructivists. From **1919** series of works entitled *Proun*: compositions of geometric planes in space. Appointed as a teacher at the Moscow Academy. Stage sets and costumes for various operas. Applies his interest in geometric principles to typography and illustration. Reputation as a poster-artist. In the same year, in the face of growing hostility from the authorities, leaves for Berlin. Links with Hans Richter, Theo van Doesburg and Moholy-Nagy, who is to spread Constructivist doctrines to the Bau-

haus. Writes many articles for periodicals. **1922-25** settles in Switzerland. Founds the ABC group and the review of the same name. **1925** with Arp, edits *The Isms of Art*. **1925-28** in Hanover. Interior décor for the modern art gallery of the Landsmuseum, destroyed by the Nazis. **1928** returns to Russia. Works as an exhibition designer. Publication of many books for children. Late works are photomontages for propaganda posters.

MORRIS LOUIS
(LOUIS BERNSTEIN)
Baltimore 1912 - Washington, D.C. 1962
Studies painting at Maryland Institute of Art, Baltimore. Moves to Washington. Works in a style broadly derived from Cubism until 1952. Becomes familiar with Pollock's painting and visits Helen Frankenthaler in her studio. Abrupt change of direction. **1954** begins to exhibit with the New Talent group in New York. Often associated with Frankenthaler and Kenneth Noland because of their shared concerns. Their work represents an attempt to move beyond the tactile values promoted by Abstract Expressionism, while at the same time avoiding the extreme formalism of Hard Edge abstraction. The method they adopt is to allow the colour to run freely over the unprimed canvas, staining rather than painting, and stressing the purely material elements of the picture. Critics have dubbed their work chromatic or Color Field Abstraction. Louis uses very dilute acrylic paints which barely cover the canvas, appearing like superimposed veils of colour. In some compositions the central portion of the canvas is left unpainted. Others consist of overlapping stripes of colour which occupy the centre, forming a column; the ribbons of colour seem to extend beyond the edge of the canvas.

AUGUST MACKE
Meschede (Ruhr) 1887 - Perthes (Champagne) 1914
Childhood in Cologne and Bonn. Studies at the Düsseldorf Academy. **1907-08** visits to Paris and exposure to French painting: Impressionism, Fauvism, and later Cubism. **1909-10** in Munich meets Franz Marc, then Kandinsky and Jawlensky. **1911** works with Kandinsky on the preparation of the Blaue Reiter *Almanac*. Nevertheless occupies a very different position from Kandinsky and Marc, remaining attached to the forms of the visible world. Broad rhythms in the manner of Matisse. **1912** in Bonn discovers the elements of a personal style in Cubism and Futurism. Greatly influenced by Delaunay whom he visits in Paris, and who visits him in Bonn. Luminosity of colours. **1913-14** small abstract compositions showing an obvious debt to Delaunay. For the major part his work continues to be in a figurative style. April **1914** travels with Paul Klee to Tunisia.

ALBERTO MAGNELLI
Florence 1888 - Meudon 1971
Technical education. Devotes himself full-time to painting without any formal art training whatsoever. **1911** association with the Futurists, Boccioni, Carrà, Marinetti, Papini and Soffici, but remains outside the group and pursues an independent line. **1914** lives in Paris. Links with Apollinaire, Max Jacob, Picasso, Gris and Léger. In Florence paints large compositions, still lifes and landscapes of highly simplified forms. **1915** increasing emphasis on formal structure leads him to abstraction. Works in brilliant zones of flat colour. **1918** reverts to figuration, using violent colour and contorted forms. Later more structured paintings of figures and landscapes in a lighter and less dramatic palette. **1933** again turns to abstraction. So-called period of "shattered stones". **1935** works of pure abstraction arrived at intuitively, founded in no explicit artistic philosophy. **1935** lives in Grasse, near

Arp, Sophie Taeuber-Arp and Sonia Delaunay. Highly deliberate formalism of strong expressive power. Also collages and montages of various materials.

KASIMIR MALEVICH
Kiev 1878 - Leningrad 1935
Attends the Kiev Academy; moves to Moscow and studies under Roeberg at the School of Painting, Sculpture and Architecture. Associates with avant-garde artists. **1908** works influenced by paintings seen in the collections of Shchukin and Morosov; initially inspired by Impressionism, subsequently Fauvism and Expressionism. **1910-12** takes part in the major exhibitions of the Russian avant-garde (**1911** "Jack of Diamonds", **1912** "Donkey's Tail", **1913** "The Target", **1915** "Tramway V"). Influence of Cubism and Futurism: geometricization pursued almost to the point of abstraction. **1913** develops the foundation of his Suprematist theories. **1915** exhibits first Suprematist works at the exhibition "0.10" in Leningrad, among them the celebrated *Black Square on a White Ground.* The paintings consist of primary forms (square, circle, cross, triangle) in bold colour. **1916** publication of manifesto *From Cubism to Suprematism.* **1919** takes Suprematism to its logical extreme in *White Square on a White Ground.* Teaching posts in Moscow and Leningrad. Work on architectural models and decorative arts projects. **1927** trip to Poland before attending a major retrospective in Germany. Selection of his writings published by the Bauhaus under the title *Die gegenstandlose Welt* (the non-objective world). Little is known about his last years in Russia.

ALFRED MANESSIER
born 1911 in Saint-Ouen (Somme)
Studies at the École des Beaux-Arts in Amiens. **1929** moves to Paris. Studies architecture at the École des Beaux-Arts but pursues his interest in painting by copying at the Louvre and attending art classes. Associa-

tion with Bissière, then teaching at the Académie Ranson. **1943** period of retreat in a Trappist monastery: much of his work betrays a religious inspiration. Around **1944** his subject matter is still recognizably derived from reality, but there is an increasing geometricization and use of pure colour. Later the expressive content of the work is conveyed exclusively in terms of line and colour. Around **1959** he adopts a more expansive and rapid style in sinuously rhythmic compositions. Other work includes non-figurative stained-glass windows (churches at Bréseux, Tousles-Saints in Basel, Saint-Pierre in Arles, the Munsterkirche in Essen, Moutier in Switzerland, Hem, Unserer Frauen Lieber in Bremen, Saint-Bénigne in Pontarlier). Also tapestries on a monumental scale.

ROBERT MANGOLD
born 1937 in North Tonawanda (New York)
1956-59 studies at the Cleveland Institute of Art, then at Yale University until 1963. **1964** first one-man exhibition at the Fischbach Gallery, New York, which includes the series *Walls.* Uses "rough" materials employed in construction: wood, plywood, cement blocks, etc., painted in flat colour. Occasional coloured projections, vertical lines dividing the surface into two zones. **1965-66** series of *Areas:* monochrome surfaces sprayed with oil-based paint, exhibiting subtle tonal variations. Subsequently the support dictates the form: shallow or steeply curving arcs of a circle. In the series *V, W, X,* explores the effects of distortion. From **1969** forms that are roughly circular, enclosed within forms that are roughly square. Shares the concerns of Minimal Art. Painting with no reference outside itself, no dimension of illusion or emotion. Interest in the specificity of the pictorial language. Exhibits regularly in Europe and in the United States.

PIERO MANZONI
Soncino (Cremona) 1933 - Milan 1963
Self-taught. **1957** first one-man exhibition at the Pater Gallery, Milan. From **1957** operates at the forefront of artistic experiment; rapidly comes to be seen as the archetypal representative of the European avant-garde. Interest in Fontana's perforated and slashed canvases, Burri's "sacking" pictures and, in particular, Yves Klein's monochromes. In **1957** executes first *Achromes,* pictures assembled by coating a piece of crumpled white cloth in plaster or soaking it in calcium sulphate. The same year joins with a number of young French and Italian artists as cosignatory of the manifesto *Contro le stile,* which demands the abandonment of every element of the traditional pictorial language. Continues to experiment with white monochromes, using a variety of techniques; materials include cotton, plaster, white canvas, glass wool and various chemicals. **1959** executes forty-five *Corpi d'Aria,* inflatable sculptures marketed under the name "the artist's breath". Later acquires a controversial reputation for various "acts" committed in a similar spirit: attaches his signature to naked women, draws an infinite line on a roll of paper contained in a box, produces boxes of "artist's shit", etc. An iconoclastic approach that anticipates many of the concerns of conceptual or ephemeral art.

FRANZ MARC
Ried (Bavaria) 1880 - Verdun 1916
Son of a painter. **1900** determines to become an artist and enrols at the Munich Academy. Art training until 1903. **1903** visits Paris and absorbs the lessons of Impressionism. In Munich, influenced by the Jugendstil movement. **1907** second trip to Paris. Admires van Gogh. **1910** meets Macke and then Kandinsky, with whom he collaborates on the Blaue Reiter *Almanac.* **1911-12** two Blaue Reiter exhibitions. Free

and expressive use of colour. **1912** works reflecting a degree of Cubist influence. Meets Delaunay and finds inspiration in his painting. **1913** uses increasingly overlapping forms. Arrives at a type of abstraction of intense lyricism. Serves in the army and is killed at Verdun in **1916**. Abrupt termination of an *œuvre* of powerful symbolism and drama, subsuming the influences of abstraction and Expressionism.

BRICE MARDEN
born 1938 in the Bronx, New York
1958-61 studies at Boston University. **1961-63** student at Yale University. Entirely self-taught as a painter. **1963** moves to New York. **1964** visits Paris. Work concerned exclusively with the nature and qualities of colour. **1966** first monochromes, single panels. In the same year first one-man exhibition in New York. Around **1968** executes compositions comprising two or three panels, juxtapositions of large monochrome surfaces. A number of canvases of monumental proportions. In his narrow concentration on subtle contrasts within the colour surface, belongs to the Minimalist tradition. Uses dots, stripes, chevrons and bands of flat colour. Also heavy impasto. More recently, intimations of a changed focus in a series of drawings entitled *Suicide Notes*: exploration of the mechanisms of self-generating forms.

AGNES MARTIN
born 1912 in Maklin (Saskatchewan), Canada
1932 settles in the United States. Attends several universities, among these Columbia University, New York. From **1940** teaches at New Mexico University. **1957** moves to New York. First one-man exhibition in **1958** at Betty Parson Gallery. In these and later works pursues an independent course, presenting an alternative to the dominant trend of Abstract Expressionism. Her work may be seen as a form of geometric purism, incorporating an insistent rhythm at times reminiscent of Op

Art. In certain respects presages the concerns of Minimalism. Paintings based on sculptures by Donald Judd. Around **1963** change of manner. Paintings of restrained delicacy, based on grids. Sometimes a simple framework against a bare canvas. Palette of varying hues of grey. In her reliance on restricted but lyrical means of expression, enjoys immense influence during the sixties. **1967** for a period ceases painting altogether, apart from silkscreen prints executed in **1973-74** in Cuba. Later paintings influenced by the radiant light and colour of the New Mexican mesa. Regarded as a leading exponent of "cool" painting.

ANDRÉ MASSON
Balagny (Oise) 1896 - Paris 1987
Studies at the Académie Royale des Beaux-Arts in Brussels. **1912** goes to Paris. Studies fresco painting at the École des Beaux-Arts. Interest in the old masters. **1922** meets Kahnweiler and starts to paint regularly. Influenced by Cubism and Juan Gris. **1923** first painting in a symbolist manner. Muted colours, sand and pigment mixtures, sinuous line. Association with the Surrealist group. Automatic drawings. Illustrations for Georges Bataille. Long period in Spain and **1934-36** in Catalonia, where he paints insects and bull-fighting scenes. **1941** flees to Martinique and then the United States, where he stays until **1945**. His violent gesturalism influences the younger generation of American painters. Numerous pastels on canvas. **1947** settles in Aix-en-Provence. Evolves a harmonious style influenced by Zen Buddhism. Breaks off his contacts with the Surrealists. Parallel activity as a draughtsman and engraver. Also numerous stage and costume designs and book illustrations.

GEORGES MATHIEU
born 1921 in Boulogne-sur-Mer
Studies law, philosophy and English at university. **1942** starts painting. Almost immediately drawn to ab-

straction. **1947** attracts attention at the Salon des Réalités Nouvelles when he exhibits works composed of blotches of colour, the pigment applied directly with the fingers, or with a rag or straight from the tube. Militantly opposed to geometric abstraction. Organizes exhibitions with Bryen and Tapié to promote his views. His stylistic approach has been described both as "psychic non-figuration" and "lyrical abstraction". Develops an increasingly calligraphic treatment of forms. Makes a positive virtue of speed of execution, in improvisations allowing gesturalism free rein. Sometimes produces works in a few minutes. Paintings of gigantic proportions. **1956** before an audience at the Théâtre Sarah Bernhardt paints in just twenty minutes a canvas twelve metres by four. Repeats the experiment in several different countries. From **1964** ceases to rely on rapidity of execution and works in a more traditional manner. His fluent graphism also finds wider application in designs for posters, coins, china, etc.

ROBERTO MATTA
born 1912 in Santiago (Chile)
Education at the College of the Sacred Heart, Santiago. Architectural studies at the Catholic University of Santiago. **1931** awarded an architect's diploma. **1933** goes to Europe to continue his studies. **1935** works as a designer for Le Corbusier on the "radial city". **1936** first drawings. Uses his architectural training in representations of forms in space. In Spain meets Lorca, who in **1937** introduces him to Dali and Breton. Active member of the Surrealist group until 1948. **1938** first paintings, which he calls "psychological morphologies", produced by techniques of automatism: explosions and fusions of matter in space. **1939** settles in New York and is again active with the Surrealists in exile. Adopts more fluid pigment and transparent forms in compositions including quasi-human figures and organic forms suspended weightless in space. After the war,

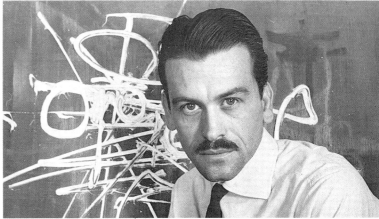

Left: Masson, 1983. Photo: Nicole Lejeune.
Above: Mathieu, 1952. Photo: Denise Colomb.

divides his time between London, Paris and Italy; increasingly uses painting as a vehicle for political protest. Like André Masson, a fertile source of new ideas for the young generation of American painters.

JEAN MESSAGIER
born 1920 in Paris
1942 studies at the École Nationale des Arts Décoratifs. Periods of work in studios run by Brianchon, Oudot and, most particularly, Desnoyer. Growing reputation as his works are presented at major exhibitions (Salon d'Automne from 1947, Salon de Mai 1948 onwards, etc.). **1946** study trip to Algeria. **1948** study trip to Italy. Discovers a new chromatic register of fluid tones. Attracted at an early stage to abstraction. **1949** finally abandons his earlier manner of analytic figuration. Compositions of aggressively original design, followed by paintings in a more serene and harmonious mode. Later embarks on a period of works of an essentially static character, with full, robustly stated volumes. Around **1960** more dynamic brushwork: a rhythmic play of light over a restricted range of transparent colours. Space evoked by gesture. More recently has turned to sculpture, taking casts from natural objects. Also open-air décors on a grand scale.

HENRI MICHAUX
Namur 1899 - Paris 1984
Jesuit education in Brussels. Embarks on medical studies, which he abandons in 1919 to become a sailor. Strongly influenced by Lautréamont, and subsequently by Asian philosophers, Paul Klee, Chirico and Max Ernst. **1926** first drawings and paintings in oils. Experiments with a variety of techniques: application of pigment in blobs or by dripping, grattage and frottage. **1927** first appearance of his characteristic "signs". Search for a personal language: sheets of paper covered in hieroglyphic squiggles. Drawings produced in part via automatic techniques. Abbreviated forms and jerky rhythms. Bestiary of fabulous creatures. **1927-36** travels all over the world, including the Far East. Studies ideograms. At this period concentrates on writing and draws very little. **1936** illustrates his own published text of *Entre centre et absence*. **1937-38** gouaches on black grounds: imaginary landscapes peopled with formless beings. Experiments with washes. Watercolours of drawn structures drenched with fluid colour. **1946** publication of *Peintures et Dessins*. Further automatic drawings. **1950-51** produces page after page covered with designs of innumerable repetitive series of ink dots. **1952-53** large

gouaches in brilliant colour. Large-format "ink paintings". From **1955** works executed under the influence of the hallucinogenic drug mescalin. Distortions of scale, microscopic graphic signs. His graphic work stands in its own right; although intimately linked to the themes of the poems, it is never merely illustrative.

LASZLO MOHOLY-NAGY
Bacsbarsod, Hungary 1895 - Chicago 1946
1914 service in the Austro-Hungarian armed forces. **1917** gravely wounded. During convalescence begins to draw portraits and landscapes. Returns to Budapest. In **1918** completes a doctorate in law. Founds the group "Ma" (Today). Influenced by the new Russian art. **1920** settles in Berlin. **1921** meets El Lissitzky in Düsseldorf. First abstract paintings. Use of unusual materials in collages and sculptures. **1922** publication in Vienna of *Buch neuer Künstler*. **1923** meets Walter Gropius, who invites him to join the Bauhaus faculty. Plays a major role in teaching from 1923 to 1928. Also edits the series of Bauhausbücher, among which are texts of his own presenting a host of original ideas concerning the use of new techniques and materials. Continues to paint in a style of pure geometric formalism but is better known for his

Above: Michaux, 1936. Photo: Yvonne Chevalier.
Right: Matta, 1957. Photo: Denise Colomb.

photograms and photomontages. **1928** returns to Berlin; designs layouts, stage and film sets, and exhibitions. **1932-36** exhibits with the Abstraction-Creation group. **1934** lives in Amsterdam. **1935** in London. Publication of photo-reportages. Starts the series of painted constructions which he calls *Space Modulators.* **1937** goes to the United States and founds his own Institute of Design. Continued activity as painter and sculptor. From **1940** sculptures in plexiglass.

PIET MONDRIAN (PIETER CORNELIS MONDRIAAN)
Amersfoort, Holland 1872 - New York 1944
Calvinist background. Two teaching diplomas in drawing. **1892-95** studies painting at Amsterdam Academy. **1895-1907** financial insecurity: work as copyist and scientific draughtsman. Naturalistic period, during which his favourite theme is the Dutch landscape. Interest in Theosophy. **1908** first visit to Domburg. Meets Toorop and is influenced by his use of Divisionism and Symbolism. **1911** moves to Paris. Experiments with Cubism. Paints a series of *Trees* in which the motif becomes increasingly abstract. Lines reduced progressively to horizontals and verticals and palette to three basic colours. **1914-18** in Hol-

land. Meets Bart van der Leck. Continues to explore abstraction. Meets Theo van Doesburg, with whom he founds the review *De Stijl* in **1917**. At this period concerned more with writing than painting. Rejects curved lines and all random interventions. **1919** returns to Paris. **1920** Léonce Rosenberg publishes *Le Néo-plasticisme.* From **1922** exclusively white backgrounds. Few exhibitions or sales of his work. **1924** ceases to write for *De Stijl.* **1930** member of Circle and Square. **1931** active in Abstraction-Creation group. Visited by experimental painters from all over the world. **1938** goes to London. **1940** settles in New York. Fragmentation of black lines into coloured segments. Experiments with more rhythmic compositions, interrupted by his death.

FRANÇOIS MORELLET
born 1926 in Cholet (Maine-et-Loire)
Self-taught as a painter. For many years classified as a kinetic artist although his concerns extend beyond that definition. Inspired originally by the decorative friezes of Islamic art. Emphasis on patterns of fluent curves leads him towards total abstraction. Rejects the notion of painting as an expression of feeling. From **1952** executes works

based on five simple pictorial principles: juxtaposition, superimposition, chance, interference and fragmentation. Titles usually descriptive of the underlying principles of construction. **1960** founder member of Groupe de Recherche d'Art Visuel (GRAV). Works requiring the active participation of the observer. **1963** one of the first to use neon tubes, which light up in a particular sequence and rhythm and create effects of interference. Light is treated as an artistic medium in its own right. Author of numerous theoretical texts.

ROBERT MORRIS
born 1931 in Kansas City (Missouri)
Art training at Kansas City Art Institute, then at California School of Fine Arts, San Francisco, and Hunter College, New York, where he later teaches. Many one-man exhibitions from **1957** onwards. Also participation in the major group shows of contemporary art. From **1964** associated with the concerns of Minimalism: one of the most prominent representatives and theoreticians of the movement, which develops its ideas out of Malevich's Suprematism and Russian Constructivism. Expression is restricted to the use of simple basic forms, designed to create an awareness in the spectator of relationships of space and

Left: Moholy-Nagy. Above: Mondrian, 1929.
Opposite, from left to right: Newman, Pollock, Smith, 1952. Photo: Hans Namuth.

volume, both internal to the work and external to it. Large-scale formats. Use of plastics and other industrial materials. Frequently works in series, intended to stress the contribution made by the viewer's changing perceptions. Monumental sculptural objects. One of first Americans to be influenced by the German artist Josef Beuys. Anti-aestheticism. With the *Felts* of the seventies, loose piles of grey felt, finds an extension of his earlier concerns in "formless" or ephemeral art, emphasizing the idea rather than the art object. Also construction of mazes and earth sculptures.

OLIVIER MOSSET
born 1944 in Bern
1964 moves to Paris. **1967** at the Salon de la Jeune Peinture, the Musée des Arts Décoratifs and the Biennale de Paris, all in the same year, the BMPT group (Buren, Mosset, Parmentier and Toroni) exhibits large canvases presenting the same limited range of "objective" forms: vertical stripes in the case of Buren, horizontal stripes for Parmentier, repeated regular brushstrokes for Toroni, and a black ring-shape of a particular size in the case of Mosset. By repeating the identical canvas again and again, the group sparks off a fundamental debate about the purposes of painting in general. The

group itself is soon disbanded, but Mosset persists with his motif of a black ring against a white ground. In **1974** a departure, with an exhibition of works in a pattern of regular stripes. Later a sequence of uniform monochromes, some of very large dimensions, among the most purely abstract contributions to contemporary art.

ROBERT MOTHERWELL
born 1915 in Aberdeen (Washington)
1937 degree in philosophy at Stanford University. **1937-38** further studies in philosophy and aesthetics at Harvard. **1938-39** visit to France. Determines to combine painting with teaching. Also continues studies in art history at Columbia University, New York, under the direction of Meyer Shapiro. Contact through him with the European Surrealists, notably Matta, who introduces him to the technique of automatic drawing. Extensive activity both as a writer and editor of writings on art. **1948** with Baziotes, Newman and Rothko co-founder of the Subjects of the Artist school, which changes its name in the following year to The Club, becoming the principal focus of activity for the avant-garde in New York. Rapidly sheds the Surrealist influence. Up to around **1950** his paintings and col-

lages indicate two main preoccupations — emotional expressivity and chromatic intensity. Around **1954** introduction of large sweeping signs, massive forms laid out in flat black. From **1960** increasing simplification of forms and colours. Large formats. **1968-74** series of *Open Canvases* in which signs have disappeared and the attention is focused on variations of the background.

BARNETT NEWMAN
New York 1905 - 1970
Son of Polish Jewish immigrants. Studies at the City College of New York. **1922-24** attends the Art Students' League. Starts painting while still working in the family garment business, of which he is not free until **1937**, following the death of his father. **1939-44** stops painting altogether. Interest in primitive art. Destroys all his past work. Earliest paintings in existence date from **1944**, when he begins to paint abstractions using a technique close to Surrealist automatic writing. Rapidly develops the characteristic vertical emphasis of his mature work; the surface is articulated as a "field" divided into two zones by a thin band of colour or strip of bare canvas, called a "zip". Formats of monumental size, exaggerated either in terms of height or width.

1948 with Baziotes, Rothko and Motherwell co-founder of the Subjects of the Artist school, later known as The Club. In the sixties first experiments with sculpture. Profoundly influential among the younger generation of American painters for whom his powerful statements of pictorial tensions supply an alternative to gesturalism.

BEN NICHOLSON
Denham (Buckinghamshire) 1894 - 1982
Son of a painter. **1911** attends the Slade School in London for one term. Largely self-trained as an artist. Numerous visits to France, Italy, Madeira and California: paintings and sketches, mostly of buildings and landscapes. From the end of the war up to 1933 works reflecting the influence of Cubism, including many still lifes. **1933** in Paris, meets Mondrian. New conception of space. Series of carved abstract reliefs consisting of superimposed rectangles and squares with very slight variations in levels, usually painted white. Paintings in a manner derived from Neo-Plasticism. Member of the group Unit One. **1933-35** active in the Abstraction-Creation movement. Joins the English group Axis. **1937** with the architect Leslie Martin and Naum Gabo edits the review *Circle*. **1939** lives in St. Ives,

Cornwall, with his wife Barbara Hepworth. Influence on younger painters within the flourishing artistic community. In **1958** settles in Brissago, Switzerland. Moves freely between abstraction and figuration, refusing to make a clear distinction between the two. Bright, flat colours give way in the later paintings to dark, muted tones. Variations of textures, achieved usually by techniques of grattage or frottage.

KENNETH NOLAND
born 1924 in Ashville (South Carolina)
Studies at Black Mountain College, North Carolina. **1948** goes to Paris. Pupil of Zadkine. **1949** first one-man exhibition at Galerie Greuze in Paris. From the late fifties is one of the principal representatives of the American school of chromatic abstraction. Pursues many of the concerns initially isolated by Rothko and Newman. In common with them, concentrates principally on the expressive power of colour, within a broader examination of the material characteristics of painting. For traditional colour values substitutes interactions between colours that are often close in tone; when these are juxtaposed they create a kind of perceptual intensity, setting up effects of optical vibration. Uses unprimed canvases

and simple repetitive geometric patterns. His radical inventions include a series of enormously long canvases painted with parallel horizontal stripes; also the so-called shaped canvases, pictures whose external form is dictated by the structure of the support. In the seventies embarks on a new period characterized by asymmetric forms lined up along opposing axes.

AMÉDÉE OZENFANT
Saint-Quentin 1886 - Cannes 1966
Classical education in Spain. **1904** returns to Saint-Quentin and attends drawing classes. **1906** goes to Paris to study architecture. **1915-17** in a series of articles published in his review *L'Elan* sets out the basic principles of Purism. **1917** develops a close association with Le Corbusier (Edouard Jeanneret). **1918** they collaborate on the Purist manifesto *Après le Cubisme*. Compositions made up of simplified forms, arrived at by strict formulae. From the starting point of real objects develops towards abstraction by eliminating all variable and chance elements, so that only the constants remain. **1920-25** with Le Corbusier founds the review *L'Esprit Nouveau*. **1925-28** work on mural paintings. **1928** publication of his text *Art. I. Bilan des Arts modernes; II. Structure d'un nouvel esprit*. **1931-38** work on a

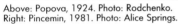
Above: Popova, 1924. Photo: Rodchenko.
Right: Pincemin, 1981. Photo: Alice Springs.

vast composition entitled *Life*. **1935-38** lives in London. Founds his own school. **1938** lives in New York. Establishes the Ozenfant School of Fine Arts. **1955** returns to France.

WOLFGANG PAALEN
Vienna 1907 - Mexico 1959
Pupil of Hans Hofmann in Munich. Painter and philosopher. From the outset paints abstract works that bear the mark of his philosophical speculations. Visits a number of European countries before settling in Paris in **1928**. **1932-35** member of the Abstraction-Creation group. **1936-40** converted to Surrealism. Paintings of visionary inspiration: mysterious ships run aground on deserted shores. Invents a Surrealist automatic technique known as "fumage", which consists in picking out the pattern of smoky traces left by a burning candle. **1939** exile in Mexico. **1942** founds the review *Dyn*; six issues are published, the last in 1944. **1945** publication in New York of *Form and Sense*. Assembles a major collection of pre-Columbian and Indian art. That interest is reflected in the orientation of his painting towards ideographic signs in unrestrained colour. Suicide in 1959.

MICHEL PARMENTIER
born 1938 in Paris
Studies at the École des Beaux-Arts in Paris, with fellow pupils Viallat, Bioulès, Kermarec, Buren *et al* – all of them products of a highly traditional system, serious contenders for the Prix de Rome, yet destined to occupy an extreme position within the avant-garde. Practises a type of gestural painting akin to Abstract Expressionism, using contrasts of black and white and a vigorous, sensual handling. For three years disappears from public view, and finally abandons painting in 1968. **1967** at the Salon de la Jeune Peinture, and in the same year at the Biennale de Paris and the Musée des Arts Décoratifs, exhibits apparently identical canvases: grey horizontal stripes against a background formed by the bare canvas. The stripes are painted with a spray gun on pleated canvas. All are thirty-eight centimetres in width. The colour chosen is unimportant: in 1966 it is blue, in 1967 it happens to be grey, in 1968 it is red. The radical stance adopted by the BMPT group (Buren, Mosset, Parmentier and Toroni) represents the first serious attempt to question the assumptions underlying French painting of the postwar era.

VICTOR PASMORE
Born 1908 in Chelsham (Surrey)
Largely self-taught as a painter. **1927** lives in London. Paints in his spare time. Early works demonstrate, successively, the influence of Impressionism, Fauvism, Cubism and finally abstraction. **1932** first one-man show in London. **1936** reverts to his earlier Impressionist manner. **1937** co-founder of the Euston Road School, a reaction against the subjectivity and idealism of the School of Paris. Works full-time as a painter. **1943-47** compositions in a Post-Impressionist manner. **1946-47** reverts to Cubist style. **1947-48** adopts geometric abstraction, becoming the leading representative of that tendency in England. **1951-52** first reliefs and three-dimensional works, using wood and plastics. **1953-61** teaches painting at Newcastle. Echoing the Bauhaus practice, devises a foundation course centred on the development of simple forms in space, published as "The Developing Process" in 1959. **1966** major retrospective at the Tate Gallery, London. Lives in London and Malta. Several works on a monumental scale, often in an architectural context.His structures address the central relationship of form and space, using stated notations.

Left: Poliakoff, 1952. Photo: Denise Colomb.
Above: Pollock, 1950. Photo: Hans Namuth.

LASZLO PERI
Budapest 1889 - London 1967
Works as a stonemason in Budapest. **1918** attends art school. Expressionist drawings. Defects while on tour with a theatre group in Czechoslovakia. Goes to Vienna then Paris. Plays an active part in the movement of opposition against the new Hungarian government and is deported by the French authorities. **1919** settles in Berlin. Drawings and sculptures in a Cubist style. **1920** short visit to Russia. First object-based motifs composed of geometrical forms. **1921** first non-objective Constructivist reliefs in concrete. Subsequently associated with the Constructivist group based in Berlin, together with his compatriot Moholy-Nagy. **1922** participates with El Lissitzky, van Doesburg and others in the International Union of Progressive Artists Congress, held in Düsseldorf. **1924-28** works as an architect for the municipal authorities in Berlin. Contributions to all the major avant-garde reviews published in Central Europe, usually reproductions of abstracts in black and white. His most distinctive feature is the achievement of monumentality by simple means. Unvarnished Constructivism. **1928** abandons abstraction for realist sculpture. **1933** settles permanently in London.

JEAN-PIERRE PINCEMIN
born 1944 in Paris
1967-68 systematic investigation of monochrome employing a variety of techniques: folding and printing the canvas, using paint-rollers, etc. Palette almost exclusively black or red. **1968-69** cut-outs and assemblies of square or diamond-shaped canvases. **1969-73** works in stripes. **1971-73** member of the Support / Surface group: a French off-shoot of American minimalism which views painting as a purely self-referential activity. Concentration on the specific nature of painting, in terms of its physical existence. For example, using techniques of collage and pliage, draws attention to the material traces left by the process, making this the overt subject of the work. In building up the layers, the glue marks and individual brushstrokes are left visible. Usually very large canvases presented without stretcher. Around **1974** experiments with new principles for alignments of two or more surfaces. Subsequent concentration on colour and chromatic effects.

SERGE POLIAKOFF
Moscow 1900 - Paris 1969
Passionately interested in music as a child. **1919** escapes post-revolutionary Russia and goes with an aunt to Constantinople. With her, travels throughout Europe. **1923** settles in Paris. Pursues an interest in painting by studying at private academies and visiting the museums. From **1930** attends the Académie de la Grande Chaumière. **1935-37** student at the Slade School in London. Earns a living as a guitarist in Russian cafés. Around **1937** first abstract works. **1938** meets Kandinsky. Association with Otto Freundlich, Sonia and Robert Delaunay. **1938-45** exhibits at the Salon des Indépendants and, once, at the Salon d'Automne. **1939** awarded the Prix Kandinsky. Growing reputation as a painter. From **1946** exhibits at the Salon des Réalités Nouvelles and the Salon de Mai. His characteristic works are studies of interpenetrating zones of colour, their shapes non-geometric but obedient to some subtle principle of harmony. The intersection of the surfaces defines the form. Subtle variations of the paint surface. Frequent use of oppositions between two pure colours.

JACKSON POLLOCK
Cody (Wyoming) 1912 - East Hampton 1956
1925 studies painting and sculpture in Los Angeles. **1927** expelled from art school. **1927** and **1929** helps his father, a farmer, with geological surveys. **1929** goes to New York

and studies at the Art Students' League under Thomas Hart Benton; reacts against his realism and emphasis on painting from nature. During the thirties discovers American Indian art. Sketches after European baroque painters: superb draughtsmanship, leaning towards tragic themes and studies of movement. From **1936** paints semi-abstract canvases of a violent Expressionist character. From **1938** murals for the WPA Federal Art Project. **Early forties** produces first major works, complex manipulations of colour. Admires Picasso and the Surrealists. Experiments with controlled automatism; invents the technique of dripping paint onto the canvas from perforated paint-cans. Relies entirely on the inspiration of the moment. **1947** achieves total mastery of his style. **1950-52** abandons colour to paint in black and white. Reverts to a type of Expressionism close to that he practised during the forties. The principal exponent of what Harold Rosenberg dubbed Action Painting: reliance on gesture and speed of execution, working with the canvas laid out flat on the floor, intense absorption in the painting process.

LARRY POONS
born 1937 in Tokyo
Studies music at the New England Conservatory. Subsequently trains at the Boston School of Fine Arts. His work may be seen as falling into two distinct periods. The first, **1962-69**, is characterized by the use of round or oval spots of colour arranged in regular grid formations against a saturated colour field. The superimposed grids create an effect of movement by leaving an afterimage in the eye. Thus, of all the chromatic abstractionists, Poons is closest in spirit to Op Art. After about **1970** a complete change of direction. In his second period practises an informal style, a development of the dripping technique invented by Pollock. Pours the colours directly onto the canvas, using large quantities of paint mixed in advance

with a thickening agent. The pigments are then allowed to run freely and intermingle. As in his earlier work his concern is to exploit to the maximum the inherent potential of colour.

LYUBOV POPOVA
Province of Moscow 1889 - Moscow 1924
1907-08 in Moscow studies painting under Stanislas Zhukovsky and Konstantin Yuon. Travels widely in Russia, making a study of church architecture and folk art. **1910** travels in Italy and develops a particular admiration for Giotto. **1912-13** works in Paris, attending studios run by Le Fauconnier and Metzinger. **1913** returns to Russia. Participates in major avant-garde exhibitions ("Tramway V"; "0.10", etc.). **1915-21** works in the new non-objective style. **1916-18** executes "painted constructions". Teaches in the state-run studios. **1921** participates in the exhibition "5 × 5 = 25". Opposed on principle to easel-painting, and turns her attention to productive applications of art: illustration, porcelain, textiles, clothing and theatre design. **1923** designs and oversees the production of clothes and textiles at the first textile factory established in the State of Moscow. **1924** posthumous retrospective in Moscow.

JEAN POUGNY
Konokkala, Finland 1894 - Paris 1956
Studies in St. Petersburg. **1911** at the suggestion of the painter Repin, goes to Paris. Attends the Académie Jullian. Converted to Cubism. **1912** returns to Russia. Member of the Union of Youth, with Malevich, Tatlin and Larionov. Associated with Suprematism. Goes back to Paris but returns to Russia at the outbreak of war, becoming an active member of the avant-garde. **1915** organizes the exhibition "Tramway V" in St. Petersburg. Following a series of *Letters* composed of broad planes of colour, executes reliefs in polychrome cardboard and wood,

also abstract compositions in Indian ink. Theatre designs and illustrations for children's books. **1917** makes a construction of a china plate attached to a plank. Teaches at the Academies of Petrograd and Vitebsk. Member of the Constructivist Realism group. **1919** leaves Russia for Finland. **1921** goes to Berlin. **1922** publication of his text *Contemporary Art*. **1923** settles in Paris. Association with Léger, Marcoussis, Severini, Ozenfant. Abandons experimental work for figurative paintings in soft color harmonies.

JUDITH REIGL
born 1923 in Kapuvar, Hungary
Studies at the Budapest Academy. Travels in Italy. Returns to Hungary. **1950** flees to the West. Four months later arrives in Paris, which becomes her permanent home. Discovers Surrealism. Drawn to the spontaneity of automatic writing. Invents a painting tool which traces furrows in the freshly applied pigment in such a way as to eliminate the possibility of conscious control or correction. Increasingly free gestural painting. **1954** first one-man exhibition at the Galerie de l'Etoile Scellée in Paris. After **1955** experiments with a type of abstraction incorporating technical errors and slips of the hand in the final picture; use of large matt backgrounds. **1955-66** four series: *Eclatements* (1955-1958); *Centre de dominance* (1958-59); *Ecriture de masse* (1959-65); *Expérience d'apesanteur* (1965-66). **1962** decides to re-use abandoned canvases lining her studio floor. Covers these in a coat of white paint and then employs a type of raclage, or scraping, to reveal areas of the underlying design. Entitles this series of paintings *Guano*. Subsequently works expressed in a sort of "linear calligraphy".

AD REINHARDT
Buffalo (New York) 1913 - New York 1967
From the age of fourteen reveals marked artistic ability, but rapidly suppresses virtuoso display to

concentrate on an austere study of pictorial means and the promotion of the doctrines of the emergent American School. Studies at Columbia University, New York, and at National Academy of Design, New York. As a painter is nevertheless largely self-taught. **1937-46** member of American Abstract Artists group. First one-man exhibition in New York in 1945. Demonstrations outside New York museums in protest against their conservatism. Also draws cartoons attacking the avant-garde for its willingness to co-operate with the commercial circuits. Experiments with works in all the major styles of the century (Cubism, Expressionism, abstraction, geometric art). Undeviating in his search for an absolute of painting. By the fifties arrives at works that are monochromes in all but name. Suppression of formal or chromatic organization. Total rejection of art as expression, in favour of "art-as-art-as-art".

BERNARD REQUICHOT
Asnière-sur-Vègre (Sarthe) 1929 - Paris 1961
Educated at various religious institutions. At the age of sixteen decides to make art his career. **1948** enters the École des Beaux-Arts in Paris. Initially works of a mystical inspiration and monumental nudes. Later paintings representing animal carcasses and skulls, in a style of Cubist fragmentation. **1955** first one-man exhibition. From this time concentrates on painting made up of signs, in a style of abstraction entirely reliant on personal inspiration. Canvases in heavy impasto, scraped or reworked with a knife. Also experiments with accumulations and obsessional juxtapositions: drawings of spirals; what he calls "illusory handwriting" based on repetitions of the letter "e", revealing animal and plant forms; "graphic traces" or "rain", streaks across the surface of the canvas; collages of "selected papers" taken from magazines, etc. In spite of the brevity of his career, his work is highly

diverse, extending also to three-dimensional collage-constructions. Also known as a poet of some originality. Suicide at the age of thirty-two.

HANS RICHTER
Berlin 1888 - Locarno 1976
1912 first contact with modernism through the Blaue Reiter group. From **1914** influence of Cézanne and Cubism. Contributes to the journal *Die Aktion* in Berlin. **1916** joins the Dada group in Zurich. After a few works in an Expressionist style, in **1917** executes black-and-white abstract paintings in a Dadaist spirit. **1918** meets Eggeling. **1919** close association between the two artists as they work on scroll paintings, exploring the rhythmic development of formal themes. Abstract elements are drawn onto long rolls of paper and developed in time and space, according to principles not unlike those governing the orchestration of a musical theme. Meets van Doesburg and contributes to *De Stijl*. **1921** first abstract film *Rhythmus 21*, an extension of the concerns of the scroll pictures. **1923-26** co-editor of the German review *G* (= Gestalt). **1941** emigrates to the United States. Teaches at City College of New York. **1944** collaborates with Max Ernst and Marcel Duchamp on the film *Dreams That Money Can Buy*, regarded now as a classic of Surrealist cinema.

BRIDGET RILEY
born 1931 in London
1949-52 studies principally in drawing at Goldsmith's College of Art, London. **1952-55** student of painting at the Royal College of Art. Interest in Seurat's Divisionist techniques. First works are mainly landscapes, revealing from the outset a concern with optical effects. **1959** a major exhibition of American art held at the Tate Gallery in London encourages her to pursue this direction and concentrate on works of pure abstraction. Within a few years is regarded as one of the principal

representatives of Op Art. Initially works exclusively in black and white: through the precise organization of simple elements, such as dots or wavy lines, sets up powerful vibrations between the elements, creating an effect in three-dimensions. **1966** introduces variations of warm or cool colours. Later uses optical devices to create effects of potent luminosity. Eliminates any element of personal handling by entrusting the execution of her work to assistants.

JEAN-PAUL RIOPELLE
born 1923 in Montreal
1938-40 studies at the École Polytechnique in Montreal. In parallel follows a correspondence course in architectural studies and practises drawing and photography. **1939-45** attends classes at the Montreal Académie des Beaux-Arts and works for a diploma in furniture design at the École du Meuble. On the teaching staff is Paul-Emile Borduas, with whom he founds the group Automatisme (1944). Influence of Surrealism and experiments with automatic writing. **1945** in Paris. Meets Wols, Bryen and Mathieu, and exhibits with them in 1947 at the Galerie du Luxembourg. **1946** first exhibition of "Automatisme" in Montreal. **1947** settles in Paris. **1948** signatory of Borduas's manifesto *Refus Global*, denouncing all forms of cultural oppression. Paintings of violent gesturalism. Association with the leading Surrealists. From **1950** uses pure colour applied straight from the tube, and from **1952** flattens the pigment with a palette knife. **1956** onwards develops a looser combination of larger masses. **1958** first sculptures. From **1960** experiments with a variety of mediums and techniques. **1970** brief return to figuration (in the *Owls* series), before resuming his former direction.

ALEXANDER RODCHENKO
St. Petersburg 1891 - Moscow 1956
1910-14 studies at Kazan School of Fine Arts. **1914** settles in Moscow. Brief period as a pupil at the Stro-

Left: Ryman, 1984. Photo: M. Nguyen, Galerie Lelong, Paris. Above: Arp, Tzara, Richter, 1917. Opposite: Russolo and the Futurists, 1912. Photo: Archives Lista.

ganov School of Decorative Arts. Abstract drawings executed with compasses and ruler. Assocation with avant-garde painters. Influence of Malevich and Tatlin. **1915** determined to be more radical than the Suprematists, promotes "non-objective" art. **1918** co-director with Rozanova of Industrial Art section of Moscow workshops. Teaches in state art schools for a number of years. **1919** in reaction to Malevich's *White Square on a White Ground* paints his own *Black on Black,* composed of black circles. Suprematist and Non-Objectivist works are shown in confrontation at a joint exhibition in Moscow. First three-dimensional constructions. **1920** organizes a major exhibition of contemporary art in Moscow to coincide with the third Congress of Comintern. **1921** participates in the exhibition "5 × 5 = 25". Signs the manifesto proclaiming the end of laboratory art and demanding that artists become engineers. The most prominent personality of the Constructivist group associated with the review *Lef.* Increasingly concerned with utilitarianism in art. **1925** designs his Reading Room for a Workers' Club. From the thirties onwards concentrates largely on photographic work.

MARK ROTHKO
Dvinsk, Russia 1903 - New York 1970
1913 emigrates to the United States with his parents. **1925** settles in New York. Starts painting. Studies under Max Weber at the Art Students' League. **1935** with Adolph Gottlieb founds group The Ten. **1936-37** works for the WPA Federal Art Project. The Expressionist figuration of the early paintings gives way to a Surrealist influence, which persists up to about **1947**: aquatic worlds peopled with biomorphic forms similar to those arrived at by Miró, Ernst and Masson. Colour takes precedence over form. **1948** with Baziotes, Motherwell and Newman, co-founder of the Subjects of the Artist school, later called The Club. Around **1950** abandons figuration altogether and ceases to mark defined contours. Works consisting in zones of colour, their forms echoing the format of the canvas. These zones finally assume the guise of large rectangles of diffuse colour. Although his compositions are in the flat plane of the canvas, because of the haloed intensity of the coloured haze the forms appear to float ambiguously in shallow space. There is a mystic quality in the silent rhythm of the colour relationships.

FRANÇOIS ROUAN
born 1943 in Montpellier
Studies at the École des Beaux-Arts in Montpellier until **1961.** Goes to Paris and works at the École des Beaux-Arts under Roger Chastel. Participates in the Salon des Réalités Nouvelles and the Salon des Jeunes d'Aujourd'hui. His painting is a type of Abstract Expressionism, stressing the fluidity of colour fields and the dynamism of colour interactions. Shows his first major work at the fourth Biennale de Paris in **1965,** a canvas in papiers collés and gouache. Subsequent experiments with works made of woven paper and woven cloth. **1967** first woven pictures, monochromes in black or white. **1968-69** takes up painting again, combining it with his weaving technique. **1971-74** in residence at the Villa Médicis. Conceives the picture surface not as a homogeneous entity but in terms of a multitude of smaller segments, usually squares. Practice of painting two canvases, cut into strips and woven together to make the finished work. Influence of craft methods, in canvases that are as much constructed as painted.

OLGA ROZANOVA

Malenki (Vladimir province) 1886 - Moscow 1918

1904-10 art training at the Boshahov and Stroganov Schools in Moscow. From **1911** lives in St. Petersburg and is an active member of the avant-garde. Association with the Union of Youth group. **1912-13** studies at the Zvantseva art school. **1911-17** participates in the Union of Youth exhibitions. From **1912** illustrates Futurist pamphlets. **1916** joins the Suprematists, following periods of experiment in Cubism and Futurism. **1916-17** member of the Supremus group. Involved with planning a journal of that name (never published). **1918** with Rodchenko co-director of the Industrial Art section of the state workshops. **1919** posthumous exhibition in Moscow. **1922** represented in the first exhibition of Russian art in Berlin.

LUIGI RUSSOLO

Portogruaro (Venezia) 1885 - Cerro di Laveno 1947

Musical studies. Self-taught as a painter. Association with avant-garde artists in Milan. Contributes to the review *Poesia*. **1909** meets Boccioni and Carrà. Active in the Futurist movement and signatory of the manifesto in **1910**. Early pictures inspired by Art Nouveau. Paintings often of women, also Futurist themes such as movement, sound, simultaneity. **1911** influenced by his musical background, and increasingly dissatisfied with works of realistic inspiration, turns to compositions founded on musical principles: interpenetration of planes, volumes superimposed in space. Extension of Futurist concerns to encompass musical expression. **1913** publishes a manifesto on the art of sounds, or "bruitism", which in several respects anticipates the development of "musique concrète". Invents the "Intonarumori" or "Rhumorium". **1913** virtually abandons painting in order to concentrate on musical research. Serves during the war as a volunteer, is wounded and obliged to undergo trepanning. After the war settles in Paris. **1922** the Futurists stage a "soirée bruitiste" at the Théâtre des Champs-Elysées. **1930** member of Circle and Square group. **1938** develops an interest in occultism and publishes a book on the subject. **1941** returns to painting, but adopts a figurative style that betrays no hint of his Futurist background.

ROBERT RYMAN

born 1930 in Nashville (Tennessee)

Studies at Tennessee Polytechnic Institute. From his first paintings, in the mid-fifties, stands apart from the dominant influences of Abstract Expressionism and emergent Pop Art. From the outset his artistic vocabulary is fully formed, consisting in painted squares of virtual monochromes. Although his point of departure may be different, is frequently categorized as a Minimalist; the comparison becomes inevitable when his paintings are viewed with others of that movement. Comes to concentrate exclusively on white monochromes. Regards his works as entirely self-referential and attempts to minimise or neutralize all elements external to the painting itself. The result is a tautological grammar of painting, most typically in the works of the mid-sixties. Formats are usually square. Variety of supports: linen or cotton canvases, paper, filter paper, tracing paper, copper, cardboard, vinyl, etc. Pigments may be oils, acrylics, vinyls, enamels or lacquers. Attention thus focuses on the texture of the support, the characteristics of the paint and the number of layers applied, the expression of horizontality or verticality, and the handling itself.

PATRICK SAYTOUR

born 1935 in Nice

1967 participates in collective exhibitions, among them the Biennale de Paris. Joins the Support/Surface group and exhibits with them from

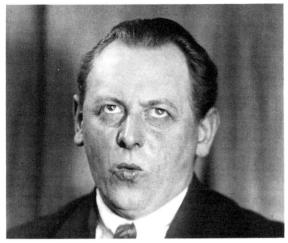

Left: Schwitters. Above: Schneider, 1983. Photo: Nicole Lejeune.
Opposite: van Doesburg and Schwitters, 1925.

1970. Profoundly influenced by research in the semiology of language, in particular the formalist theories developed by the avant-garde group associated with Philippe Sollers's review *Tel Quel*. Seeks a logical analysis of the constituent elements of plastic expression, leading to the final elimination of figured form. Rejects the traditional network of distribution of art objects. Dismisses aesthetic criteria. Numerous acts of intervention in the natural environment. Disbandment of group in 1972. **1975** first one-man show at the Galerie Eric Fabre, which continues to exhibit his work. Teaches at the École des Beaux-Arts in Nîmes. Lives in Aubars (Gard).

MIRIAM SCHAPIRO
born 1923 in Toronto
Father works as an industrial draughtsman. **1937-41** attends Erasmus Hall High School in Brooklyn, New York. **1943-49** studies at Iowa State University. Meets Philip Guston and models for him. Becomes Lasansky's first assistant. Exhibition of engravings. **1950-52** moves with her husband Paul Brach to Columbia (Missouri) and teaches drawing to children. **1952-55** returns to New York. Various exhibitions. **1957** shows work at the "New Talent Exhibition" staged by the Museum of Modern Art, New York.

1958 first one-man show. Continues to work on engravings. **1966-67** teaches at the Parsons School of Design in New York City. **1967** moves to La Jolla (California) and teaches in the art department of the University of California at San Diego. Becomes active within the movement of women artists and collaborates on several books. **1974** with Robert Zakanitoh organizes the first meeting in New York of what comes to be known as The Pattern and Decoration Group. Later helps to set up the Los Angeles Museum of Contemporary Art.

OSKAR SCHLEMMER
Stuttgart 1888 - Baden-Baden 1943
Studies at the Stuttgart Academy under Adolf Hölzel. **1911** in Berlin encounters modern French and German painting. Initially works in a Cubist manner, influenced by Cézanne, but subsequently is more interested in the techniques of Seurat. Geometric landscapes in muted tones. **1915** figuration is further simplified to a geometric pattern of straight and curved lines. **1920** joins the staff of the Bauhaus; in Berlin heads the sculpture department, in Dessau runs the theatre design course. Reliefs in cement and later in wire; increased concern with spatial values. Also stages gala events, creating the décors and performing

as a dancer. Seeks a theatre revival which will integrate all the arts. Paintings based on correspondences of pure, bright colours. **1929-32** teaches in Breslau. **1932-33** teaches in Berlin. Introduces diagonals within his compositions. Influence of his friend Otto Meyer-Amden. **1933** goes to Eichberg in southern Germany to escape the Nazi threat; conditions of life are harsh. Paintings of less rigorous construction, darker colours, figures emerging from a background which retains the marks of the brushstrokes. Sense of mysticism.

GÉRARD SCHNEIDER
Sainte-Croix, Switzerland 1896 - Paris 1986
Childhood in Neuchâtel; early training in decorative arts. **1916** moves to Paris. **1916-18** studies at the École des Arts Décoratifs. **1918-20** attends the École des Beaux-Arts and works under Cormon. **1920** returns to Neuchâtel. First one-man exhibition. **1923** settles permanently in Paris. Works as a picture restorer. **1926** shows at the Salon d'Automne and in **1936-39** at the Salon des Surindépendants. Torn between Cubism and Surrealism. Shortly before the war, first experiments in abstraction. **1944** concentration on abstract work. From **1946** exhibits at the Salon des Réalités

Nouvelles and the Salon de Mai. His early non-figurative compositions consist in groups of forms which, although heavily outlined, are not geometric in character. Later colour takes over, in vast panels. Gestural spontaneity in a calligraphic style. His method is to sketch a few motifs on the canvas and elaborate these in successive stages. Even in the titles there is no reference to external reality.

KURT SCHWITTERS
Hanover 1887 - Ambleside, England 1948
Education in Hanover. **1909-14** studies at the Dresden Academy. Earns his living as a portrait painter. **1914** army service. **1918** returns to Hanover. Produces drawings in a semi-abstract style, reflecting the influence of German Expressionism and Cubism, and later Kandinsky and Marc. **1919** first paper collages. First series of relief paintings made of pieces of junk, which he calls *Merz*. Contacts with Dada. Association with R. Hausmann and H. Höch. **1922** visits Holland. Meets van Doesburg who introduces him to the ideas of De Stijl. Accompanies him on a Dada tour of Holland. Links with El Lissitzky. Contributions to many reviews including *Der Sturm*. **1923-32** publishes his *Merz* magazine, a voice for Dada and

Constructivist views. **1924** starts building his first *Merzbau,* an environment assembled out of a heterogeneous collection of rubbish, often picked up in the street. Works on this over a period of ten years. **1924** at the Bauhaus gives the first public reading of his poem *Sonate in Urlauten.* **1930** member of Circle and Square and in **1932** of Abstraction-Creation. When the Nazis take power, exile in Norway. Builds a second *Merzbau* in Lysaker. Goes to England. Third *Merzbau* in Ambleside.

WILLIAM SCOTT
born 1913 in Greenock, Scotland
Parents are of Irish and Scottish descent. Grows up in Enniskillen in Northern Ireland. Studies at the Belfast School of Art. **1931-38** student at the Royal Academy in London. **1937-39** lives abroad, mainly in France and Italy. **1942** first one-man exhibition in London. **1946-56** professor at the Bath Academy of Art. Influences are many and various (including Piero della Francesca and Bonnard, van Dyck and Cézanne). From **1945** begins to develop an original style, broadly schematic in its approach. Is thus one of the first of the English painters to make use of a contemporary artistic vocabulary. Compositions are mainly still lifes but also austere

studies incorporating human figures, verging at times on abstraction, notably in the period from **1953** onwards following a visit to the United States. Nevertheless always retains a symbolic link with reality. Also executes large mural paintings. Lives in London and Somerset.

TONY SMITH
born 1912 in South Orange (New Jersey)
Studies at the Art Students' League in New York and in **1938** at the New Bauhaus in Chicago. **1938-39** clerk of works on several of the houses designed by Frank Lloyd Wright. **1940-60** runs his own architectural practice; dissatisfied with architecture, concentrates on sculpture. From **1946** also teaches at several major institutions. With Robert Morris, is one of the first to isolate the concerns of Minimal Art. As with the Hard Edge school of painting, the movement represents a reaction against the profligacy of Abstract Expressionism. With its emphasis on disciplined structure and the use of elementary forms it may also be seen as a continuation of the theories of Mondrian's Neo-Plasticism and of Constructivism. In particular promotes the return to simple expression within "primary structures", fundamental geometric forms often of monumental propor-

Above: Soto. Photo: André Morain.
Right: Soulages, 1954. Photo: Denise Colomb.

tions, in monochrome. **1966** first one-man exhibition at Hartford Atheneum; by the following year enjoys a major reputation as a sculptor.

JESUS RAPHAEL SOTO
born 1923 in Ciudàd Bolivar, Venezuela
1942 studies art at Caracas Academy. Influence of Cubism. Interest in Kandinsky, Malevich, Mondrian. **1947-50** director of art school at Maracaibo. **1950** settles in Paris. Annual contributions to the Salon des Réalités Nouvelles. Paintings based on the repetition of units arranged to set up a vibratory rhythm. Goes on to study effects of superimposition of simple units, in particular the optical blend produced by mounting perspex sheets painted with spiral patterns one slightly above the other. **1955** participates in the influential exhibition "Mouvement" held at the Galerie Denise René in Paris. Subsequently moves on to related works on a monumental scale. From **1969** explores the "dematerialization" of space, creating kinetic environments, mobiles, screens with projecting metal rods and wires, etc. Develops certain ideas of Suprematism and Neo-Plasticism. In these works the spectator's presence is crucial since the optical effects of dissolving

space are provoked by his change of viewpoint.

PIERRE SOULAGES
born 1919 in Rodez
Starts painting at an early age. Interest in the ancient monuments and megalithic stones of the Rouergue. **1938** in Paris discovers Cézanne and Picasso. Determines to study painting independently, outside the academic system. Copies at the Louvre. Dramatic landscapes, snow scenes with gnarled trees. During the war returns to Aveyron. **1946** settles in Paris. Begins to exhibit his work. Abandons figuration and graphism and produces his first abstract signs, black or brown marks against a light background, the pigment applied with leather scrapers. Robust, emphatic handling. Interplay of tensions between light and dark. Space treated as a unified whole. Intense, focused expression. Exploitation of internal dynamics of vertical, horizontal and diagonal rhythms. Stark simplicity of structure becomes accentuated over the years, culminating in pure pictorial signs of imposing intensity in canvases of enormous size.

NICOLAS DE STAËL
St. Petersburg 1914 - Antibes 1955
1919 accompanies aristocratic parents to exile in Poland. **1921-22** death of both parents. Paints first watercolours at about sixteen years of age. Jesuit education; regarded as a brilliant pupil. **1933** trains at the Royal Academy in Brussels. Top prize for painting. Visits Holland, France, Spain and Italy. **1938** settles in Paris. Particular interest in Cézanne, Matisse, Braque and Soutine. Drawings at the Louvre. In Morocco, starts to paint from nature. Army service in Tunisia. **1940** demobilized, settles in Nice. Meets Delaunay and Magnelli, who introduce him to modern art. **1943** returns to Paris. Association with Braque and Lanskoy. Moves rapidly towards abstraction, at first largely in drawings. **1948-52** period of abstract paintings. Initial emphasis on curving line, then simplification of forms. Flattens pigment with a palette knife, later a trowel. Broad surfaces of paint in intense colours. **1952** series of *Footballers* marks the beginning of a return to modified figuration. Violent colour and impasto. Experiments with collage. Numerous gallery exhibitions and purchases of his work by museums. Moves to Ménèrbes in the Vaucluse and in **1955**, shortly before his death, to Antibes.

194

Left: Nicolas de Staël, 1954. Photo: Denise Colomb.
Above: Stepanova.

FRANK STELLA

born 1936 in Malden (Massachusetts)

Studies painting at Princeton University. **1958** settles in New York, where he works as a house-painter. Meteoric career following a major exhibition at the Museum of Modern Art in **1960**. Works grouped in series, systematic explorations of aspects of colour and proportion. Initially influenced by Jasper Johns's *Stars and Stripes,* creates austere works in black or grey stripes, later in colour, in which white strips of bare canvas echo the line of the edge of the support. So-called deductive structure, which finds its ultimate application in the shaped canvas. Associated with Post-Painterly Abstraction, typified by the concern to create autonomous painting which has no reference outside itself. Following the period of monochromes, works in a much more varied and arbitrary manner. **1959-60** large black paintings. **1960** first one-man exhibition at the Castelli Gallery. In the same year, canvases in shiny metallic paint. **1966** irregular *Polygons.* **1967** *Protractors*: segmentations of geometric shapes in brilliant colours. More recently, abandonment of repetitive geometric effects for luxuriantly coloured bas-reliefs of a highly complex visual structure.

VARVARA STEPANOVA

Kovno 1894 - Moscow 1958

1911 studies at the Kazan School of Fine Arts. Meets her future husband Rodchenko. **1912** goes to Moscow. Studies under Ilya Mashkov and Konstantin Yuon. Attends the Stroganov School. **1914** exhibits at the Moscow Salon. Her career begins at the time Constructivism is giving way to Suprematism. Represented at most of the major exhibitions during the twenties. **1920-25** employed by INKHUK. **1921** works shown at "5 × 5 = 25". **1922** theatre designs and costumes. **1923** with Popova, Rodchenko and others produces fabric designs for the first textile works in the State of Moscow. **1923-29** active in association with Mayakovsky on the review *Lef.* **1924-25** teaches in the textiles department of the state workshops. **1925** takes part in the Exposition Internationale des Arts Décoratifs et Industriels Modernes, in Paris. In the mid-twenties concentrates on typographical work, poster design and stage sets. In the thirties engages in propaganda work for the periodical *USSR in Construction.*

CLYFFORD STILL

Grandin (North Dakota) 1904-1980

Art studies at Spokane University in Washington State. **1933-41** teaches at Washington State College, Pullman. Early paintings influenced by Surrealism. Moves to San Francisco. War service working in local factories. **1946-50** teaches at the California School of Fine Arts, San Francisco. Plays a decisive role in the development of Abstract Expressionism but rejects gesturalism. At this period regards himself as belonging to a distinct "Pacific School" of American painters. Highly visionary works, which seem to push out beyond the canvas edge, expressive of continuity and movement away from the centre. **1950** settles in New York. Teaching posts at Hunter College and Brooklyn College. Works explore the interactions of colour expressed in jagged indentations and vertical shapes set against strongly contrasting monochrome backgrounds.

WLADISLAW STRZEMINSKI

Minsk, Belorussia 1893 - Łódź 1952

Trains as an artist in the Moscow state workshops established after the October Revolution, and at INKHUK, the Institute of Artistic Culture. Links with Malevich, who influences his early works. **1922** returns to Poland and takes a leading role in the activities of the avant-garde. **1924** member of the BLOK group. **1926** joins the Praesens

group. **1929** with his wife, the sculptor Katarzyna Kobro, and the painter Stazevski, founds the "a.r." movement (Revolutionary Artists). All his major work dates from the period **1925-34:** abstract geometric compositions, often strict monochromes, with distinctive impasto surfaces built up from successive applications of layers of pigment. The intention is to represent painting in terms of its fundamental material qualities. With his wife, a founder member of the Unovis movement. **1936** onwards concentrates for the most part on theological studies. **1945-50** teaches at the school of plastic arts in Lódź. Also responsible for fabric and furniture designs and stage sets.

SOPHIE TAEUBER
Davos 1889 - Zurich 1943
Studies in the applied arts in Saint-Gall, Munich and Hamburg. **1915-19** teaches textile design at the École des Arts et Métiers in Zurich. **1915** meets Hans Arp, whom she marries in 1921. Active within the Dada movement. **1916** onwards non-figurative paintings in a geometric style. Constructs puppets, works on stage sets and fabrics. Mural paintings and stained-glass windows in Strasbourg. **1926-27** participates in the decoration of the café-cinema L'Aubette, with Arp

and van Doesburg. **1928-40** lives with Arp in Meudon in a house built to her own design. **1930** participates in Circle and Square exhibitions and **1933** those of the Abstraction-Creation group. Abstract paintings of geometric forms. Member of the Swiss group Die Allianz. Founds the review *Plastique* of which four issues are published, between 1937 and 1939. Spends the war years in Grasse, where she executes a number of lithographs, and in Zurich. Works characterized by their bare formal simplicity.

PIERRE TAL COAT
Clohars-Carnoët (Finistère) 1905 - St-Pierre-de-Bailleul (Eure) 1985
Vocation as a painter from an early age. Initially works for a manufacturer of ceramics in Quimper, painting designs on china. **1924** moves to Paris. Pursues his artistic education independently, outside the academic system. His pre-war paintings tend towards either monumentality and simplification of forms or alternatively a type of Expressionist realism. During the war is greatly influenced by Matisse, then Picasso. Begins to extend his artistic vocabulary to encompass the concerns of modern painting. Increasingly geometrical forms and distortion of objects. Concerned as much to achieve expressive power as with

formal innovation for its own sake. A palette of largely pale colours with occasional patches of brightness. Around **1949** minimalistic compositions in muted tones, inspired by a love of the Chinese painting of the Sung dynasty. Also adopts its characteristic motifs, rocks, mountains in the rain, etc. **1961** visits the Dordogne. Embarks on a period of large canvases featuring rough appoximations of signs in a restricted palette.

ANTONI TÀPIES
born 1923 in Barcelona
Studies law. **1946** decides on a career as a painter. Until **1948** concentrates on collage, using scraps of newspaper, card, wire, etc., to create emblematic forms. In his early paintings uses grattage and graffiti-like figures in combination with earthy pigments. **1948** with the painters Ponç, Tharrats and Cuixart, the poet Brossa and the critics Puig and Cirlot, co-founder of the group and magazine *Dau Al Set,* waging a campaign against the cultural isolation imposed on Catalan art. The group remains active for three years. Works consisting of abstract signs marked onto backgrounds of subtly varying tone values. The graduations of grey are occasionally punctuated by patches of green or bright red impasto with a fabric-like

Left: Tobey, 1966. Photo: Daniel Frasnay.
Above: Tatlin, Malevich, Kliun, 1916.

texture, obtained by impressions of pieces of cloth. **1950-51** period in Paris. **1953** visit to New York. From **1954** returns to his investigations of matter, combining oils with a variety of substances such as powdered plaster. Vast surfaces marked with impressions, incisions and reliefs. Works of increasing power and sobriety, founded in the tension between materials and signs, entirely abstract and yet bearing the mark of the Catalan soil from which they spring.

VLADIMIR TATLIN
Kharkov 1885 - Novo Devitch 1953
Begins studies in painting in **1909** at Moscow School of Architecture, Sculpture and Painting. Influenced by the Russian icon tradition and Cézanne. **1912** close association with Larionov, primitivist paintings. Trip to Paris. Visits Picasso's studio and sees Cubist assemblages which change his conception of art. Back in Russia makes his first "painting reliefs", using a variety of materials and eliminating all figurative subject matter. Thus engages on the course that leads ultimately to Constructivism. In the winters of **1913** and **1914** shows his reliefs in his studio, and in **1915** at the "Tramway V" exhibition in St. Petersburg. In the same year begins to make "counter-reliefs", constructions without base or mount-

ing, designed to be suspended across the angle of two walls. Presents these at the exhibition "0.10" in St. Petersburg. Influences the Dadaists in Western Europe. **1917** collaborates on the decoration of the Café Pittoresque in Moscow. Teaches in the workshops set up to provide artistic and technical training. Becomes the focus of the Productivist group, which campaigns for art to be used for utilitarian purposes. **1919** designs *Monument to the Third International* (the Tatlin Tower), one of the first buildings conceived on abstract principles. **1920** goes to Leningrad and from **1922** teaches at the Institute of Artistic Culture. **1927** returns to Moscow and resumes his teaching activities in the state workshops. Subsequently several décors for theatre and a resumption of figurative painting.

MARK TOBEY
Centerville (Wisconsin) 1890 - Basel 1976
Self-taught as a painter. **1907** goes to Chicago and earns his living as a fashion illustrator. **1912** settles in New York. Paints portraits. **1922** moves to Seattle and teaches at the Cornish School. **1925-26** travels extensively in Europe and the Near East. **1931-38** lives in England. **1931** visits Mexico. **1935** travels in the Far East. Studies Chinese cal-

ligraphy. **1935** paints the first of his "white writings", patterns of calligraphic markings in white Indian ink. Initially these works have a reference point in the real world, being schematizations of the forms of an Oriental city. Later they are entirely abstract. In parallel continues to execute drawings from nature. **1939** returns to Seattle. Works characterized by meticulous execution, delicate colours. Concentrates almost exclusively on watercolour, tempera and pastel. Pictures in small formats, covered in a dense fog-like pattern of signs.

NIELE TORONI
born 1937 in Muralto, Switzerland
1959 settles permanently in Paris. **1967** shows work in association with the BMPT group (Buren, Mosset, Parmentier, Toroni) at the Salon de la Jeune Peinture, an exhibition staged by the Musée des Arts Décoratifs and at the Biennale de Paris. On the latter occasion the group presents a slide show designed to question every aspect of artistic activity. They propose a return to the ontological reality of painting in its most basic physical manifestation. There are thus similarities with the American Minimalists and also with the Support/Surface group in France. Toroni uses a number 50 brush on a white surface, applying the paint at

197

Left: Vasarely, 1967. Photo: Denise Colomb.
Above: Ubac, 1954. Photo: Denise Colomb.

30 centimetre intervals. His support may be made of canvas, cotton, paper, oilcloth, or it may even be a wall or patch of ground, usually white. His activities with the BMPT group take on a polemical character, attacking the notion of form itself and protesting against the exalted value placed on artistic creativity. The aim of the group is to reduce the act of painting to the status of a simple mechanical gesture.

JOAQUÍN TORRES-GARCÍA
Montevideo 1874 - 1949
1891 goes to Barcelona to study mural painting at the School of Fine Arts. Decorations rather in the manner of Puvis de Chavannes for various public buildings, notably the churches of San Augustin and Divina Pastora and the Palace of the Generalitat. **1906** collaborates with Gaudi on stained-glass windows for the cathedral of Palma, Majorca. **1910** visits Paris and Brussels, where he comes under the influence of Cubism and Futurism. Returns to Montevideo. **1920-22** period of residence in New York. **1924** settles in Paris. **1929** meets Michel Seuphor and in the same year, in association with him, founds the group Circle and Square. **1930** takes an active role in the organization of the International Exhibition staged by the group in Paris. **1934**

returns to Montevideo. Working independently, continues publication of the review *Cercle et Carré*. Opens a celebrated school of art. In Montevideo is responsible for a number of innovative decorative schemes and a monument in the city's Rodo Park (the *Cosmic Monument*). Gives several lectures in which he promotes the cause of non-figurative art. **1944** publication of an important text entitled *Universalismo Constructivo*. Apparently draws much of his inspiration from pre-Columbian art, used in combination with elements of contemporary European painting, notably certain aspects of Cubism, Neo-Plasticism and the work of Paul Klee. Works of true abstraction confined to the period of his association with Circle and Square.

CY TWOMBLY
born 1928 in Lexington (Virginia)
Studies at the Boston Museum School, then at the Art Students' League in New York. Later attends Black Mountain College, North Carolina, where he works in association with Motherwell and Franz Kline. From the outset his painting is influenced by Abstract Expressionism. Uses a technique he describes as "psycho-improvisation" in compositions exhibiting a crude, almost childishly naïve calligraphy, execut-

ed in all-over space. Towards the end of the fifties moves on to large bare canvases which have the look of old walls, bearing occasional scrawls of graffiti, numbers, letters and vague approximations to human figures. Later works characterized by a denser profusion of signs, the surface occupied by scribbles of automatic writing which take the form of spirals and wavy lines. Canvases prepared with a white or black ground, overlaid with markings in chalk or white colour, sometimes worked with the fingers or with crayons. The emphasis in his compositions on the written sign is indicative of an urge to find expression for philosophical and metaphysical preoccupations, a desire to incorporate within the painted surface an embryonic suggestion of verbal significance or speculation.

RAOUL UBAC
Malmédy, Belgium 1910 - 1985
Initially intends to pursue a career in forestry. **1929** settles in Paris. Enrols for a humanities degree at the Sorbonne but soon abandons his studies to frequent the studios of Montparnasse and the Académie de la Grande Chaumière. Travels extensively in Europe. Around **1934** becomes associated with the Surrealist group. Following the example of Man Ray, concentrates principally

Left: Bram van Velde, 1980. Photo: Michel Nguyen, Galerie Lelong, Paris.
Above: Viallat, 1982. Photo: Jean-Philippe Reverdot.

on photography. Also executes collages. At the same time learns the technique of burin engraving under William Hayter. From **1942** begins to develop a strong personal style. Abandons Surrealism. Begins work on large drawings in pen and ink or pencil. Around **1945** first gouaches and slate sculptures, also paintings in oils. The realistic manner of his early works is rapidly replaced by an innovative exploration of the concerns of non-figuration. Both paintings and sculptures typically exhibit striations and furrows, and zones of stratification. Landscapes and still lifes expressed in terms of their various constituent layers. Works of great calm and restraint. Concentration on the qualities of materials, especially those of an earthy consistency and texture: casein, plastic cement, slate dust, etc.

ANDRÉ VALENSI
born 1947 in Paris
Works sharing the general concerns of the Support/Surface group, of which he is a member. The movement emerges in France around **1970**, essentially as an offshoot of the American tradition of abstraction represented in the all-over compositions of Pollock and subsequently the work of Newman, Reinhardt, Rothko, etc. The members of the group envisage painting en-

tirely in terms of its material existence. Thus their work is self-referential; the picture is viewed as no more than the sum of its constituent parts: surface, colour, texture. Major works include canvases that are cut and sewn in such a way as to juxtapose on a single surface both the front and back of the canvas, stained in advance with colour. Emphasis on the interaction of pigment and the texture of the support. Paint is viewed not as a covering layer but as a medium of penetration whose effects may be modulated at will.

VICTOR VASARELY
born 1908 in Pécs, Hungary
Studies medicine, then spends a year at the Podolini-Volkmann Academy in Budapest. **1928** student at the Mühely Academy of Applied Arts, set up by Alexander Bortnyik as the Hungarian equivalent of the Bauhaus. **1930** settles in Paris. Employed as a commercial artist and decorator. In parallel executes works in a Constructivist style, mainly graphics, black-and-white drawings. Later paintings composed of superimposed sheets of cellophane; so-called "multi-dimensional" effects of transparency and depth. **1944** co-founder of the Galerie Denise René. Preoccupation with surface animation; writes

on the back of his canvases the type of light in which they should be viewed. One of the principal exponents in Europe of "cool abstraction". **1955** embarks on kineticism, abstract painting exploiting optical effects to give an impression of movement. Participates in the exhibition "Mouvement". Publication of his *Manifeste jaune*. **1960** introduction of brilliant tones of colour. **1970** publication of his text *Plasti-Cité*. Rejects the myth of the unique work of art; promotes the use of methods of mass production to create multiple editions of paintings. **1970** founds the Vasarely Didactic Museum at Gordes, in southern France.

BRAM VAN VELDE
Zoeterwoude, near Leiden 1895 - Grimau 1981
Childhood in Leiden and The Hague. Apprenticed to a decorating firm. **1924** settles in Paris. For a long period lives a life of almost total seclusion. Early works are figures and landscapes in a spirited style influenced by Fauvism, brilliant colours used to accentuate forms. From around **1928** still lifes of increasingly free compositional structure. **1940** large gouaches from which all figurative reference has disappeared. Dynamic interactions of abstract forms contained

From left to right: Germain, Vieira da Silva, Zao Wou Ki, Mathieu, Pierre Loeb, Riopelle, Paris, 1953. Photo: Denise Colomb.

within heavy coloured outlines. In the war years ceases to paint altogether. **1946** first one-man exhibition. Loosely organic forms in complex combinations of line and colour. Interpenetrating zones of transparency subjected to a violent underlying distortion. Each work is the product of a long period of tormented introspection.

CLAUDE VIALLAT
Born 1936 in Nîmes
Studies at the École des Beaux-Arts in Montpellier. **1958** moves to Paris and completes his training at the École des Beaux-Arts. **1964** teaches at the École des Arts Décoratifs in Nice. Associated with the Nice School of painters. **1967** appointed to the École Nationale d'Art Décoratif in Limoges, where he remains for several years. One of the founder members of the Support/Surface group. Although his association with the group is of short duration, his work is very typical of its concerns. Distinguished from an early stage by a strong decorative sense, in direct line of descent from Matisse. Concentration on the material elements of painting. Undeviating repetitions of the same basic motif in large unmounted canvases, suspended freely in space. Application of colour by staining, dyeing, painting with brushes, and other techniques; use of stencils. Also experiments with knots, cord and string. Mid-seventies departs from the strict principles of his earlier works to explore other methods of liberating painting from the restraints of frame and stretcher.

MARIA ELENA VIEIRA DA SILVA
born 1908 in Lisbon
Wealthy family background. From **1919** taught drawing and painting by private tutors. **1924** studies sculpture. **1928** moves to Paris. Pupil of Bourdelle and Despiau at the Académie de la Grande Chaumière. **1929** studies painting at the Académie Scandinave under Dufresne, Friesz and Waroquier. Later trains with Léger and learns engraving in

William Hayter's studio. **1930** marriage to Hungarian painter Arpad Szenes. **1932** studies under Bissière at the Académie Ranson. Meets Jeanne Bucher, who from **1933** exhibits her work. Greatly influenced by the paintings of Torres-García. **1936** commissions for murals in Lisbon and Rio de Janeiro. **1939** returns to Lisbon. **1940-47** settles in Rio de Janeiro. Meets Torres-García. Mastery of personal style: figures and objects that retain their identity within hallucinatory perspectives of chessboard motifs. **1947** returns to Paris. Meets Pierre Loeb, who exhibits her work. Highly developed spatial organization of line and soft, light colour; themes are the labyrinthine worlds of *Towns* and *Libraries*.

FRIEDRICH VORDEMBERGE-GILDEWART
Osnabrück 1899 - Ulm 1962
From **1919** studies in architecture and sculpture in Hanover. Earliest paintings in a Constructivist style; rigorous geometrical combinations of primary elements. **1924** founder of the "K" group. Subsequently associated with the De Stijl group based in Leiden. **1925-26** and **1929** visits to Paris. **1930** member of Circle and Square group. **1932** founder member in Paris of Abstraction-Creation. **1936-37** visit to Berlin. **1938** visit to Zurich. Settles in Amsterdam. Takes Dutch nationality. From **1948** runs the Duwaer publishing house. **1954** moves to Ulm. Professor at the Hochschule für Gestaltung. Various constructions under the title *Compositions*. Work is broadly an extension of the concerns of Neo-Plasticism. Nevertheless employs a highly varied palette and his combinations of forms include not only squares but triangles and even irregular polygons. Author of numerous texts and articles.

WOLFGANG WOLS
Berlin 1913 - Paris 1951
Born Alfred Otto Wolfgang Schülze. Childhood in Dresden. Exceptional ability as a violinist. In Frankfurt as-

sists Frobenius on an anthropological study of music. Brief period at the Bauhaus in Dessau before fleeing Nazism. **1932** settles in Paris. Adopts the pseudonym Wols. Lives by selling his watercolours. Links with Miró, Calder, Tzara and Ernst. **1933** settles in Barcelona, before returning to France. **1937** official photographer at the International Exhibition in Paris. When war breaks out is interned in various camps. **1940** on his release settles in Cassis, then in **1942** in Dieulefit, where he is helped by the collector Pierre-Henri Roché. First exhibition in New York. **1945** returns to Paris. Period of extreme poverty and anguish. Begins to paint fantastic visions of towns and crowds. Moves progressively towards abstraction. Explosions of paint and atomized forms that seem to reflect cosmic and microscopic investigations of matter, with elements of calligraphy and gesturalism. Engravings for illustrations of books by Sartre, Kafka, Paulhan, de Solier, Artaud, Bryen. Dies just as his work begins to achieve recognition.

ZAO WOU KI
born 1921 in Peking
1935 enters the Hang Chow School of Fine Arts, where he later teaches, in **1941-47**. **1948** settles in Paris. Paints in a figurative style influenced by Paul Klee, and in **1953** turns to abstraction. Exhibits regularly at the Salon de Mai. Subsequent works reflect a renewal of interest in Chinese landscape painting and calligraphy. His delicate and subtle art is founded in the ancient Oriental tradition of inner contemplation and graphic spontaneity. Paintings evoking the constantly changing face of nature over the days and seasons, of a deliberate tranquillity far removed from Western dynamism. Moves progressively to a pure calligraphy of impulsive signs. Also a practised engraver, responsible for illustrations of books by Henri Michaux, André Malraux and René Char.

ILLUSTRATIONS

We are indebted to the following organizations and individuals for their assistance in making reproductions available for publication: the galleries Ariel, Franka Berndt, Jeanne Bucher, Durand-Dessert, Jean Fournier, Daniel Gervis, Yvon Lambert, Baudoin Lebon, Lelong, Protée, Regards, Denise René, Daniel Templon, Patrice Trigano, 1900-2000, Galerie de France and Artcurial; the Musées des Beaux-Arts of Le Havre and Calais, the Musée d'Art et d'Industrie de Saint-Étienne, Capc in Bordeaux and the Magasin in Grenoble; also Martin Barré, Patrick de Haas, Arrigo Lessana, Ghislain Mollet-Viéville, François Morellet and Alexis Poliakoff.

Josef Gipstein Agam
129 : *Transformable Picture,* 1954.
© SPADEM, 1988.

Josef Albers
84 : *Violin-pegs,* 1935, gouache, 36.5 × 20.5 cm.
Josef Albers Museum, Bottrop.
99 : *Homage to the Square : Ritardando,* 1958.
Private collection.
© ADAGP, 1988.

Pierre Alechinsky
124 : *Swimming,* 1955. Private collection.
© ADAGP, 1988.

Karen Appel
124 : *La Nurse,* 1950, oil on canvas.
Galerie Ariel collection, Paris.
© SPADEM, 1988.

Hans Arp
70 : *Dada Collage,* 1918. Private collection.
71 : *Enak's Tears (Terrestrial Forms),* 1917,
painted wood relief, 86.2 × 58.5 × 6 cm.
Museum of Modern Art, New York.
71 : *Travel Kit of a Da,* 1920, partly painted wood,
27.5 × 39 cm.
© ADAGP, 1988.

Giacomo Balla
32 : *Flight of Swifts,* 1913, charcoal and coloured crayon
on paper, 54 × 85 cm.
Private collection.

Martin Barré
150 : *76-77-D-170-160,* 1976-77, 170 × 160 cm.
Henies-Onstads Kunstsentret, Oslo.
© SPADEM, 1988.

Jean Bazaine
120 : *Noon, Trees and Rocks,* 1952, 100 × 81 cm.
Courtesy Galerie Lelong, Paris.
© ADAGP, 1988.

Max Bill
133 : *Construction with 10 Rectangles,* 1940-43,
oil on canvas, 75 × 90 cm. Kunstmuseum, Bern.
© ADAGP, 1988.

Julius Bissier
94 : *3 February 1959,* 1959.
Private collection.

Camille Bryen
110 : *Crinane jaune (no. 41),* 1953, oil on canvas,
100 × 81 cm. Musée d'Art et d'Industrie,
Saint-Étienne.
© ADAGP, 1988.

Daniel Buren
146 : *Photo souvenir,* 1968, 150 × 131 cm.
Courtesy Ghislain Mollet-Viéville, Paris.

Alberto Burri
118 : *Sabbia,* 1952.
Private collection.

Pol Bury

128 : *Mobile Plane 2*, 1954, painted metal.
Courtesy Galerie Denise René, Paris.
© SPADEM, 1988.

Louis Cane

147 : *Untitled*, 1974, oil on canvas, 306 × 600 cm.
Courtesy Galerie Daniel Templon, Paris.
© SPADEM, 1988.

Carlo Carrà

33 : *Interventionist Manifesto*, 1914.
Private collection.
© SPADEM, 1988.

Paul Cézanne

18 : *Trees at the Edge of a Road*, 1900-04,
watercolour and pencil, 46.7 × 30.5 cm.
Galerie Beyeler, Basel.

22 : *Fishing*, 1904-06, watercolour and pencil,
12.5 × 22 cm. National Museum of Western Art,
Tokyo.

22 : *Foliage*, 1895-1900, watercolour and pencil,
44.8 × 56.8 cm. Museum of Modern Art, New York.

23 : *Mont Sainte-Victoire*, c. 1900, watercolour
and pencil, 29 × 44.5 cm.
Artus Club, San Francisco.

23 : *Mont Sainte-Victoire*, 1902-04, watercolour
and pencil, 47.5 × 61.5 cm.
National Gallery of Ireland, Dublin.

23 : *Mont Sainte-Victoire Seen from Les Lauves*,
1904-05. Galerie Beyeler, Basel.

Carlos Cruz-Diez

130 : *Physichrome no. 1*, Caracas, 1959, 50 × 50 cm.
Courtesy Galerie Denise René, Paris.

Alan Davie

125 : *The Martyrdom of St. Catherine*, 1956,
183 × 244 cm. Courtesy Artcurial, Paris.

Jean Degottex

116 : *Suite la rose (IV)*, 1959, Indian ink and watercolour
on paper, 50 × 65 cm. Courtesy Galerie de France,
Paris. Photo: F. Walsh.

Robert Delaunay

28 : *Window*, 1912-13, oil on canvas,
111 × 90 cm. Musée National d'Art Moderne,
Pompidou Centre, Paris.

30 : *Simultaneous Disc*, 1912.
Private collection.
© ADAGP, 1988.

Marc Devade

146 : *Untitled*, 1971, acrylic on canvas, 200 × 180 cm.
Courtesy Galerie Regards, Paris.

Jean Dewasne

132 : *Paris-Paris*, 1952, oil on canvas, 140 × 195 cm.
Courtesy Galerie Denise René, Paris.
© SPADEM, 1988.

Daniel Dezeuze

149 : *Cut Fragments of Tarlatan*, 1972, 1033 × 29 cm.
Courtesy Galerie Yvon Lambert, Paris.

Theo van Doesburg

62 : *Rhythms of a Russian Dance*, 1918, oil on canvas,
135.9 × 61.6 cm. Museum of Modern Art,
New York.

65 : *Arithmetic Composition*, 1930, oil on canvas,
101 × 101 cm. Private collection, Basel.
© SPADEM, 1988.

César Domela

87 : *Composition A VIII*, 1923, oil on panel,
691 × 183 cm. Collection, Ascona,
Switzerland.
© ADAGP, 1988.

Jacques Doucet

125 : *Time of Re-Creation*, 1948, painting and collage,
45 × 65 cm. Jean Pollack collection, Paris.

Jean Dubuffet

112 : *Landscape with Bat*, 1952, 97 × 130 cm.
Courtesy Galerie Jeanne Bucher, Paris.

112 : *Terre courde*, 1959, 71 × 109.2 cm.
Courtesy Galerie Jeanne Bucher, Paris.

113 : *Mire G 49 Kowloon*, 1983, acrylic on paper,
mounted on canvas, 134 × 100 cm.
Courtesy Galerie Jeanne Bucher, Paris.

Marcel Duchamp

34 : *The Bride Stripped Bare by the Bachelors*, Munich,
summer 1912, crayon and wash on paper.
Private collection.

34 : *Two Nudes : One Strong and One Swift*, Neuilly,
1912, crayon on paper. Private collection.

66 : *Study for the Chocolate Grinder, no. 2*, Paris, 1914,
oil and crayon on canvas. Staatsgalerie, Stuttgart.

68 : *You-Me (Tu m')*, 1918, oil on canvas with bottle
brush, 70 × 312 cm. Yale University Art Gallery,
New Haven.
© ADAGP, 1988.

Viking Eggeling

73 : Photogram from the film *Diagonal-Symphonie*,
1921-24. Document: Patrick de Haas, Paris.

Max Ernst

71 : *Dadaville*, 1923-24, 66 × 56 cm.

93 : *Grey Forest*, 1926.

93 : *False Positions*, 1925, frottage and crayon on
paper, 43.5 × 27.5 cm. Courtesy Artcurial, Paris.

94 : *Snow Flowers*, 1929, oil on canvas, 130 × 130 cm.
Galerie Beyeler, Basel.
© SPADEM, 1988.

Maurice Estève

120 : *Sioule*, 1956. Private collection.
© ADAGP, 1988.

Alexandra Exter

54 : *Non-objective Composition*, 1918, 64 × 45 cm.
Wilhelm Hack Museum, Ludwigshafen.
Archives Nakov, Paris.

Jean Fautrier

111 : *Sweet Woman*, 1946, whiting, glue, pigment and oil
on canvas, 97 × 145.5 cm. Musée National d'Art
Moderne, Pompidou Centre, Paris.

111 : *Hostage: Head, no. 1,* 1944. Private collection.
111 : *Little Square,* 1958, oil on paper backed with canvas, 45 × 55 cm.
© SPADEM, 1988.

Lucio Fontana
128 : *Slashed Canvas,* 1960.

Sam Francis
103 : *Blue Figure,* 1960, 231 × 200 cm. Courtesy Galerie Jean Fournier, Paris. Photo: Piotr Trowinski.

Helen Frankenthaler
138 : *Mauve District,* 1966, acrylic on canvas, 262.6 × 407 cm. Museum of Modern Art, New York.
138 : *Blue Caterpillar,* 1961, 297.3 × 378.5 cm.

Natalia Goncharova
50 : *Rayonism,* 1917, oil on paper. Courtesy Galerie Franka Berndt, Paris.
© ADAGP, 1988.

Arshile Gorky
88 : *Landscape-Table,* 1945, oil on canvas, 92 × 121 cm.
Musée National d'Art Moderne, Pompidou Centre, Paris.
98 : *Agony,* 1947, oil on canvas, 101.6 × 128.2 cm. Museum of Modern Art, New York.

Adolph Gottlieb
98 : *Descending Arrow,* 1956, oil on canvas, 243.5 × 182.4 cm. Museum of Modern Art, New York.

Raymond Hains
134 : Untitled, 1961, 94 × 100 cm. Arrigo Lessana collection, Paris.

Simon Hantaï
145 : Untitled, 1962, 265 × 215 cm. Courtesy Galerie Jean Fournier, Paris. Photo: J. Hyde, Paris.

Hans Hartung
108 : Untitled, 1956-59, 180 × 137 cm. Courtesy Galerie de France, Paris.
109 : Untitled, 1924, black chalk on paper, 34.3 × 32.7 cm. Courtesy Galerie Daniel Gervis, Paris.
115 : *T 1936-10,* 1936, oil on canvas, 130 × 289 cm. Courtesy Galerie Daniel Gervis, Paris.
© ADAGP, 1988.

Stanley William Hayter
120 : *Yellow Flight,* 1953, 150 × 120 cm. Courtesy Artcurial, Paris

Jean Hélion
85 : *Tensions,* 1932, oil on canvas, 50.1 × 49.8 cm. Musée des Beaux-Arts, Le Havre. Photo: Routhier.
© ADAGP, 1988.

Hans Hofman
99 : *Cathedral,* 1958, 188 × 122 cm. Private collection.

Johannes Itten
80 : Colour studies : spring, summer, autumn, winter.

Alexej Jawlensky
40 : *Symphony in Black and Red,* 1929, oil on cardboard, 37.5 × 28 cm. Kaiser Wilhelm Museum, Krefeld.
40 : *Twilight,* 1916, oil on cardboard, 36 × 27 cm.
© ADAGP, 1988.

Jasper Johns
134 : *Flag,* 1954-55, encaustic, oil and collage on canvas, 107.3 × 153.8 cm. Museum of Modern Art, New York.

Asger Jorn
124 : *I'm Browned Off with the Sun,* 1961, oil on canvas, 162 × 130 cm. Jean Pollack collection, Paris.

Wassily Kandinsky
36 : First abstract watercolour, 1910, watercolour and Indian ink on paper, 49.6 × 64.8 cm. Musée National d'Art Moderne, Pompidou Centre, Paris. Nina Kandinsky Donation.
38 : *In the Forest,* 1911, woodcut, 5.8 × 5.5 cm. Musée National d'Art Moderne, Pompidou Centre, Paris.
38 : *Brightly Coloured Field,* 1911, woodcut, 5.6 × 6.6 cm. Musée National d'Art Moderne, Pompidou Centre, Paris.
39 : Drawing for *Composition III,* 1910, Indian ink, 25 × 30.4 cm. Musée National d'Art Moderne, Pompidou Centre, Paris.
39 : Drawing for *Composition IV,* 1911, pencil and Indian ink, 24.9 × 30.5 cm. Musée National d'Art Moderne, Pompidou Centre, Paris.
39 : Drawing, 1923, Indian ink, 25.2 × 36.4 cm. Musée National d'Art Moderne, Pompidou Centre, Paris.
41 : *Landscape with Tower,* 1908, oil on cardboard, 74 × 98.5 cm. Musée National d'Art Moderne, Pompidou Centre, Paris.
41 : *Romantic Landscape,* 1911, oil on canvas, 94.3 × 129 cm. Städtische Galerie im Lanbachhaus, Munich.
41 : *Impression IV (Gendarme),* 1911, oil on canvas, 95 × 107 cm. Städtische Galerie im Lanbachhaus, Munich.
42 : *Lyrically,* 1911, oil on canvas, 159.5 × 250.5 cm. Kunstsammlung Nordrhein-Westfalen, Düsseldorf.
42 : *Black Lines I,* 1913, oil on canvas, 129.4 × 131.1 cm. Solomon R. Guggenheim Museum, New York.
43 : *Improvisation 26 (Rowing),* 1912, oil on canvas, 97 × 107.5 cm. Städtische Galerie im Lanbachhaus, Munich.
44 : *Improvisation 14,* 1910, oil on canvas, 74 × 125.5 cm. Musée National d'Art Moderne, Pompidou Centre, Paris. Nina Kandinsky Donation.
44 : *Painting with a Black Arch,* 1912, oil on canvas, 189 × 198 cm. Musée National d'Art Moderne, Pompidou Centre, Paris.
46 : Study for the almanac of *Der Blaue Reiter,* 1911, watercolour, 29 × 21 cm.
47 : *The Last Judgement,* 1912, watercolour and Indian ink, painted on glass, 33.6 × 45.3 cm. Musée National d'Art Moderne, Pompidou Centre, Paris.

81 : *Thirteen Rectangles,* 1930, oil on cardboard,
69.5 × 59.5 cm. Musée National d'Art Moderne,
Pompidou Centre, Paris.
82 : *On White II,* 1923, oil on canvas, 105 × 98 cm.
Musée National d'Art Moderne, Pompidou Centre,
Paris.
83 : *Upward Tension,* 1924, pencil, Indian ink, brown ink
and watercolour, 48.7 × 33.7 cm. Musée National
d'Art Moderne, Pompidou Centre, Paris.
Nina Kandinsky Donation.
© ADAGP, 1988.

Ellsworth Kelly
141 : *Two Panels Yellow and Black,* 1968,
233.7 × 294.6 cm.

Paul Klee
47 : *Composition,* 1914, oil on cardboard,
26.7 × 21.6 cm. Kunstmuseum, Basel.
47 : *View of the Harbour at Hammamet,* 1914,
22 × 27 cm. Private collection, Switzerland.
82 : *Hovering, Before the Ascent,* 1930, oil on canvas,
84 × 84 cm.
Klee Foundation, Bern.
© ADAGP, 1988.

Yves Klein
135 : *Anthropometry from the Blue Period,* 1960, pigment
and synthetic resin on paper, mounted on canvas,
155 × 281 cm. Musée National d'Art Moderne,
Pompidou Centre, Paris.
135 : *Monochrome IKB,* 1960, pigment and synthetic
resin on canvas, mounted on wood,
199 × 153 × 2.5 cm. Musée National d'Art
Moderne, Pompidou Centre, Paris.
© ADAGP, 1988.

Franz Kline
102 : *Painting Number 2,* 1954, oil on canvas,
204.3 × 271.6 cm. Museum of Modern Art,
New York.

Ivan Kliun
52 : Untitled, 1916, gouache. Courtesy Galerie Franka
Berndt, Paris.

Gustav Klucis
78 : *Axonometric Construction, c.* 1920, oil on canvas,
66 × 47 cm. Thyssen-Bornemisza collection,
Lugano, Switzerland.
© SPADEM, 1988.

Willem de Kooning
102 : *Woman I,* 1950-52, oil on canvas,
192.7 × 147.3 cm, Museum of Modern Art,
New York.
102 : *Night Square,* 1950-51, oil on canvas,
76.2 × 101.6 cm. Private collection.

Franz Kupka
31 : *Around a Point,* 1911, oil on canvas,
194 × 200 cm. Musée National d'Art Moderne,
Pompidou Centre, Paris.
31 : *The Cathedral,* 1913, oil on canvas, 180 × 150 cm.
Courtesy Galerie Louis Carré, Paris.
© ADAGP, 1988.

Mikhail Larionov
50 : *Rayonism,* 1912, pastel. Courtesy Galerie Franka
Berndt, Paris.
© ADAGP, 1988.

Bart van der Leck
63 : *Composition 1916-4 (Mine Triptych),* 1916,
oil on canvas; centre panel: 113 × 110.5 cm;
side panels: 113 × 56 cm. Gemeentemuseum,
The Hague.
64 : *Composition,* 1918-20, oil on canvas,
101 × 100 cm. Stedelijk Museum, Amsterdam.
© SPADEM, 1988.

Fernand Léger
30 : *Contrast of Forms,* 1913, oil on canvas,
100 × 81 cm. Musée National d'Art Moderne,
Pompidou Centre, Paris.
30 : *The Discs,* 1918, oil on canvas, 240 × 180 cm.
Musée d'Art Moderne de la Ville de Paris.
© SPADEM, 1988.

Sol LeWitt
142 : *Pyramids,* June 1986. Magasin, Centre National
d'Art Contemporain, Grenoble. Photo: Q. Bertoux
and D. Quarella.
150 : *Wall-Relief,* 1972, 194 × 194 cm. Courtesy Galerie
Daniel Templon, Paris.

El Lissitzky
76 : *Proun 4B,* 1919-20, distemper on canvas,
70 × 55.5 cm. Thyssen-Bornemisza collection,
Lugano, Switzerland.

Morris Louis
139 : *Beta Lambda,* 1960, acrylic on canvas,
262.6 × 407 cm. Museum of Modern Art, New York.

Kasimir Malevich
48 : *Yellow Suprematism,* 1917, oil on canvas,
106 × 70.5 cm. Stedelijk Museum, Amsterdam.
Archives Nakov, Paris.
51 : *Suprematist Painting, Black Rectangle, Blue Triangle,*
1915, oil on canvas, 66.5 × 57 cm. Stedelijk
Museum, Amsterdam.
51 : First exhibition of Suprematist paintings, Petrograd,
1915.
51 : *Suprematism no. 50,* 1916, 66 × 97 cm. Stedelijk
Museum, Amsterdam. Archives Nakov, Paris.
52 : *Suprematism,* 1915-16, oil on canvas,
101.5 × 62 cm. Stedelijk Museum, Amsterdam.

Man Ray
70 : *The Rope Dancer Accompanies Herself with Her
Shadows,* 1918, aerograph, ink and watercolour
on paper, 33.4 × 44.5 cm.
Private collection.

Piero Manzoni
132 : *Achrome,* 1959, china clay on pleated canvas,
140 × 120.5 cm. Musée National d'Art Moderne,
Pompidou Centre, Paris.

Franz Marc
45 : *Genesis II,* 1912, wood engraving, 23.9 × 19.9 cm.
Museum of Modern Art, New York.

45 : *Landscape with Animals and Rainbow,* 1911,
glass painting.
47 : *Bull Resting,* 1913, tempera, 40 × 46 cm.
Private collection.

Masoero
33 : *From the Aeroplane,* 1935, aerial photograph,
dimensions and whereabouts unknown. Archives
Lista, Paris.

André Masson
90 : *Battle of Fishes,* 1926, mixed media on canvas,
36.2 × 73 cm. Museum of Modern Art, New York.
90 : *Villagers,* 1927, sand, glue and oil on canvas,
81 × 65 cm. Musée National d'Art Moderne,
Pompidou Centre, Paris. L. and M. Leiris Donation.
91 : *Soleils furieux,* 1925, automatic drawing,
pen-and-ink.
© SPADEM, 1988.

Henri Matisse
24 : *The Church Tower, Collioure,* 1905, watercolour.
Private collection.
24 : *Notre-Dame,* 1914, oil on canvas, 147 × 94.5 cm.
Museum of Modern Art, New York.
25 : *The Piano Lesson,* 1916, oil on canvas,
245 × 212 cm. Museum of Modern Art, New York.
25 : *The Moroccans,* 1916, oil on canvas,
181.3 × 279.4 cm. Museum of Modern Art,
New York. © SPADEM, 1988.

Roberto Matta
94 : *Untitled,* 1947, 200 × 210 cm. Patrice Trigano
collection, Paris.
© ADAGP, 1988.

Henri Michaux
117 : *Movement,* 1950, Indian ink, 32 × 24 cm.
Courtesy Galerie Baudoin Lebon, Paris.
117 : *Face,* 1958, gouache, 49.5 × 32.5 cm. Courtesy
Galerie Baudoin Lebon, Paris.
© ADAGP, 1988.

Joan Miró
91 : *The Family,* 1924, drawing, 74.1 × 104.1 cm.
Museum of Modern Art, New York.
92 : *Untitled,* 1925, painting, 116 × 89 cm. Courtesy
Galerie Lelong, Paris.
92 : *Untitled,* 1927, painting, 130 × 95 cm. Courtesy
Galerie Lelong, Paris.
© ADAGP, 1988.

Laszlo Moholy-Nagy
78 : *Composition A XX,* 1924, oil on canvas,
135 × 115 cm. Musée National d'Art Moderne,
Pompidou Centre, Paris.
78 : *Composition A 19,* 1927.

Piet Mondrian
58 : *Composition in a Square with Red, Yellow and Blue,*
1921-19, oil on canvas, 143.5 cm diagonally.
National Gallery of Art, Washington.
60 : *Still Life with Ginger Jar II,* 1912, oil on canvas,
91.5 × 120 cm. Gemeentemuseum, The Hague.
60 : *Apple Tree in Blossom,* 1912, oil on canvas,
78 × 106 cm. Gemeentemuseum, The Hague.

61 : *Composition with Lines,* 1917, oil on canvas,
108.4 × 108.4 cm. Rijksmuseum Kröller-Müller,
Otterloo.
62 : *Composition in Colour A,* 1917, oil on canvas,
50 × 44 cm. Rijksmuseum Kröller-Müller,
Otterloo.
63 : *Composition. Checkerboard, Bright Colours,*
1919, oil on canvas, 86 × 106 cm.
Gemeentemuseum, The Hague.
64 : *Composition with Yellow Lines,* 1933, oil on canvas,
113 cm. diagonally.
Gemeentemuseum, The Hague.
126 : *Broadway Boogie-Woogie,* 1942-43, oil on
canvas, 127 × 127 cm. Museum of Modern Art,
New York.
© SPADEM, 1988.

Claude Monet
20 : *Haystack, Snow Effect, Morning,* 1891, oil on canvas,
65 × 92 cm. Museum of Fine Arts, Boston.
20 : *Haystack, Snow Effect, Overcast,* 1891, oil on canvas,
65 × 92 cm. The Art Institute of Chicago.
20 : *Haystack, Thaw, Sunset,* 1891, oil on canvas,
65 × 92 cm. Private collection.
21 : *Waterlilies, Sunset,* 1916-23, oil on canvas,
197 × 600 cm. Musée de l'Orangerie, Paris.
21 : *Weeping Willow (Tangled Foliage),* c. 1923, oil on
canvas, 110.5 × 100 cm. Galerie Beyeler, Basel.
© SPADEM, 1988.

François Morellet
130 : *Untitled,* 1952, oil on wood, 40 × 70 cm.
Hofmann collection, Mönchengladbach.
131 : *2 Lattices of Perpendicular Lines,* 1952, acrylic on
wood, 60 × 60 cm. Liliane and Michel Durand-
Dessert collection, Paris. Photo: Adam Rzepka.

Robert Motherwell
103 : *Elegy for the Spanish Republic no. 34,* 1953-54,
oil on canvas, 203.2 × 254 cm. Albright-Knox Art
Gallery, Buffalo.

Barnett Newman
104 : *Ulysses,* 1952, 330.2 × 127 cm.
Private collection.
105 : *Vir Heroicus Sublimis,* 1950-51, oil on canvas,
242.2 × 513.6 cm. Museum of Modern Art,
New York.

Ben Nicholson
86 : *Painting (Trout),* 1924.

Kenneth Noland
139 : *Navajo,* 1971, 259 × 443 cm. Courtesy Galerie de
France, Paris.
140 : *Untitled,* 1960, acrylic on canvas, 91 × 91 cm.
Ludwig Museum, Cologne.
140 : *Horizontal Stripes III-27,* 1978, 127.1 × 85.2 cm.
Museum of Modern Art, New York.
141 : *Erin,* 1970, acrylic on canvas, 355 × 103 cm.
Courtesy Galerie Daniel Templon, Paris.
Photo: A. Morain, Paris.

Michel Parmentier
146 : Works of 1966 (blue), 1968 (red), 1984 (black).
Exhibition at Galerie Durand-Dessert, Paris, 1984.

Victor Pasmore

85 : *Square Motif (Indian Red), no. 1,* 1959.
Musée des Beaux-Arts, Calais.

Laszlo Peri

79 : *Spatial Construction in Three Parts,* 1923,
painted wood, black and reddish-brown:
part 1: 60 × 68 cm; part 2: 55.5 × 70 cm;
part 3: 58 × 68 cm.

Francis Picabia

35 : *Behold the Daughter Born of No Mother,* 1916-
17, watercolour, gouache, silver metallic paint,
pencil and ink on cardboard, 75 × 50.7 cm. Musée
National d'Art Moderne, Pompidou Centre, Paris.

68 : *Music Is Like Painting,* 1914-17, watercolour and
gouache on wood, 122 × 66 cm.
Private collection.

69 : *Hydraulic Press,* 1921-22, watercolour on paper,
59.7 × 72.5 cm.
Courtesy Galerie 1900-2000, Paris.
© ADAGP, SPADEM, 1988.

Pablo Picasso

26 : *Violin,* 1913-14, charcoal and collage,
62 × 47 cm. Museum of Modern Art, New York.

27 : *Man's Head with Hat,* 1913, charcoal, 64 × 27 cm.
Private collection.
© SPADEM, 1988.

Serge Poliakoff

122 : *Yellow and Black,* 1952, oil on canvas,
130.3 × 89 cm. Musée National d'Art Moderne,
Pompidou Centre, Paris.

123 : *Composition,* 1950, oil on canvas, 100 × 81 cm.
© ADAGP, 1988.

Jackson Pollock

96 : *Eyes in the Heat,* 1946, oil on canvas,
137.2 × 109.2 cm. The Peggy Guggenheim
Collection, Venice.

100 : Drawing, 1947, 47.6 × 63 cm. Private collection.

100 : *Gothic,* 1944, oil on canvas, 215 × 142.2 cm.
Museum of Modern Art, New York.

101 : *Convergence,* 1952, oil on canvas, 237.5 × 396 cm.
Albright-Knox Art Gallery, Buffalo.

101 : *Greyed Rainbow,* 1953, oil on canvas,
182.8 × 243.8 cm. The Art Institute of Chicago.

Liubov Popova

55 : *Non-objective Composition, c.* 1916, 35.5 × 31 cm.
Wilhelm Hack Museum, Ludwigshafen.
Archives Nakov, Paris.

Ad Reinhardt

106 : *Blue Painting,* 1953, 190.5 × 71.1 cm. The Museum
of Art, Carnegie Institute, Pittsburgh, Pennsylvania.

Hans Richter

72 : Photogram of the film *Rythmus 23,* 1923-25.
Document: Patrick de Haas, Paris.
© ADAGP, SPADEM, 1988.

Bridget Riley

132 : *Orient IV,* 1970, acrylic on canvas, 59 × 53 cm.
Private collection.

Jean-Paul Riopelle

115 : *Follow the Guide,* 1969, oil on canvas,
130 × 289 cm. Courtesy Galerie Trigano, Paris.
© ADAGP, 1988.

Alexander Rodchenko

57 : Untitled, 1921, coloured crayon. Courtesy
Galerie Franka Berndt, Paris.

57 : *Non-objective Composition,* 1917, gouache on
paper, 28 × 19 cm.
Private collection.
Archives Nakov, Paris.

Mark Rothko

105 : *White and Green in Blue,* 1957, oil on canvas.
Private collection, New York.

107 : *White Stripe,* 1958, oil on canvas, 206 × 232 cm.
Private collection.

Luigi Russolo

32 : *Sensations of Bombardment,* 1926, oil on canvas,
65 × 100 cm.
Private collection.
© SPADEM, 1988.

Oskar Schlemmer

80 : *The Nightingale's Song,* 1929, collage on paper,
glue, black crayon on black paper, 44.2 × 65 cm.
Staatsgalerie, Stuttgart.
© SPADEM, 1988.

Gérard Schneider

115 : Untitled, 1960, oil on canvas, 130 × 162 cm.
Courtesy Galerie Trigano, Paris.
© ADAGP, 1988.

Kurt Schwitters

74 : *Merz 600 Leiden,* 1923, collage.
Kunsthalle, Hamburg.

74 : *Disjointed Forces,* 1923, assemblage,
Kunstmuseum, Bern.

74 : *Revolving,* 1919, assemblage, 122.7 × 88.7 cm.
Museum of Modern Art, New York.

75 : *Merz Picture with Candle,* 1925-28,
assemblage, 27 × 27 cm.
Musée d'Art et d'Histoire, Geneva.
© ADAGP, 1988.

William Scott

110 : *Composition,* 1955.
Private collection.

Gino Severini

32 : *The Armored Train,* 1915, oil on canvas,
116.8 × 87.8 cm. Museum of Modern Art,
New York.

Jesus Raphael Soto

129 : *Spiral,* 1955, plexiglass. Courtesy Galerie
Denise René, Paris.
© ADAGP, 1988.

Pierre Soulages

116 : Untitled, 1956, painting, 195 × 130 cm. Courtesy
Galerie de France, Paris.
© ADAGP, 1988.

Nicolas de Staël
123 : *Composition in Pale Green,* 1948.
Private collection.
123 : *The Small Footballers,* 1952. Musée des Beaux-Arts, Dijon.
© ADAGP, 1988.

Frank Stella
136 : *Hyena Stamp,* 1962, 195.5 × 195.5 cm. Tate Gallery, London.
142 : *Marquis of Portago,* 1960. Private collection.
142 : *Parczezew,* 1972, mixed media, 290 × 280 × 10 cm. Courtesy Galerie Daniel Templon, Paris. Photo: André Morain.
143 : *Naguchi's Okinawa Woodpecker,* 1978, mixed media on canvas, 152 × 220 cm. Courtesy Galerie Daniel Templon, Paris.

Varvara Stepanova
56 : *Construction,* 1921, collage on paper, 35.8 × 22.8 cm. Private collection, U.K. Archives Nakov, Paris.
© SPADEM, 1988.

Clyfford Still
98 : *Untitled,* 1951, oil on canvas, 238 × 208.3 cm.

Wladislaw Strzeminski
84 : *Architectonic Composition 13c,* 1929, oil on canvas, 96 × 60 cm.

Sophie Taeuber-Arp
86 : *Aubette,* 1927, relief, oil on pavatex.
© ADAGP, 1988.

Pierre Tal Coat
121 : *Vein of Flint,* 1959, 97 × 299 cm. Courtesy Galerie Lelong, Paris.
© ADAGP, 1988.

Antoni Tàpies
118 : *Collage with Rice,* 1969, painting, 89 × 116 cm. Courtesy Galerie Lelong, Paris.
119 : *Rectangle and Oval,* 1976, painting, 82 × 65 cm. Courtesy Galerie Lelong, Paris.
© ADAGP, 1988.

Vladimir Tatlin
53 : *Synthetico-Static Composition,* 1914-15, tempera, oil on wood, metal and cloth on wood panel, 70 × 50 cm. Private collection, Switzerland.
53 : *Non-objective Composition,* 1916, tempera on wood, 52 × 39 cm. National Gallery, Berlin.
© SPADEM, 1988.

Jean Tinguely
134 : *Metamatic,* 1959. Moderna Museet, Stockholm.

Marc Tobey
95 : *Composition on Blue,* 1955, tempera, 60.5 × 91 cm. Courtesy Galerie Jeanne Bucher, Paris. Photo: Luc Joubert.
95 : *The Search,* 1954, tempera, 18 × 27.5 cm. Courtesy Galerie Jeanne Bucher, Paris. Photo: Luc Joubert.
© ADAGP, 1988.

Niele Toroni
147 : *Untitled,* 1970, brushmarks repeated at regular (30 cm) intervals on oilcloth. Exhibition at the Galerie Yvon Lambert, Paris, 1970. Photo: A. Morain, Paris.

Cy Twombly
144 : *Mars and the Artist,* 1975, collage, oil, crayon and pencil on paper and cardboard, 14.2 × 127.4 cm. "Légendes" exhibition, Capc, Bordeaux, 1984. Photo: Delpech.

Victor Vasarely
129 : *Ilile-Couple,* 1952. Private collection.
© SPADEM, 1988.

Bram van Velde
122 : *Composition,* 1955.
© SPADEM, 1988.

Claude Viallat
148 : *Untitled,* 1969, mixed fibres, mordant dyes, 450 × 210 cm. Courtesy Galerie Jean Fournier, Paris. Photo: Adam Rzepka.

Maria Elena Vieira da Silva
122 : *Noon,* 1958. Private collection.
© ADAGP, 1988.

Friedrich Vordemberge-Gildewart
79 : *Construction in Red,* 1924, oil on canvas, 160 × 120 cm. Private collection.

Wolfgang Wols
114 : *The Butterfly's Wing,* 1947, oil on canvas, 55 × 46 cm. Musée National d'Art Moderne, Pompidou Centre, Paris.
114 : *Untitled,* 1949, painting. Private collection.
© SPADEM, 1988.

Léon Zack
121 : *Untitled,* 1954-55, oil on canvas, 146 × 97 cm. Courtesy Galerie Protée, Paris. Photo: S. Veignant, Paris.
© SPADEM, 1988.

BIBLIOGRAPHY

GENERAL WORKS

Books

Osborne, H. *Abstraction and Artifice in Twentieth-Century Art.* Oxford: Clarendon Press, 1979.

Pohribny, A. *Asbstrakte Malerei.* Freiburg: Herder, 1978.

Seuphor, M. *L'Art abstrait,* 4 vols. Paris: Maeght éditeur, 1971-74.

Turowski, A. *Existe-t-il un art de l'Europe de l'Est ?* Paris, 1986.

Vallier, Dora. *L'Art abstrait.* Paris: Librairie Générale Française, 1980.

Catalogues

Abstraction Création 1931-1936, Munster, Westfalisches Landesmuseum für Kunst und Kulturgeschichte, April 2-June 4, 1978; Paris, Musée d'Art moderne de la Ville de Paris, June 16-Sept. 17, 1978.

Abstraction: Towards a New Art, London, Tate Gallery, Feb. 6-April 13, 1980.

Contrasts of Form: Geometric Abstract Art 1910-80, New York, MoMA, 1985.

Origini dell'astrattismo: verso altri orizzonti del reale, Milan, Italy, Palazzo Reale, Oct. 18, 1979 - Jan. 18, 1980; Silvana Editore, 1979.

Paris-Moscou, Paris, Centre Pompidou, 1979.

Paris-New York, Paris, Centre Georges-Pompidou, 1977.

Paris-Paris: créations en France 1937-1957, Paris, Centre Georges-Pompidou, May 28-Nov. 2, 1981.

Tendenzen der zwanziger Jahre; 15. Europaische Kunstausstellung Berlin 1977, Berlin, Neue Nationalgalerie, 1977; Dieter Reimer, 1977.

The Planar Dimension: Europe 1912-32, New York, Salomon R. Guggenheim Museum, 1979.

Von Konstruktivismus zur konkreten Kunst, Berlin, Neue Nationalgalerie, 1977.

BAUHAUS

Books

Bauhaus 1919-1928, edited by H. Bayer, W. Gropius, with a preface by A. H. Barr. London: Secker and Warburg, 1975.

Humblet, C. *Le Bauhaus.* Lausanne: L'Age d'homme, 1980.

Poling, C. V. *Color Theories of the Bauhaus Artists.* New York: Columbia University, 1973.

Richard, L. *Encyclopédie du Bauhaus.* Paris: Somogy, 1985.

Whitford, F. *The Bauhaus.* London: Thames and Hudson, 1984.

Wingler, H. M. *The Bauhaus: Weimar, Dessau, Berlin, Chicago.* Boston: M.I.T. Press, 1969.

CONSTRUCTIVISM

Books

Bowlt, J. E. *Russian Art of the Avant-Garde: Theory and Criticism 1902-1934.* New York: The Viking Press, 1976.

Conio, G. *Le Constructivisme russe : textes théoriques, manifestes, documents.* Lausanne: L'Age d'homme, 1987.

Gray, C. *The Great Experiment: Russian Art. 1863-1922.* London: Thames & Hudson, 1962.

Lodder, C. *Russian Constructivism.* New Haven, London: Yale University Press, 1983.

Nakov, A. *L' Avant-garde russe.* Paris: Hazan, 1984.

Russian Avant-Garde Art. The Georges Costakis Collection. New York: Abrams, 1981.

Catalogues

Constructivism in Poland, 1923-1936: Blok, Praesens, Museum Sztuki, Lodz, 1973.

Malewitsch-Mondrian: Konstruktion als Konzept. Hanover, Kunstverein, 1977.

Russian Women-Artists of the Avant-Garde 1910-1930. Cologne, Galerie Gmurzynska, Dec. 1978-March 1979, edited by K. Rubinger.

The Avant-Garde in Russia 1901-1930: New Perspectives, Los Angeles County Museum of Art; Cambridge, M.I.T. Press, 1980.

DADA

Books

Foster, S. C., Kuenzli, R. E., eds. *Dada Spectrum: The Dialectics of Revolt.* Madison: Coda Press; Iowa City: University of Iowa, 1979.

Lemoine, S. *Dada.* Paris: Hazan, 1986.

Richter, H. *Dada: Art and Anti-Art.* London: Thames and Hudson, 1985.

Sanouillet, M. *Dada à Paris.* Nice: Centre XXᵉ Siècle, 1980.

DE STIJL

Books

Jaffe, H. L. *De Stijl.* London: Thames and Hudson, 1970.

Jaffe, H. L. *De Stijl, 1917-1931: The Dutch Contribution to Modern Art.* Amsterdam, 1986.

Lemoine, S. *De Stijl.* Paris: Hazan, 1986.

ABSTRACT EXPRESSIONISM

Books

Lucie-Smith, E. *Late Modern: The Visual Arts since 1945.* New York, Washington: Praeger, 1969.

Peinture américaine, texts by Catherine Francblin, Jacques Henric, Catherine Millet, Marcelin Pleynet, Severo Sarduy, Guy Scarpetta, Philippe Sollers. Paris: Galilée, Art Press, 1980.

Rose, B. *American Art since 1900: A Critical History.* New York, Washington: Praeger ("World of Art" Series), 1967.

Stich, S. *Made in USA: An Americanisation in Modern Art, the '50s and '60s.* London: University of California Press, Ltd, 1987.

Tuchman, M. *The New York School: Abstract Expressionism in the 40s and 50s.* London: Thames and Hudson, n.d.

INFORMAL

Books

Bony, A. *Les Années 50.* Editions du Regard, 1982.

Grenier, J. *Entretiens avec dix-sept peintres non-figuratifs.* Paris, 1963.

Ragon, M., Seuphor, M. *L'Aventure de l'art abstrait.* Paris: Robert Laffont, 1956.

Restany, P. *L'Aventure de l'art abstrait: de l'esthétique à l'éthique: 1945-1965.* Paris: Skira, 1982.

Xuriguera, G. *Les Années 50: peinture, sculpture, témoignages.* Paris: Arted, 1984.

Catalogues

L'Art en Europe. Les Années décisives 1945-1953. Geneva: Skira, 1987. Musée d'art moderne de Saint-Etienne.

Les Années 50. Paris: Centre Georges Pompidou, 1988.

MINIMALISM

Books

Battcock, G., ed., *Minimal Art: A Critical Anthology.* New York: E. P. Dutton, 1968.

Burnham. *Great Western Salt Works: Essays on the Meaning of Post-Formalist Art.* New York: Braziller, 1974.

Muller, G. *The New Avant-Garde: Issues of the Seventies.* New York: Praeger, 1972.

Catalogues

Develing, E., Lippard, L. et al. *Minimal Art.* Dusseldorf: Stadtiche Kunsthalle, 1968.

Foley, S. *Unitary Forms: Minimal Sculpture by Carl Andre, Don Judd, John McCraken, Tony Smith.* San Francisco, Museum of Modern Art, 1970.

Friedman, M., Guay, P., Pincus-Witten, R., *A View of a Decade: 1966-1976/Ten Years.* Chicago, Museum of Contemporary Art, 1970.

AMERICAN PAINTING

Books

Arnason, H. H. *Robert Motherwell.* New York: Harry N. Abrams, 1982.

Ashton, D. *About Rothko.* New York: Oxford University Press, 1983.

Ashton, D. *Yes But... A Critical Study of Philip Guston.* New York: Viking Press, 1976.

Coplans, J. *Ellsworth Kelly.* New York: Harry N. Abrams, 1972.

Franz, E. *Jackson Pollock.* New York: Abbeville Press, 1983.

Fried, M. *Morris Louis.* New York: Harry N. Abrams, 1970.

Moffett, K. *Jules Olitski.* New York: Harry N. Abrams, 1981.

Moffett, K. *Kenneth Noland.* New York: Harry N. Abrams, 1977.

Namuth, H., Krauss, R., O'Connor, F. V. *L'Atelier de Jackson Pollock.* Paris: Collection Macula, 1978.

Rose, B. *Helen Frankenthaler.* New York: Harry N. Abrams, 1971.

Catalogues

Adolph Gottlieb, 1903-1974 : A Retrospective, Washington, Corcoran Gallery of Art, 1981.

Barnett Newman: The Stations of the Cross, New York, The Solomon R. Guggenheim Museum, 1966.

Clyfford Still, New York, The Metropolitan Museum of Art, 1979-80.

Franz Kline: 1910-1962, New York, Whitney Museum of American Art, 1979-80.

Hans Hofmann: 1880-1966, Fort Worth Art Museum, 1985.

Jackson Pollock: A Catalogue Raisonné of Paintings, Drawings and Other Works, 4 vols. New Haven and London: Yale University Press, 1978.

Jackson Pollock, Paris, Musée national d'art moderne, Centre Georges-Pompidou, 1982.

Mark Rothko 1903-1970: A Retrospective, New York, The Solomon R. Guggenheim Museum, 1979.

Mark Tobey Retrospective, Dallas, Museum of Fine Art, 1968.

Willem de Kooning Retrospective Exhibition, New York, Whitney Museum of American Art, 1983-84.

William Baziotes: A Memorial Exhibition, New York, The Solomon R. Guggenheim Museum, 1965.

ALBERS

Books

Comringer, E. *Joseph Albers: son œuvre et sa contribution à la figuration visuelle au cours du XXᵉ siècle.* Paris: Dessain et Tolra, 1972.
Search Versus Research: Three Lectures by Josef Albers at Trinity College, April 1965. Hartford, Conn.: Trinity College Press, 1969.

Catalogues

Joseph Albers: A Retrospective, New York, Salomon R. Guggenheim Museum, 1988.

ARP

Catalogues

Arp, Wurttembergischer Kunstverein, Stuttgart, G.F.R., 1986.
Arp 1887-1966, Musée d'art moderne de Strasbourg, 1986.
Jean Arp: le temps des papiers déchirés, Paris, Musée national d'art moderne Georges-Pompidou, 1983.

ROBERT DELAUNAY

Books

Delaunay und Deutschland. Cologne: Dumont, 1985.
Spate, V. *Orphism: The Evolution of Non-Figurative Painting in Paris 1910-1914.* New York: Oxford University Press, 1979.

Catalogues

Robert/Sonia Delaunay, Tokyo, National Museum of Modern Art, 1979.

SONIA DELAUNAY

Catalogues

Robert et Sonia Delaunay, Paris, Musée d'art moderne de Paris, 1985.
Sonia Delaunay: A Retrospective, Buffalo, New York, Albright-Knox Art Gallery, Feb.-March 1980.

VAN DOESBURG

Books

Baljeu, J. *Theo van Doesburg.* New York: MacMillan, 1974.
Doig, A. *Theo van Doesburg: Painting into Architecture, Theory into Practice.* Cambridge, New York: Cambridge University Press, 1986.

KANDINSKY

Books

Arnold Schœnberg - Wassily Kandinsky: Letters, Pictures and Documents, edited by J. Hahl-Koch, translated by J. C. Crawford. London, Boston, 1984.
Kandinsky, W. *Regards sur le passé et autres textes 1912-1933.* Introduction by J. P. Bouillon. Paris: Hermann, 1974.
Polling, C. V. *Kandinsky's Teaching at the Bauhaus: Color Theory and Analytical Drawing.* New York: Rizzoli, 1986.
Tio Bellido, R. *Kandinsky.* Paris: F. Hazan, 1987.
Washton-Long, R. C. *Kandinsky, the Development of an Abstract Style.* Oxford: Clarendon Press, 1980.
Weiss, P. *Kandinsky in Munich: The Formative Jugendstil Years.* Princeton University Press, 1979.

Catalogues

Kandinsky, Paris, Musée national d'art moderne Georges-Pompidou, 1984.
Kandinsky. Catalogue raisonné de l'œuvre peint: 1900-1944, Paris, K. Flinker, 1982.
Kandinsky in Munich 1896-1914, New York, Solomon R. Guggenheim Museum, Feb.-April 1985.
Kandinsky: Russian and Bauhaus Years, New York, Solomon R. Guggenheim Museum, 1983.

KLEE

Books

Geelhaar, C. *Paul Klee et le Bauhaus.* Neuchâtel: Ides et Calendes, 1972.
Glaesemer, J. *Paul Klee The Colored Works in the Kunstmuseum Bern - Paintings, Colored Sheets, Pictures on Glass, and Sculptures.* Kornfeld, 1974.
Kagan, A. *Paul Klee and Music.* Ithaca, New York: Cornell University Press, 1983.
Naubert-Riser, C. *Paul Klee "les Chefs-d'œuvre".* Paris: Hazan, 1988.
Verdi, R. *Klee and Nature.* New York: Rizzoli, 1985.

Catalogues

Die Tunisreise: Klee, Macke, Moilliet, ed. E. G. Guse, Stuttgart, Gert Hatje, 1982.
Klee et la musique, Paris, Musée national d'art moderne, Centre Georges-Pompidou, 1985.
Paul Klee, New York, MoMA; Boston, distributed by New York Graphic Society Books/Little, Brown and Co., 1987.
Paul Klee: das Fruwerk 1883-1922, Munich, G.F.R., Städtische Gallery Lenbachhaus, Dcc. 12, 1979-March 2, 1980.

F. KUPKA

Catalogues
Frank Kupka, Cologne, Galerie Gmurzynska,
Feb.-April 1981.
Frank Kupka 1871-1957: A Retrospective,
New York, Solomon R. Guggenheim Museum,
1975.

EL LISSITZKY

Catalogues
*El Lissitzky, 1890-1941: Catalogue for an
Exhibition of Selected Works from North
American Collections, the Sprengel
M. Hanover and the Staatliche Galerie
Moritzburg Halle,* Cambridge, Harvard
University Art Museum, 1987.

MALEVICH

Books
Malevich. Cahiers 1, ed. J. C. Marcadé. Lausanne:
L'Age d'homme, 1979.
Zhadova, L. A. *Malevich: Suprematism and
Revolution in Russian Art 1910-1930.*
New York: Thames and Hudson, 1982.

Catalogues
Malevich, Paris, Musée national d'art moderne
Georges-Pompidou, 1980.
*Malevich: Catalogue Raisonné of the Berlin
Exhibition 1927,* Amsterdam, Stedelijk
Museum, 1970.

MOHOLY-NAGY

Books
Passuth, K. *Moholy-Nagy.* London:
Thames and Hudson, 1984.

MONDRIAN

Books
Bois, Y. A., *L'atelier de Mondrian: recherches et
dessins.* Paris: Macula, 1982.
Champa, K. S. *Mondrian Studies.* Chicago:
University of Chicago Press, 1985.
Jaffe, H. *Mondrian.* New York: Abrams, 1986.
Lemoine, S. *Mondrian et De Stijl.* Paris: Hazan,
1987.
*The New Art - the New Life: The Collected Writings
of Piet Mondrian.* Boston: G. K. Hall, 1986.

Catalogues
Mondrian: The Diamond Compositions,
Washington, D. C., National Gallery of Art,
July-Sept. 1979.
Mondrian und De Stijl, Cologne, Gmurzynska
Gallery, 1979.

RODCHENKO

Books
Karginov, G. *Rodchenko.* London:
Thames and Hudson, 1979.
Khan-Magomedov, S. *Rodchenko: The Complete
Work.* Boston: M.I.T. Press, 1986.

OSCAR SCHLEMMER

Books
The Letters and Diaries of Oskar Schlemmer.
Middletown: Wesleyan University Press, 1972.

Catalogues
Oskar Schlemmer, Baltimore, Maryland, Baltimore
Museum of Art, Feb.-April 1986.

SCHWITTERS

Books
Elderfield, J. *Kurt Schwitters.* London:
Thames and Hudson, 1985.
Schmalenbach, W. *Kurt Schwitters.* Munich: Prestel,
1984.